Power from the Waves

Power from the Waves

DAVID ROSS

Incorporating and expanding on
Energy from the waves
by the same author

Oxford   New York   Tokyo
OXFORD UNIVERSITY PRESS
1995

Oxford University Press, Walton Street, Oxford OX2 6DP

Oxford   New York
Athens   Auckland   Bangkok   Bombay
Calcutta   Cape Town   Dar es Salaam   Delhi
Florence   Hong Kong   Istanbul   Karachi
Kuala Lumpur   Madras   Madrid   Melbourne
Mexico City   Nairobi   Paris   Singapore
Taipei   Tokyo   Toronto
and associated companies in
Berlin   Ibadan

Oxford is a trade mark of Oxford University Press

Published in the United States
by Oxford University Press Inc., New York

A catalogue record for this book is available from the British Library

Library of Congress Cataloging in Publication Data

Ross, David, 1925–
Power from the waves / David Ross.
Incorporating and expanding on Energy from the waves by the same
    author.
Includes bibliographical references and index.
1. Ocean wave power.   2. Electric power production–Great Britain.
I. Ross, David, 1925–   Energy from the waves.   II. Title.
TK1457.R672 1995   333.79'4–dc20   95-242370   CIP

ISBN   0 19 856511 9

Typeset by Hewer Text Composition Services, Edinburgh
Printed in Great Britain by Bookcraft Ltd, Midsomer Norton, Avon

Foreword

Dr D.A. Elliott
Director, Open University Technology Policy Group

Over the last decade or so, renewable energy technology has moved from the margins to the mainstream. Whereas once it was the dream of Utopians, now we have British Trade and Industry Ministers talking of a £2.5 billion market for the UK renewable energy industry, and the government's Renewable Energy Advisory Group estimating that renewable sources could contribute perhaps 20 per cent of the UK's electricity requirement by the year 2025.

Although some work had been done earlier, the UK entered the renewable energy field seriously in 1974, following the first oil crisis. A total of some £230 million has been spent on a range of research and development projects. Wave power was initially seen as one of the front runners and some £15 million was spent on it before the 'deep sea' wave programme was wound up in 1982. The decision to abandon deep sea wave power was the focus of much debate, in which the author of this book, David Ross, took a vigorous part. His earlier book, *Energy from the waves*, first published in 1979, provided unique coverage, for the general reader as well as for students of renewable energy, of the technology involved in capturing the energy of the waves and of the historical and political development of this novel technology. He has since followed the twists and turns of the debate over wave power and, while his investigative journalism and campaigning style have not endeared him to the energy establishment, his vigorous exploration of the policy issues has provided us with a fascinating account of decision-making processes.

The policy issues are, if anything, more urgent now than ever. With nuclear power widely seen as an unviable option, the development of renewable energy technologies, along with conservation techniques, is one way in which we can respond to the threat of global warming and other environmental problems.

Clearly, some of Ross's analysis is contentious; but then the topic is controversial, with interpretations of facts often still being in dispute. For example, in terms of the economics, all we have are estimates of likely costs, often based on purely conceptual systems, framed in contemporary short-term financial accounting contexts which usually ignore wider environmental considerations. Given this situation, it would probably be impossible to produce a totally independent and impartial review of the issues, or a 'final conclusion' on wave power. The jury is still out.

Accepting this limitation (although he is clearly a partisan for wave energy), Ross provides us with a unique insight into the issues of the technological decision-making process, an insight which may help us decide on the issues ourselves.

Preface

The story which follows is a moral tale, the triumph of good over bad. It takes us all the way from the development by a Japanese naval commander of a method of turning the energy of the waves into a stream of air, to the invention of an Edinburgh engineer who turned the capture of wave energy into a mechanical problem which he could solve. Then came the building in Norway, India and the Inner Hebrides of small stations on the shore. And on 2 August 1995 the launch took place of the first power station designed to stand alone on the seabed, away from the coast, generating smoke-free electricity from the renewable energy of the waves.

It is a story which resembles that of the Pied Piper of Hamelin: the comfortable, established burghers summoned him to rid their city of the rats and then when the pest and their fear had gone they lost enthusiasm for paying him his due. It was much the same in Britain. In 1976, there was enthusiastic official backing as the government contemplated the prospect of an Arab oil boycott or at least a drastic rise in the price of oil (which happened).

The mood changed when it was discovered that the energy 'gap', forecast to arrive in the mid-1990s, was going to be delayed. The North Sea and Alaska oil reserves came on-stream. So the comfortable burghers snapped shut their cheque books, turned away, and tried to pretend that we could go on burning oil, coal, and particularly gas without heed, and that global warming and growing pollution were not happening. We were even subjected to a propaganda campaign on behalf of 'clean gas', ignoring the millions of tonnes of carbon dioxide it adds to the atmosphere.

But why wave power? Because the sea covers more than 70 per cent of the world's surface. Engineers and scientists have discovered how to harvest its power in this generation. It can provide vast amounts of electricity without cooling towers, without pollution, without any risk of the 'fuel' running out, because the waves go on for ever . . .

So why has it been largely ignored for so long? There are a mixture of reasons. Money is the main one. But wave power is not about saving money: it is about saving the world. It was nuclear power that was supposed to be dirt cheap.

And it is ironic that the British wave energy programme, which dominated the scene from 1976 until 1982, was masterminded from, of all places, Harwell, the home of nuclear power. It was assigned there on the grounds that both sources were 'alternatives'. And the work was given to the Energy Technology Support Unit (ETSU), a subsidiary of the Atomic Energy Authority (AEA).

The years passed and ETSU rejected wave power as being hopelessly expensive, both now and in the future. And then came the OSPREY, to be based in Dounreay at the site of the fast breeder reactor, which had also been abandoned by the government. And it was the AEA, the parent body from Harwell, which was happy to offer its facilities, its people and its backing to wave power.

'Sweet are the uses of adversity, which like the toad, ugly and venomous, wears yet a precious jewel in his head', as Shakespeare wrote.

London   D.R.
August 1995

Acknowledgements

Ever since I started writing about wave energy in 1976, I have received all the assistance I have sought from everyone in the wave energy family, in all countries where it is being researched and developed. To all who have contributed to my understanding, I wish to say, 'Thank you'.

There are two people who have figured prominently: Clive Grove-Palmer and Tom Thorpe. Both were appointed and employed by ETSU, which may at times have felt that it was the undeserving recipient of many of my criticisms. I do indeed believe that it was too responsive to Treasury demands that a young technology should be assessed in terms of absurd costings, and that at times it appeared to be an agent of government policy. But perhaps ETSU will note that two of its officials and three of its publications are singled out by me for particular praise. I have always respected the pioneering work that ETSU has done, which is why I feel particular sadness about the way it has been misused.

The other person whom I must single out, at the risk of appearing unfair to others, is Stephen Salter. His brilliance as an engineer and scientist is recognised. What may not be so obvious is his enormous decency in the way that he patiently and tirelessly educates everyone from visiting journalists to MPs (who are sometimes even less aware of the issues) and helps overseas delegates at international conferences when, for instance, difficulties with the English language risk diminishing the value of the contributions that they are making. In addition, his own writing about wave energy is superlative.

There are others who have helped, many of whom are cited in the book, plus Roger Pope, Derek Todd, and Godfrey Bevan of the Department of Energy (as was); George Elliot and Ray Hunter of the NEL; Les Duckers and Peter White from Coventry; Tim Beaumont from the CEGB (as was); Meric Srokosz of the Institute of Oceanographic Sciences; John Twidell from de Montfort University, Leicester; Roger Price, who was always eloquent if critical, and Malcolm Cloke, both from ETSU; staff of Pergamon and Oxford University Press; the Norwegians (from Tapchan, OWC and Trondheim); Dave Elliott and Godfrey Boyle of the Open University; Frank Cook, MP; advisers and helpers at Friends of the Earth, Greenpeace, the Council for the Protection of Rural England, the Parliamentary Group for Alternative Energy Strategies, and many others.

I am also endlessly grateful to Tamara, my wife, who has lived for nearly 20 years with the waves roaring through our home and has nevertheless found time to turn from her own subject, philosophy, to read and comment on my manuscript, even though her mother country is Switzerland, one of the few which has nothing to gain from the story I have told.

Contents

Introduction 1

On 29 April 1976, the Chief Scientist of the Department of Energy, Dr Walter Marshall, announced in London that the British Government was to spend just over £1 million on investigating the possibility of harvesting the energy of the waves. It was the beginning of a long struggle—against nature, against engineering and scientific problems, and against the established powers in the energy and political worlds. But wave energy has won through. In Norway and the Inner Hebrides, pioneering wave power stations have been built. Others are under construction now (1995) off Dounreay in the north of Europe and the Azores in the south. Others are working or in preparation in Japan, India, and Indonesia. They are only a start, small in capacity compared with what is to come.

The ultimate prize is an inexhaustible source of non-polluting energy which has still to be achieved on a large scale. But the story so far is one of a triumph of science and engineering. The difficulties which had to be overcome were immense but the major problems have been solved. Progress since the early days, the mid-1970s, when the world was galvanised by a growing energy crisis, has been remarkable. We have learned an astonishing amount. We know how the waves behave and what has to be done to capture their elusive motion and turn it into useful energy. We know how to absorb a fluctuating supply and use it so that the lights do not go out or even flicker. Now what is needed are governments, utilities, and industries with the capital and the will to turn today's pioneering wave power devices into major energy providers, and start out seriously on the road to generating energy without the pollution that comes from burning gas, oil, coal, wood, and rubbish. There is no such thing as smoke-free smoke and the person who first rubbed two sticks together has a lot to answer for.

The damage this does has been evident since the Industrial Revolution, when smoke turned central England into the black country. Only the descriptions vary. It started life as fog and became a pea-souper, then smog, then acid rain, global warming, and the greenhouse effect. We are aroused from time to time by a conference or a learned paper or an alarming symptom of environmental change. There is a moment of headline panic. Society recognises that something must be done, but then loses interest because solutions are not easy.

Nuclear power has tried to present itself as a clean alternative, but has proved unacceptable because of regular emissions of radioactivity into the atmosphere and the sea, and because there is no agreed method of dealing with nuclear waste or with power stations awaiting decommissioning; and the memory of Chernobyl and other nuclear accidents has meant that most societies have turned their backs on that option.

But is wave energy the answer? It is not intended to be exclusive. For those countries blessed with vast, empty countryside, wind power may be a suitable renewable source. In equatorial regions, solar power may be the appropriate technology. There is also a good case to be made for tidal and other forms of hydroelectric power where the topography permits. But for many countries it is the waves that provide the best hope of developing a major energy source with no environmental objections to overcome. And the waves contain the amount of energy the world needs. Anyone who has stood on the deck of a ship and watched the ceaseless, tireless stirring of the sea exploding in a useless waste of froth must have wondered whether we could capture that perpetual motion and turn it into something useful. To ignore it is a crime against nature.

But how much useful energy is available? Is it a significant resource? The answer is that the waves contain about as much energy as the world is using today. To avoid any misunderstanding, let me repeat—*energy*, not just electricity. The best estimates, to which I shall return, put the figure for wave power at 1 terawatt (TW), the equivalent of the world's electricity production, from the waves arriving at the coast, and at 10 TW for the power in the open sea. That is comparable with the world's power consumption. A terawatt is 1000 gigawatt (GW) or 1 000 000 megawatts (MW). For comparison, an industrialised country such as Britain has a grid capacity of around 50 GW.

Let us return to that fateful day in April 1976, when the search got under way. A reporter was injudicious enough to ask Walter Marshall whether wave energy would be safer than nuclear power. Looming and ominous, Marshall—who happened also to be the most prominent nuclear scientist in the country and has since been rewarded with a peerage—replied sternly that he did not accept that nuclear power was dangerous. The exchange foreshadowed the future history of wave energy. It was to be, to a very great extent, a struggle between rival groups of competing energy producers, with the nuclear lobby in the forefront.

The British announcement was, I submit, one of the more significant announcements of our time in the field of energy. It implied that we might be able to obtain electricity from cold sea water, far away from land, without the need to use up finite resources or add to pollution. I say 'might' because at that time the whole operation was little more than a theory, born out of desperation at the height of an energy crisis. It is difficult, 20 years later, to recall just how ignorant the public (and many of the experts) were.

It is also difficult to appreciate what was the central purpose of the programme. Listening to official opinions, in and out of Parliament, one could gain the impression that it was all about reducing the cost of electricity by a few pence. This is a false impression that has grown up because, certainly in Britain and in most other countries too, the dominant idea on the official energy scene is that cheap is beautiful. But that was not the main concern in 1976. All the western countries were terrified that we were about to run into an energy famine. The Arab–Israeli war of 1973 had resulted in the Middle Eastern countries discovering the oil weapon. There were fears that they would refuse to supply the western countries which had supported Israel.

For Britain and Norway, the North Sea had scarcely come on stream as a source of crude oil, and it was uncertain how fruitful it would prove. Alaska also had still to be exploited. There was real fear that the West would find itself without oil for transport or for power stations, where it was burnt extensively. To rely on coal meant handing power to one group of workers, something that was much to the forefront of official thinking in Britain particularly, where the miners had just brought down the Heath government (in 1974). As to nuclear power, it was providing problems and not much electricity. Demand for energy was rising sharply, so alternative sources were desperately needed.

The question of cost was a secondary issue, raised largely at the start by the culture of the Central Electricity Generating Board (CEGB). It was beholden by Parliamentary statute to produce electricity as economically as possible and this had become its credo. It dedicated much effort to proving that whatever method it had chosen was the cheapest. It argued that nuclear power was 'too cheap to meter' and used this argument as justification for spending vast amounts of money on it. And so when wave energy became a possibility, it naturally turned first to the question of cost and found a ready audience in governments which had watched in horror as the price of oil rose, first in response to the Arab–Israeli war of 1973. A barrel of oil which had cost $1.80 in 1970 rose to $2.90 by mid-1973, and to $11.65 by December of that year. It was later to reach $45 for brief periods, after the overthrow of the Shah of Iran in 1979. That was the sort of problem which transfixed governments. But the real crisis, which is still with us, is far worse than that: it is that we are consuming 65.5 million barrels of oil a day, the inheritance of countless millions of years, and using up coal and gas in a wild, irresponsible splurge.

As to money, let us try to keep our minds on the fact that it was nuclear power that was supposed to be dirt cheap. Wave energy is not about saving money; it's about saving the world.

The first consideration must remain: can we find ways of illuminating and warming and empowering our lives without pollution and without running out of fuel? The 'energy gap', the excess of demand over supply which was accepted as a fact in the 1970s, and was due to paralyse the nation by the mid-1990s, remains a likely prospect although the date has slipped. But given the speed at which we are using up fossil fuels, and the collapse of the nuclear industry in most countries, the world is going to encounter a famine of useful energy within the lifetime of today's children if we do not change our pattern of production and consumption. We need desperately to develop renewable sources, however uncertain the need may appear at times. The question of cost is a luxury.

So let us return to the official British announcement. The revolutionary idea of using the ceaseless movement of the waves to generate electricity had (and still has) an immediate appeal, particularly in a country such as Britain, surrounded by water. The sea has fed us. It has saved us from invasion. Could it now be the means of lighting up and heating our living rooms and driving our factories and trains?

This was the prospect raised by Marshall's announcement, and it should have been greeted with official cries of delight. But Whitehall tried to play it down. It was announced formally in the House of Commons by the Under-Secretary, Alex Eadie, and not the Minister.[1] The statement referred to 'a varying and partly unpredictable supply of electricity', as close as the Civil Service could get to saying that it was not much use.

From then on, the attacks on wave energy never ceased. The main argument was that energy generated by the waves was too expensive and always would be so. The authorities used all the weaponry of government: secrecy, dubious statistics, massaged reports, and above all absurd methods of calculating costs. They priced the components of a wave power station at an impossibly high level. They treated experimental prototypes as though they were production units and gave them little credit for reduced costs from serial production and competitive tendering. And they imposed the Treasury trick of a high discount rate, which discriminates unfairly against capital-intensive technologies which have most of their expenditure in the early stages when the power station is built and installed, and then benefit later on from the flow of free 'fuel'. And when all of this proved inadequate, the government set up a committee with terms of reference which ensured that it would find against wave power.

One brief example will help to make the general point: in August 1991 the government set up the Renewable Energy Advisory Group and gave it the following terms of reference: 'Consistent with current government financial support for renewable energy to review strategy to stimulate the development and application of renewable energy technologies . . .'[2] The sentence reads painfully. Something has gone wrong. Read it again slowly and you will realise that the sentence must have started at the phrase, 'To review strategy to stimulate the development . . .' etc. The Department of Energy decided that this was too open an invitation to a group of largely independent experts and added the opening nine words, 'Consistent with current government financial support for renewable energy . . .' This confined the group to juggling with details of the government's parsimonious budget for renewables and prevented it from suggesting anything requiring a larger outlay.

This is obvious from the construction of the sentence: no one would normally start a sentence in such a backhanded way, and whoever made the insertion forgot to add in a comma after the word 'energy'. Who can have been responsible? We do not know but John Guinness had been appointed only two months earlier as Permanent Under-Secretary with overall control of the Department. He was later to take early retirement in order to become chairman of British Nuclear Fuels. He was and remains an ardent nuclear enthusiast and would not have invited a group appointed by the democratically-elected politicians to comment on his Department's pattern of expenditure, with its strong bias in favour of nuclear power. He—or whoever on his staff wrote the words—did not do so. Instead, the members of the committee became his prisoners.

It would be misleading to think of wave energy as simply an aspect of anti-nuclear feeling. Indeed, in 1976 there was a widespread view, even among many environmentalists, that nuclear energy was welcome: atoms for peace, not war, as campaigners put it. So wave energy needed to establish its own credibility. It had to demonstrate that the day when we needed to boil water to make steam to generate electricity had been overtaken, and that we could now go forward to the idea of obtaining most of our power from cold water, just as in the days of the water wheel, before James Watt. But on that day in 1976, when the oil crisis was at its height, and the prospect of an 'energy gap' was frightening the western world, such considerations were nugatory and luxurious.

Marshall was speaking on behalf of a Labour government which showed no particular enthusiasm for wave energy but it does deserve credit for having initiated the programme. After the first year, the grant was increased to a modest £2.5 million. A year later it scarcely rose, this time to £2.9 million, but with the Minister, Tony Benn, making the announcement himself.

The smallness of this third 'drop in the ocean', as one commentator called it, was defended by Benn on the grounds that 'the limitation to making faster progress is not the level of funding but the state of the technologies involved'. This was what he had been told by his civil servants but it was not quite true. Wave energy researchers could have built full-scale prototypes in the sea at that time if they had been encouraged to go ahead on the understanding that the first devices would be experimental and hazardous. The devices might not even survive for long in heavy seas but that would have been understood. They might not be highly efficient at converting the primary into useful energy but, as Stephen Salter, the best-known of the wave energy inventors, said at the time: 'Efficiency itself is of no concern when the gods pay for the waves'.

Improvements could have been introduced later. For the present, what was needed in my view was a demonstration in the open sea that we had a new source of ever-lasting energy available. Sir Hermann Bondi, who succeeded Marshall as Chief Scientist, told me that he shared this point of view. 'You sound like one of my memos,' he told me. We needed a 'green sea site', as he put it in his Hungarian English, to test the real sea because the sea always had a trick up its sleeve. But sadly the wave energy pioneers were not pressing him. They had a programme of work, funded by government. It was accepted everywhere that the need for energy would grow. We were heading for an energy gap. There was no reason to imagine that the government would suddenly change direction. I can claim to have been the solitary dissident at the Heathrow Hotel conference in 1978 who questioned the pace of development.[3] The wave energy research teams were happy to have a programme of work backed by government. And looking back at those halcyon days, one can understand.

Since then, some £15 million has been spent by Britain on research into wave power. Other countries, particularly Norway and Japan, have made significant contributions. There has been one spectacular mishap in Norway and the low efficiency which was forecast has been demonstrated in a prototype on a Scottish island. There have been numerous obstacles erected by those who did not wish wave energy well. But they have been surmounted and it has survived and grown.

It has been a long and difficult journey. It required mastery of many disciplines ranging from oceanography to mechanical, electrical, chemical and civil engineering, embracing physics, chemistry, mathematics, marine biology, and accountancy on the way. All of that was within the reach of the teams of researchers, engineers and scientists who, for the past 20 years, have tackled the problems in Harwell, Edinburgh, Bergen, Tokyo, Lisbon, Belfast, Cork, Glasgow, Madras, Bristol, Coventry, Southampton, and other centres. What proved more difficult were the obstacles that emerged from the establishment. These included politicians and civil servants, supported by scientists and engineers similar in background to the wave power people but different in one significant respect: they represented the existing sources of energy and they had no wish to see a newcomer with enormous popular appeal moving in on their domain.

Wave energy was seen by them as a greater threat than other renewable sources because, from the start, it was intended as a major supplier to the Grid. Instead of the 'small is beautiful' concept of most other renewables, with their image of new cottage industries with localised technology, it envisaged 2000 MW power stations at sea. They would be equal in capacity to the largest conventional and nuclear stations and they would have an advantage: they aroused no environmental objections at a time when concern about pollution and the countryside were entering the popular arena.

There was not, in my view, a 'conspiracy' against wave power, but there was an instinctive defensive reaction by people who had interests in other energy sources; and once they had made a point, they were not prepared to surrender it and from then on they fought to defend what was, as the record shows, an unworthy position. It has been an ugly spectacle, a classic example of how the establishment defends itself against an intruder that threatens its preserve.

The story that follows has lessons for everyone who may seek to develop a new idea that challenges stability and threatens mediocrity. What follows is an account of the ultimately triumphant war on two fronts fought by the wave energy family, a group of some 300 men and perhaps half a dozen women. It was a struggle against nature, against reaction, against prejudice, and against Mammon.

References

1. Eadie, A. (29 April 1976). *Official report* (Hansard). **910**, columns 150–1, written answers. HMSO, London.
2. Holdgate, M., Archer, M., Bellak, J., Bondi, Sir Hermann, Goldsworthy, P., Leach, G., Lindley, D., Oppenheimer, P., Sainsbury, J., and Wolfendale, A. (1992). *Renewable energy advisory group*, Energy paper Number 60. Appendix 1, A1. Department of Trade and Industry.
3. ETSU (1979). *Proceedings, wave energy conference, Heathrow Hotel, London, November 22–23, 1978*. HMSO, London.

2 How and why it started

349.

12 juillet 1799.

BREVET D'INVENTION DE QÙINZE ANS,

Pour divers moyens d'employer les vagues de la mer,
comme moteurs,

Aux sieurs GIRARD père et fils, de Paris.

La mobilité et l'inégalité successive des vagues, après s'être éle-
vées comme des montagnes, s'affaissent l'instant après, entraînant
dans leurs mouvemens tous les corps qui surnagent, quels que
soient leur poids et leur volume. La masse énorme d'un vaisseau
de ligne, qu'aucune puissance connue ne serait capable de soulever,
obéit cependant au moindre mouvement de l'onde. Qu'on suppose
un instant, par la pensée, ce vaisseau suspendu à l'extrémité d'un
levier, et l'on concevra l'idée de la plus puissante machine qui ait
jamais existé.

C'est principalement sur ce mouvement d'ascension et d'abais-
sement des vagues, qu'est fondée la théorie des nouvelles machines
que nous proposons.

L'application en est aussi simple que l'idée première. Nous avons
imaginé plusieurs moyens d'utiliser cette force; mais le moins
compliqué de tous consiste à adapter ou à suspendre à l'extrémité

13 *

Fig. 2.1 The first patent for a wave energy device, dating from 12 July 1799.

The motion and successive inequality of waves, which after having been elevated like mountains fall away in the following instant, take into their motion all bodies which float on them. The enormous mass of a ship of the line, which no other known force is capable of lifting, responds to the slightest wave motions. If for a moment one imagines this vessel to be suspended from the end of a lever, one has conceived the idea of the most powerful machine which has ever existed . . .

The words were written originally in French, in a style which echoed the majesty of the project: 'La mobilité et l'inégalité successive des vagues, après s'être élevés comme des montagnes. . . .' Those words were filed on 12 July, 1799, as the first-ever patent for a wave energy device, by a father and son named Girard in Paris. Nothing is known of the outcome, if any, of the project. The idea was to build a gigantic lever, with its fulcrum on the shore and with a 'body', the ship of the line as the Girard inventors called it, floating on the sea. As the body rose and fell 'to a greater or lesser height according to the magnitude of the waves', the lever would work up and down and 'could be applied to pumps, to bucket wheels, etc., or directly to mills, fulling machines, tilt hammers, saws, etc.'. Attached to the application were a series of beautifully-drawn designs showing the floating vessel as a pontoon or flat boat. It was an invention similar to the project which Sir Christopher Cockerell was to build and test on the Solent—an articulated raft.

The patent was discovered and translated by Alan E. Hidden, an engineer at Queen's University, Belfast, which has emerged as one of the most successful centres for wave energy research *and* development. It was here that Professor A.A. Wells, FRS, designed a turbine, named after him and used all over the world from Norway to Japan for wave energy. It accepts air from below and above, as the waves rise and fall, and continues to revolve in the same direction. It was also here that Trevor Whittaker became Professor Wells' first student and went on to build Britain's first working wave energy station on the shore of the island of Islay in the Inner Hebrides (see Chapter 10). And it was the same Professor Wells who was the scientist who played the major role in designing the OSPREY (Ocean Swell Powered Renewable Energy), the first wave power station in the open sea (see Chapter 12).

Alan Hidden also uncovered the fact that Thomas Edison, the great inventor who gave us electric light bulbs, almost invented wave energy. He considered using dynamos moored in harbours and powered by the waves to provide warning lights, and while crossing the Atlantic in August 1889 he would sit on deck by the hour and watch the waves. 'It made me perfectly savage to think of all that power going to waste,' he commented[1]. Nothing came of it at that time but, a century later, we can say to Edison: 'Welcome to the club.'

The Girards did not vanish entirely. One can find references to a turbine which bears their name and which contributed to the development of the watermill. But it was to be a long time before engineering techniques and scientific understanding of the waves were to enable us to reach a point where wave energy became a practical possibility.

It was 174 years later, in the depressing winter of 1973, that Mrs Margaret Salter turned on her husband and said: 'Stop lying there looking sorry for yourself. Why don't you solve the energy crisis?' Stephen Salter, an engineer at Edinburgh University, had 'flu. The Arab–Israeli war had brought the oil crisis to a head and we had all become aware that energy was likely to prove at best expensive and possibly scarce. The Arabs might boycott the West; they would at least put up the price and create chaos with our economies. And, as so often happens, it was the increase in price that helped to concentrate the public's attention most wonderfully. When petrol went up from 30p a gallon towards a forecast level of £1, everyone suddenly realised that we were in trouble. The crisis was rather more than some doomwatcher crying out that the end was near.

Just how serious the long-term crisis really is will provide material for numerous discussions until such time as the lights go out, if they ever do. Most futurologists are devoted to graphs which extrapolate a picture of the distant future from fairly recent events. They need not be taken too literally. We know that demographers are unable to prepare our schools for a rise or drop in the birth-rate even five years ahead. They tend to assume that last year's trend will continue indefinitely. We know that town planners can actually offer large sums of money to induce people to leave the inner cities because they are becoming over-crowded and then, within a few years, appeal to them to come back. We know that the Treasury is regularly wrong in its calculations. And we must take into account the fact that most of the forecasts of our fuel consumption were based on the belief that growth would maintain itself at a steady 3.5 per cent.

Let us assume that the forecasts are going to prove hopelessly wrong, in whichever direction you prefer. We are still left with the incontrovertible fact that we are using up our fossil fuels at a rate that cannot be sustained indefinitely. Even if there is nil growth, even if the Third World does not industrialise, the world will one day find itself without oil, coal, gas, or uranium. And in the meantime, by using up those fuels, society will be polluting the air. And it will be condemning tens of thousands of human beings to spending their working life in uncivilised conditions underground, digging up coal and uranium. It is surely obvious that as this process continues, energy will become dear and scarce. At best, we will be forced to ration our use of energy or we can press forward heedlessly and leave it to our grandchildren to work out the consequences.

There is little doubt that society would choose the easy option and let the future take care of itself if the only consideration was a series of warnings. Happily, the increases in price in the 1970s provided the missing element in making the crisis real.

It is important to understand the significance of this development. If there had not been this awareness of the situation, chiefly inside the Government but also backed by a public feeling of anxiety, then the stray remark by Mrs

Salter—if, indeed, she would ever have uttered it—would have had no fruitful outcome. Salter's Duck, if it had ever been invented, would have joined the long list of devices filed in the Patents Office in London and in other countries, and that would have been that.

But, because of the price of oil in 1973, Mrs. Salter's suggestion may go down in history as being as significant as the day when, nearly 200 years ago, James Watt is reputed to have noticed the power of steam lifting the lid of a kettle and set off to invent the steam engine. This may well be a myth. There are authorities who claim that it is one of those nice fictions which has grown up, just as (in a similar area) there is no consensus about whether King Canute believed that the waves would obey his command. But there is no doubt that Mrs Salter is the mother of modern wave energy devices. She is a psychologist, also at Edinburgh University, and she had rightly assessed her husband's reaction. He did not explode in fury as he nursed his wretchedness. Instead, he went off to his study and began work. His wife, he said later with a touch of sour humour, showed 'callous indifference' to his misery. Instead, she gave him a precise objective: 'What she wanted', Salter told me in his laboratory, 'was something which would provide the vast amounts of energy needed, would be clean and safe, would work in winter in Scotland and would last for ever.' He added drily: 'It is a good thing for an engineer to have the design objective clearly specified.' It is an even better thing to note that since that day Salter, and other engineers working on similar projects, have been doing successfully just what the good lady demanded.

To spell it out in a sentence: we could be on the verge of a new industrial revolution in which we shall be able to obtain all the energy we need from the ceaseless motion of the waves.

It is not a new idea. Since M. Girard and his son put their plan in writing, there have been more than 340 patents filed in Britain alone. Most of them, like the Girard scheme, are based on ideas that were not then, and in many cases are still not, practicable. But all of them have been inspired by what all of us have seen and felt. Anyone who has stood on the deck of a ship or a pier, or on a beach, must have been fascinated by the ceaseless, wasted surge of energy as the waves roll and break again and again in an apparently purposeless stream of excitement.

We have all been brought up to know that the water wheel was a main source of power before the steam engine. It is logical to conclude that a water wheel, poised in the ocean, could do the same job. There is a snag: despite their appearance, the waves go up and down in a peculiar motion which we shall study in detail later. They do not move in the way that a millstream or river does, flowing down a hillside and driving a wheel. The tide does flow in that way but it has disadvantages.

This is a convenient point at which to explain why I am writing about wave energy and not about some of the other renewable sources, and perhaps why some of the engineers and scientists engaged in wave energy research and development are so loyal to a discipline that is not the easiest.

For me, the key phrase is 'appropriate technology'. I live on an island, surrounded by some of the world's most fruitful waves, and it seems to me a crime against nature to fail to make use of this gift. The same applies, to a varying extent, to many other countries, including all those in western Europe with a west-facing coastline and Australia, New Zealand, North and South America, South Africa, Japan, India, and such islands as Mauritius. Naturally, other non-polluting sources, such as wind, solar, and tidal, should be pursued for those regions where they are suitable. Equally, there is a strong case for using energy as efficiently as possible by employing measures of energy management, peak load-shedding, and insulation.

Nothing helpful should be excluded when we are contemplating a vast range of demands, from sophisticated grids equipped to handle varying loads without interruption, to developing countries where most of the people have never known the luxury of switching on an electric light.

But I have learned to be wary of governments which, when they are urged to invest in wave energy, immediately direct attention to other alternatives. A classic case, discussed in detail in Chapter 8, was the attempt to justify abandoning research into wave energy in 1982 by lauding the virtues of Hot Dry Rock geothermal energy. This, in its turn, was abandoned in 1991.

Wind farms were for a time regularly praised by the British Government and the CEGB as the preferred way of generating electricity. Its advocates inside the energy establishment were well aware that it would not be easy in a crowded island such as Britain to find sites that did not arouse controversy over noise and visual intrusion, and prevent the wind becoming a major contributor to the Grid, which is required to supply up to 50 000 MW at times of peak demand.

While writing this chapter, I was approached by a leading campaigner for wind power who said how much she was longing for wave energy to be developed because she and her environmentalist organisation were being torn by the growing controversy over wind turbines. It is an issue which has been seized upon by the nuclear lobby, despite its own abysmal record of industrial pollution in such sites as the Romney Marshes (Dungeness), the Lake District (Sellafield), and Sedgemoor (Hinkley Point).

What of basing the wind turbines at sea? There have been plans to station them in inshore waters, for example in the Wash, and the CEGB had plans for a pilot plant off Wells-next-the-Sea in Norfolk. With privatisation, that was abandoned, along with most other research. There is one genuine objection: if you are going to incur the expense of going to sea, then it is common sense to harvest the waves, which are a concentrated form of wind power. Ideally, perhaps we could do both but it is not practical politically, at a time when money is tight. One has to choose.

Wind turbines do have great value in the right circumstances. There is a major role for wind power in countries with lots of room, particularly if they lack useful coastlines. Russia is an obvious choice. And in crowded countries such as Britain they can be introduced, if it is done sensitively, on a moderate scale, with considerable local consultation, supplying 'free' electricity and relieving people of total dependence on the Grid. The approach by big business, attracted in Britain by government subsidies, whose core business is not generating electricity, has not been helpful. There is a need to farm the wind while recognising that it cannot be done on the same scale as in countries less densely populated.

The same applies to tidal power, which is a natural partner for wave (and wind) energy because its timing is certain. It, too, arouses controversy because of environmental concerns. Most of these have been effectively answered, in my opinion, by such experts as Clive Baker in his book *Tidal power*[2], and by the splendid report by Sir Hermann Bondi on a Severn Barrage.[3] But there is plainly room for continuing disagreement in which well-meaning environmentalists will oppose such plans. This hampers development.

Solar energy is wonderful for countries blessed with a suitable climate, which include many in the Third World. It is less appropriate between the latitudes 40° and 60° north and 30° and 50° south, where there is more wave power than sunshine, but even here it is useful for passive heating.

What of energy efficiency and conservation? Naturally, everyone (except the suppliers of electricity and gas) is in favour of reducing the growing demand for artificial heating and freezing, and is opposed to the wasteful use of electricity and other energy sources. So sensible measures to reduce demand are welcome.

But we are talking about a *growing* demand which will increase ever more rapidly in the industrialised countries, and later in the Third World as those countries emerge from poverty and become industrialised. Much of the gain from more economic use of energy will be needed just to reduce the rate of increase. Even in developed countries, there is a real need for better insulation to enable millions of people to live in greater comfort, to live better and longer. Welcome as that is, it does not necessarily reduce energy demand significantly. We cannot escape from the fact that the civilised world has an enormous energy demand which will have to be met from new generating capacity.

Considering electricity alone, which is what wave energy provides, in Britain we use up to 50 000 MW at peak periods and this is officially forecast to grow to 76 500 MW by the year 2000[4]. If demand is reduced marginally by sensible economies, fine. Any reduction in demand, as a result of insulation, conservation, energy management, and peak-load lopping, is helpful; but nothing can remove the need for a civilised society to generate a vast amount of electricity.

The intelligent energy policy is to employ the appropriate renewables. Solar-cell-generated electricity has been used on mobile refrigerators in the tropics to enable medicines to be taken to remote areas. Wind pumps have been introduced by Intermediate Technology to bring water to African villages. In the Mediterranean, where the waves are small and the sunshine is plentiful and the winds are often fulsome, you would use wave energy only for small-scale generation and the other renewables to supply the local grid. There is no sense in which one is superior to another in all circumstances. Choices have to be made according to the locality. And in much of the world, for an industrialised or developing country with a good seaboard and a favourable wave climate, there is nothing better than the waves.

Offshore wave energy is the only renewable to have been certified by the Department of Energy as presenting no difficult dilemmas for society: 'No major deleterious environmental effects of the converters themselves could be identified, provided that the converters are well offshore'.[5]

References

1. Clark, R.W. (1977), Edison: *The man who made the future*. Macdonald and Jane's, London.
2. Baker, A.C. (1991). *Tidal power*. Peter Peregrinus, London.
3. Bondi, H. (1981). *Tidal power from the Severn estuary*. Energy Paper 46.
4. National Grid Company (1994). *Seven year statement*. NGC, Coventry.
5. Dawson, J.K. (1979). *Wave energy*. Energy paper number 42, 89. HMSO. London.

What is a wave? 3

When Stephen Salter began his studies late in 1973, he set out first to visit the Institute of Oceanographic Sciences (IOS), a bleak collection of buildings on a side road somewhere between Witley and Wormley in Surrey. Everyone involved in wave energy followed the same path, seeking out Laurence Draper who showed unlimited patience in spelling out the basic facts about the waves, a subject on which he is one of the foremost experts in the world, to the growing stream of inventors and experts in other disciplines such as mechanical, constructional and electrical engineering, and to me. Draper has the gift of simplicity. He needed it less for that first visitor, as Salter is a physicist. But the waves are an esoteric branch of physics.

Salter's first need was information. He then needed a suitable site for experiments to find out just how much wave energy there was available, and Draper knew how to find it. He telephoned to Rear Admiral D.A. Dunbar Nasmith, CB, DSC, in Inverness, where he was Deputy Chairman of the Highlands and Islands Development Board (now Highlands and Islands Enterprise). It was not easy. It will be appreciated that there are problems in launching oneself into this topic. 'You see, Admiral, there is a scheme to get electricity from the waves and we would like to use your beaches . . .'

Unknown to Draper, the Admiral had a visitor in his office at the time who was to prove a key figure. Father Calum MacLellan was the priest in charge of St Mary's at Benbecula in the Outer Hebrides and his parish was to prove the most suitable site for the first tests. The sea in that area is beautifully rough and therefore productive; and a major industry is lobster fishing, which means that trawlers stay away and would not therefore be fouling the Waverider Buoy which Salter and Draper planned to tether off shore to obtain accurate measurements of the waves. Benbecula is the island where the Reformation stopped half way and the southern half is correspondingly fierce in its Catholicism. Without Father MacLellan, a foreigner had no hope.

But on that day, the only concern was to obtain the support of the Admiral, who gave it readily, and remained a keen enthusiast. Draper, and a colleague, John Driver, an expert on wave recording instruments, set off for the Outer Hebrides. They were met by an Army colonel from the nearby rocket range and he, like practically everyone else who first encounters the idea, was intrigued. He took his own car and drove the two men over the area looking for a suitable site. Father MacLellan's parish was the answer. But how could one win the cooperation of the local villagers, who were suspicious of any outsiders, let alone a crackpot pair of boffins who wanted to plant bits of machinery in the lobster beds?

'It was then that Father MacLellan entered the scene', Draper told me. 'It is not too much to say that the villagers are devout Roman Catholics and Father MacLellan's word is law. He is an impressive man, a person with whom we rapidly developed a friendship based on respect, and if we had not been able to reach agreement with him, it would not have been on. But at short notice he had interrupted his busy schedule and hurried over to the military base where we discovered that he was on good terms with the Admiral and so had heard about us before we arrived, and he said he felt sure that it was a worth-while project.'

Father MacLellan confirmed this to me while retaining a cautious attitude. 'There is nothing wrong with putting down an instrument to find out whether wave energy is going to be a feasible proposition', he said. 'And I do not believe it is contrary to God's purpose. But if it does become feasible, one would have to consider very carefully in case it changes the whole environment and interferes with the lobster fishermen. Our information was that they wanted one single buoy. There is no possible objection to that. But they wanted to be sure that lobster fishermen would not be picking it up and looking at it and that it might disappear. They have lost other buoys.'

With the assurance of acceptance, the two men began the first scientific study of the waves close to the west of the Outer Hebrides.

How does a wave travel? It was, as in so many other areas, Leonardo da Vinci who was an early explorer. He noted that when the wind blew across a field of corn, it looked as though there were waves of corn running across the field. In fact, the individual heads of corn were making only a slight movement and when the wind dropped they were back almost where they had started. A more common description nowadays is to compare it with the movement in a skipping rope. You waggle one end and a wave *form* travels to the other end.

In a seminal address to the Royal Society of Arts in March 1975, one of the great pioneers of wave energy, A.N. Walton Bott, whose scheme for Mauritius was a precursor of the Norwegians' most successful device, and who was the first practical engineer to tackle the problem in modern times, said:

The visible effect can be seen from the motion of a floating bottle or ball which, as the wave passes, describes a circular motion returning to approximately its original position. I have never yet been able to think of a suitable mechanical analogy but perhaps the pushing by hand of a ridge in a carpet from the centre to a wall edge is somewhere near; for a wave does move across the carpet but every strand of pile remains firmly in position . . .

Each water particle describes a circular path in a vertical plane at right angles to the wave line, the diameter of these orbits diminishing rapidly with water depth at right angles to the wave line, ultimately becoming zero.[1]

It is essential to grasp the concept that the waves are not tides or currents. It has been possible to identify waves arriving in Cornwall as having originated in the Antarctic but this does not, of course, mean a current of icy water cutting across the Gulf Stream.

The seaman divides waves into two main types—those generated by a local wind and known as the wind sea, and those which come from remote storms and arrive in the form of a swell sea. In layman's terms, it is the difference between a busy sea of lively bobbing waves and a long, sweeping, rolling sea. These are Bott's water particles turning in diminishing circles. And then: 'the wave rears up until it catches its feet, so to speak, on the ocean floor and falls head over heels as it crashes on a reef or beach'.

Most of our knowledge of wave energy is recent. There were some studies over the past 150 years, but no real development until, as in so many other activities, the needs of warfare provided an incentive for government expenditure. It had been the same with steam power: the Napoleonic wars increased the cost of animal feedstuffs and made steam more economic than horses. It had been the same with nuclear power: Sir John Anderson, the Minister in charge, noted: 'In four years, our scientists solved a problem that in peace might have taken 25–50 years.' And with the waves, it was the need to invade continental Europe in 1944 which suddenly aroused interest and a readiness to spend money.

Fleets of landing craft had to be put ashore in Normandy. An artificial harbour called the Mulberry had to be towed across the Channel and installed. There was little satisfactory information available. I recall an appeal going out from the Ministry of Information for holiday snapshots showing the beaches of northern Europe. The Admiralty set up a Research Laboratory Group W (the mysterious letter stood for Waves but it was secret, see?).

That unit became the nucleus of the National Institute of Oceanography and has now been re-christened the IOS. It is run by the Natural Environment Research Council. Another organisation, about which more later, is the Hydraulics Research Station at Wallingford, in Oxfordshire, now HR Wallingford Ltd., which is dedicated to checking the validity of engineering designs for harbours, ship moorings, and so on. It had a plan of its own for wave energy, reflecting its involvement in the civil engineering side. The IOS covers basic research into the oceans, from the character of the waves and the behaviour of the water, including tides, to marine biology, chemistry, and the geology of the seabed.

The bespectacled physicist in charge of those early IOS studies on wave energy, Laurence Draper, somewhat improbably owes his involvement to an interest in rock climbing. He was a student at Nottingham University in the early fifties, after being a scientific assistant with ICI. He felt little inclination to return there and had not much idea of what he would do with his degree. But he was a keen mountaineer and one day read in a climbing magazine the obituary of a talented climber named P.J.H. Unna. Not long after, he was reading the scientific journal *Nature* and came across an article on the waves by P.J.II. Unna. IIe thought that if one mountaineer could be fascinated by the waves, surely another could be, too. Later, he came across a report that the newly-formed NIO was measuring waves, so he wrote to them, to ask if they would like a helping hand in the holidays.

They had never before had a holiday relief but the idea appealed. He spent a summer with them and the director invited him to come back when he had his degree. He did just that. On this completely illogical, unscientific happening, linking the mountains and the sea, may depend much of our energy future today.

Draper now looks back coolly at the primitive efforts of Research Laboratory Group W as they wrestled with the problem of crossing to Normandy. 'They got it right in 1944', he told me, 'but only just. They failed to fully understand the problem of swell.' Some of the chaps in the landing craft would agree, feelingly. Trust the Navy, as we used to say in the RAF.

He was at the centre of what he happily called 'one of today's growth industries, the systematic collection of instrumentally-measured wave data'. He and his colleagues became world leaders in knowledge of what is called 'the wave climate'. The Institute of Oceanographic Sciences' methods are used world-wide. The Department of Energy was well aware of its importance and supported it. Britain was the first country to have a map of predicted extreme waves right round the coast. That map provided the basis of all North Sea oil operations and was able to save the Americans from what, in Draper's opinion, would have been certain catastrophes. They were convinced that their experience in the Gulf of Mexico would serve them well in the North Sea. In particular, they were rather over-confident because they had the experience of coping with hurricanes. 'But', as Draper told them, 'hurricanes move very fast and so they do not produce the biggest waves. They asked us what would be the biggest that they should expect if the platforms were to be there for 50 years so we looked at the wave data and came up with a figure of 17 m. The Americans seemed to think that we were just trying to cover ourselves. They thought that 12 m would be the biggest. The difference in cost then was about £4 million for every 10 ft (nearly 4 m) on each platform. But they have since seen waves bigger than that themselves and the oil platforms would probably have fallen apart if they had followed their own instincts. Even so, there have had to be restrictions placed on the use of the early platforms, which have to be evacuated in rough weather, and which have had second platforms built alongside to take people off.'

It is worth pausing to appreciate that a wave 17 m high is the size of, say, a five-storey block of flats. The waves off the Outer Hebrides, where wave energy generators will probably be based, can exceed 24 m, the 'worst' sea in the world, probably worse even than Cape Horn, and therefore the best for our purposes.

The science of wave climatology has grown spasmodically, usually as a poor and almost unknown relation of other branches of science and engineering. It was needed for wartime landings and then came increasing demands for information for the building of lighthouses, pipelines, break-waters, harbours and, in recent years, oil platforms, hovercraft, and hydrofoil services. And now comes wave energy, its needs arising to justify the collection of all this once-purposeless information, like feathers folding into a dove's tail.

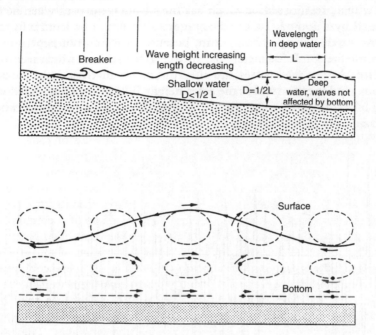

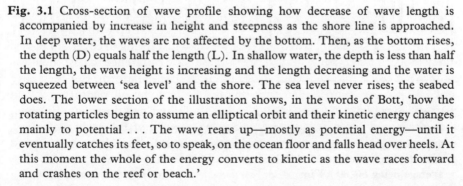

Fig. 3.1 Cross-section of wave profile showing how decrease of wave length is accompanied by increase in height and steepness as the shore line is approached. In deep water, the waves are not affected by the bottom. Then, as the bottom rises, the depth (D) equals half the length (L). In shallow water, the depth is less than half the length, the wave height is increasing and the length decreasing and the water is squeezed between 'sea level' and the shore. The sea level never rises; the seabed does. The lower section of the illustration shows, in the words of Bott, 'how the rotating particles begin to assume an elliptical orbit and their kinetic energy changes mainly to potential . . . The wave rears up—mostly as potential energy—until it eventually catches its feet, so to speak, on the ocean floor and falls head over heels. At this moment the whole of the energy converts to kinetic as the wave races forward and crashes on the reef or beach.'

The information has been built up with the aid of three main types of wave recorder, on the seabed, on the surface, and in ships. It is available so that a civil engineer can collect a graph from which it is easy to read off the expected wave height in any area, provided certain basic and easily obtainable information is available.

One of the first recording devices was the spark plug recorder. A series of spark plugs, each with a horizontal electrode, are stationed in a vertical line with the plugs a few inches apart. As the sea water rises and falls, the plugs under water are shorted and it is easy to collect a record. It is ingenious but not as sensitive as others which are designed to register a difference as small as 0.25 mm (1/100th of an inch). One such development is underwater measurement with a pressure sensor which has the advantage that it is less likely to be damaged by shipping. Its disadvantage is that it can be used only in fairly shallow water, down to about 12 m, because waves do not penetrate too far down into the sea. It is a metal box, sitting on the seabed, which records water pressure. As a wave crosses the site, the depth increases and so does the pressure, and the box records the extra height. The information is recorded on a graph or a cassette, either in the box itself or back on shore to where the information is relayed by cable.

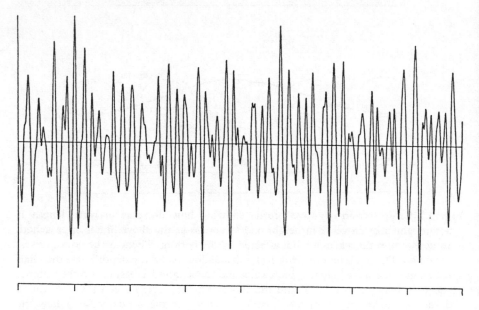

Fig. 3.2 Typical wave record, taken over 8 minutes. (For another way of representing wave climate see the scatter diagram in Appendix 1.) For deep water waves approaching our western shores, the power level varies from practically zero on calm days up to over 10 000 kW in some of the largest deep sea waves, with the yearly average being 60–80 kW/m.

A more sophisticated device, which can be used in deep water, is the Shipborne Wave Recorder which was invented as long ago as 1951 by an IOS scientist, M.J. Tucker. A pressure sensor is mounted inside a stationary ship, such as a weather or light ship, below the waterline. Then a hole is bored in the side. As the water deepens and shallows outside the ship, the pressure sensor records the changes. But it has to be coupled with an accelerometer which registers the movement of the ship itself. Then the two measurements are added together automatically and the graph prints out a picture of the waves on the site. This became the main wave-recording workhorse of the IOS.

It was put first on one of the IOS research ships but they are required for many duties and are moving around all the time. The same applies to weather ships—for instance, the best known site, Station India (in the North Atlantic, despite her name) would be served by half a dozen ships with turns of duty of four weeks on and two weeks off. Nevertheless, one of the Meteorological Office's vessels, *Weather Explorer*, was fitted with a recorder in 1953 and by 1965 she and her successors had amassed enough information at Station India for the wave climate there to be known quite well. In fact, these measurements became the basic information on which the wave energy potential of the Atlantic was calculated. Subsequently, Trinity House gave permission for one of its Light Vessels to be used, but as they remain on station for three years at a time they have to make a special trip into dry dock to be fitted because, as Mr Draper remarked, Trinity House is rather strict and doesn't like chaps drilling holes below the water line while ships are at sea. Meanwhile, a replacement ship has to be provided. That costs money. So, up to that point, it had all been done on a string-and-Scotchtape basis.

It was then that, once more, Defence came to the rescue. The military needed information about the waves for radar research. There was no shortage of money. A Light Vessel called the *Morecambe Bay*, stationed in the Irish Sea, was swiftly called in and a replacement sent out. Trinity House and the IOS worked fast and within six weeks had installed their recorder and the ship went back on station. The experiment was intended to last for a few months and, indeed, once the military had the information they needed, they were happy to let the IOS have their bits of equipment back. But the IOS were in no hurry. They had realised that for the first time they were receiving instrumentally-measured details of the wave climate at an offshore location.

The main purpose of the exercise at that time was to enable the man in charge, Professor J. Darbyshire, to develop a method of forecasting the height of waves by what is known as 'hindcasting'. If you know the strength of the wind and the distance and length of time over which it has blown, you can calculate the height of the waves. But data had to be obtained before the method could be developed.

As soon as the IOS realised how valuable were its first consistent records from a permanent site, it approached Trinity House for more facilities. It obtained permission to remove the recorder from the Irish Sea and install it on the Smith's Knoll Light Vessel in the southern North Sea in 1959. Another set of records was obtained. Then records were collected from the Helwick Light Vessel in the Bristol Channel and from the Sevenstones Light Vessel off Land's End. Eleven other Light Vessels were eventually employed, and several are still operational today.

The IOS did encounter one area that proved unexpectedly difficult. There is no Light Vessel in deep water off Scotland because, as Draper put it, 'there are all those nice little islands to put lighthouses on'. But he stumbled by chance on a reference to a Norwegian Rescue Vessel. The British had once been asked to contribute to the cost of it and had refused and everyone concerned from then on had ignored its existence. Draper wrote to the Norwegians and explained what he was trying to do. And he was able to add that the information he obtained would almost certainly be of use to them. Happily, they proved to be less narrow in their views than the British and a recorder was installed in 1969 and proved to be a vital source which has contributed greatly to the safety of the platforms built in both the British and the Norwegian sectors since then.

Subsequently, another recording instrument has been in increasing prominence. It is a Dutch invention called the Waverider Buoy, a bright yellow and orange sphere, 80 cm in diameter, moored to the seabed and tethered (literally) by a piece of elastic. There are dozens of them now functioning, one of them in the sea off Benbecula. They transmit their information over a radio link and their only disadvantage is that they can be damaged easily by shipping or by curious seamen. The aerial is particularly susceptible to light-fingered gentlemen.

The work of collecting data had started by a happy accident but it was to prove timely. The discovery of North Sea oil was round the corner and the oil companies were soon desperate for information. It was provided for them but it is worth noting that their gratitude has not taken the most practical form. Some of the companies still want their environmental data free, which drives the more enlightened ones who pay for their own studies to act as though they were afraid that a playback of information might help their rivals and to treat their knowledge as a commercial secret. They were all beneficiaries of the sort of information that only governments would have subsidised in the days when its practical advantages were not apparent. But—business is business, once the assets have been gained at public expense. And it was also at public expense that the next major steps forward in the science of wave recording were made. They changed the nature of the task.

Most people would assume that instruments in or on the sea would be the best and most obvious place to collect information about the waves. But in 1946 the Admiralty Research Laboratory decided to gain a bird's eye view of the scene and opened the way to a completely different and, eventually, much more rewarding approach. It mounted a radar unit in a Lancaster bomber and sent it out over the Irish Sea to fly over the waves at a height of 25–30 metres—not much higher than the highest possible wave peaks.

'Flying so low across the Irish Sea in winds up to Force 7 was hazardous and often extremely uncomfortable,' record three scientists from the Natural Environment Research Council.[2] 'Some indications of variations in wave height and period with fetch were obtained but the programme was curtailed, apparently because of the high cost. Nearly 20 years passed before the technique was used again, by the US Naval Oceanographic Office, from a Lockheed Super Constellation flying at an altitude of 152 m.'

And then, in the 1970s, an altimeter was installed on space satellite GEOS-3 and it provided some (incomplete) wave data on seasonal variations during its three-year lifespan. A significant breakthrough came in 1978 when the US satellite Seasat provided data for the whole of its 100-day mission, the first global measurements of significant wave height in a continous operation, which the earlier satellites had been unable to provide.

The launch of the European Space Agency satellite, ERS-1 in 1991 also with an altimeter aboard, was the next step.[3] It contained a radar altimeter giving wind speed, wave height, and sea surface topography data. Five or six satellites with wave sensors aboard are expected to be in orbit during the 1990s. This will increase significantly the amount of wave data available. 'One radar altimeter sampling every 7 km will produce as many estimates of significant wave height in a single day as a waverider sampling every three hours does in 20 years.'[2]

The primary purpose of a satellite's radar altimeter is to measure the satellite's altitude but scientists realised that it was possible to analyse the return signals and arrive at estimates of significant wave height. These are complementary to the measurements taken on the surface from ships and buoys, which can record wave length and period as well as height. Altimeters can record only the height, which is the most important feature but does not give a full picture of a sea state. Against this, the satellites cover a much larger area and in that way have transformed the operation of measurement. One advantage of satellite measurement is noted by Challenor: there is no tendency 'to under-sample regions of extreme waves as occurs, for example, with ship measurements'.[4]

Satellites have provided some support for the view, first expressed by Draper[5] in 1988 that wave heights in the North Atlantic had been increasing, a fact which is still intriguing the wave energy community. At one site, a weather ship recorded a rise of 40 per cent between 1962 and 1985. One optimistic explanation offered tentatively by Salter is that ships may have been more cautious in making illegal discharges and oil, as we know, tends to calm troubled waters; there will also have been a halt to leakages from ships destroyed during World War II.[6] Another possible explanation is that there has been a shift in the pattern of the winds that generate the waves and that this shift in wind patterns may be a response to global warming. Most scientists think that there has not been sufficient time to decide whether it is part of a trend over the whole region.[3] Whatever the explanation, it is good news for wave energy because it means that there is more of it about.

Challenor notes that in 1986 the highest mean significant wave heights of 4.5–5 m were observed in the southern ocean in winter and during the southern summer the values there remained high, dropping only to 4.5 m.

In the northern hemisphere wave heights also reached 4.5 m. (between October and December in the Atlantic and between January and March in the Pacific). But during the northern summer the values for both oceans dropped to around 2 m. The area, too, of high wave heights is greater in the south. This means that wave energy inputs all the year round are available to large areas of the southern parts of South America, South Africa, Australia, and New Zealand, giving them even greater potential than the northern hemisphere.

The pictures could not have been obtained by conventional means; only the arrival of satellites has made such observation possible. It is particularly helpful for the southern hemisphere, as shipping movements in the areas south of the land masses are not as frequent as in the northern hemisphere.

The significance of the height of a wave is that it gives an accurate indication of its power. The wave consists of kinetic and potential energy—in simple language, the energy available for release as the wave falls (potential) and the energy contained in the moving water (kinetic). Research has shown that both are roughly equal, so the height is an excellent indication of how much energy it represents. The formula for calculating wave power is shown in Appendix 1, Wave language. The information is obtained from readings over fixed periods, typically for about 1000 seconds, or just over a quarter of an hour, every three hours. You want to describe the wave climate for the whole year at one site but you would have hundreds of thousands of waves to consider so you try to reduce it to something typical by choosing 1000 typical representative waves. One three-hour recording is taken and the data recorded is measured electronically and analysed to calculate a representative wave which has the 'average' height and period of all the waves during the three hours' measurement. This is then plotted as one of the thousand representative waves on a chart called a scatter diagram (see Appendix 1, p.197). It shows on the left-hand upright the significant wave height in metres and on the base the period between waves in seconds. The frequency of occurrence of each combination of wave height, and the time between waves, is plotted for the duration of each recording and that produces the representative wave—the average wave with respect to power. In a year you have hundreds of thousands of waves and you try to reduce them to something typical.

On the specimen scatter diagram, an experienced researcher will note at a glance that there have been, for example, 37 representative waves with a height of 5 m and a period of 9.5 seconds but only six representative waves with a height of 8 m and a period of 10.5 seconds. The longest period is 13.5 seconds for 10 waves of 2.5 m. There are not many waves below 2 m. There were several waves of eight seconds, one of them 8 m high but two others of the same period only 4 m in height. These readings will tell the researcher what sort of sea it is—rollers or an excited local sea.

Ultimately, because we are dealing with power, we want to know how many kilowatts this will generate across every metre of wavefront. For deep water waves approaching the western shores of the UK, the power level varies from practically zero on calm days up to over 10 000 kW in some of the largest deep sea waves, with the yearly average being 60–80 kW/m. This variation in power level poses problems for the designer: the average power captured by his device might be 80 kW/m but the device has to withstand the battering of some extreme, infrequent waves over 100 times the average power level.

A third key factor is the frequency with which the waves arrive. This depends to some extent on the length of what is called 'the fetch', the uninterrupted distance over which the wind has been blowing across the sea before reaching the point of interest. A long fetch, with waves generated by storms far away, produces swell, the long period waves or rollers which roar in majestically on, for instance, the western side of the north Atlantic.

There are also the local seas, sometimes called storm waves, and the local features produced as the waves approach the shore and the depth is reduced. Here the shallow waves become subject to friction from the seabed, to refraction which turns them from their normal path, and to diffraction as they avoid barriers to their forward movement. They lose energy from some interruptions to their freedom and gain it from others which focus their power on to 'hot spots', the best sites to station shoreline wave energy converters.

But the main centres to capture the power of the waves must be out at sea, where the rollers arrive after crossing a thousand or more miles of fetch. It has to be a straight line without interruption from land. This, combined with knowledge of the wind speed, enables scientists to forecast wave heights by the method of hindcasting. Records exist going back 100 years of winds over the sea. By knowing the expected wind speed at any season, the distance of the fetch and the length of time that the wind has blown, it is possible for anyone with a minimum of technical knowledge to read-off on a chart the predicted wave height. One can also read-off another chart the wave period, the time it takes between the arrival of one crest and the next.

This period can vary from 2 seconds to above 20. And by reading backwards from the time interval between the arrival of waves of different period, it is possible to discover where the waves originated. Thus it is possible to say occasionally that a wave reaching Cornwall originated in Antarctica.

Sea waves are unlike radio waves which always travel at the same speed. In the same severe storm, there will be waves with periods from 2 seconds up to 20. The longer the period between waves, the faster they travel. So waves with 20 seconds between them travel faster than those with 19 seconds. If you are a long way from the source of the storm which first whipped up the sea, then the waves of a 20 second period will arrive first, having outpaced the waves of 19 seconds, which will have outpaced those of 18 seconds, and so on. The further the waves have travelled, the greater will be the lead of the longer period wave over the shorter. It is like two planes taking off at the same time, one going at 300 km/hr and the other at 600 km/hr. Just after take-off, they are close together. As the distance gets greater, the gap between them grows.

If you know these facts, and the time difference between their arrivals at some other point, you can work out how far away they started. An example from the IOS charts will help to demonstrate this. Take a wind speed of 50 knots and a fetch of 100 km. Then what is known as the 'significant wave height' will be 6 m. Assume the same windspeed of 50 knots and a fetch of 1000 km, then the 'significant wave height' will be 8 m. It is obvious to anyone who has ever done an algebraic equation that armed with any two of these three facts, one can find the third. But it took a long time and extraordinary talent to reach this point, which is going to prove vital to all our futures.

I have deliberately over-simplified the problem. How, for instance, do the waves in a storm vary so much in height? Mr Draper's answer gives some indication of the difficulties that he and his colleagues and predecessors have had to grapple with:

Each one of the waves was generated by the same wind over the same water and at the same time, and yet they come in sizes over a range of more than 10 to 1 in height. The explanation is that waves are remarkably short-lived creatures, no storm wave ever exists as an identifiable entity for more than about two minutes. Even the 80-foot monster has a very short moment of glory and if one could follow its progress it would be seen to diminish in size and within a couple of minutes it would subside into the random jumble of the sea, never again to reappear in that form. This behaviour is a consequence of the fact that wave energy in the sea is locked in a very wide range of wave components, each with its own height and period.

The key to the problem is that each component travels at a rate determined by its period, so that the faster components (which have the longer periods) will continually overtake the slower ones. Consider, for a moment, the simple case of a wave system consisting of two components travelling at slightly different speeds. As the crest of one component overtakes the other one, a bigger wave will temporarily appear. Similarly, as a crest overtakes the other component's trough the sea will be relatively placid. In a real sea there are not just two but millions of wave components (an infinite number if one takes it to its mathematical limit), each travelling along at its own pre-ordained speed. Just occasionally, purely by chance, a very large number of components will all be trying to overtake each other at one point in space and time, and the unfortunate mariner who happens to be there too will be able to report an enormous wave.[3]

One begins to see the problem of identifying—the problem. That is one reason why the engineers and scientists grappling with wave energy are even today, when the need for more energy is starker than ever before, tending to caution. The most elaborate tests, in laboratories or lakes or sheltered coastal waters, can never reproduce the fury of the open sea.

Yet it is a fact that, even before they knew what they were facing, Victorian engineers were able to build harbours, breakwaters, and piers which could survive the sea for 150 and more years. The surge wave which swept away part of Margate pier in January, 1978 was evidence not that the sea was irresistible but that what civil engineers could do in 1800, in providing a structure that would last until 1978, can be eminently better done now.

One must not be unfair: a pier, like an oil platform, is designed to allow the sea the minimum resistance while wave energy generators will need to absorb and process its energy. They will, therefore, be subject to greater stress. But technology has advanced a long, long way since those seaside piers, and even the North Sea oil platforms, were erected.

I have used the phrase 'significant wave height' and it is defined by the scientists as 'the average height of the highest one-third of the waves'. This formula has been reached after studying the print-outs of wave recorders. And the extraordinary thing is that the most modern data, obtained by the sophisticated electronics that have been developed in the last 20 years, confirm the old mariners' stories about the waves they survived. As Draper puts it, 'If the heights of 99 consecutive waves are measured, the significant height is the average height of the 33 biggest and it is this height which is very close to the figure which an experienced seaman would give if one were to ask him to estimate the wave height.'

Thus, in 1839, a Captain Robert Fitz-Roy reported a wave 18 m high in the Atlantic and an American naval ship, the *Rampapo*, claimed to have survived a wave of 34 m in the Pacific in 1933. Fantasies, one might have said—until recently. But now we have an authenticated report of a 27 m wave hitting a drilling rig off Vancouver Island in the Pacific and in 1971 a wave of 26 m was experienced by the weather ship *Weather Reporter* out in the North Atlantic with a shipborne wave recorder to confirm it. So the old salts, with just their eyes to rely on, have had their tales confirmed by modern science. Instincts are not always wrong.

On the other side of the coin, Draper has a cold douche of water to throw over a hallowed myth. There are, he has noted, such things as 'freak' waves which exist for a brief moment as countless wave components come together. They rarely come singly. Their usual appearance is one huge wave followed by a few slightly smaller, stretching over a distance of hundreds of feet, 'all following each other obediently in a regular procession along the Loch before disappearing as they get out of phase (or diving for food, if you prefer it)'. And he adds, as a good scientist must: 'It should be pointed out that such a plausible explanation cannot prove that the Loch Ness Monster *is* just a figment of its disciples' imaginations. . . .'[5]

When he wrote that, in 1971 in *Motor Boat and Yachting*, he could not have guessed that within seven years there would be a major project, equipped with all the latest technological equipment, based on the shores of the Loch for the purpose of launching a string of wave energy devices, and with the prospect of discovering, as an accidental by-product of research designed for a different purpose, if there really is a monster around.

References

1. Bott, A.N. Walton (1975). Power plus proteins from the sea. *Journal of the Royal Society of Arts*. **CXXIII**. 486–503.
2. Carter, D.J.T., Challenor, P.G., and Srokosz, M.A. (1988). Satellite remote sensing and wave studies into the 1990s. *Int. J. Remote Sensing*, **9**, 1835–46.
3. Marine Sciences (1992). *Eye on the Earth*. Natural Environment Research Council, Swindon.
4. Challenor, P.G., Foale, S., and Webb, D.J. (1990). Seasonal changes in the global wave climate measured by the Geosat altimeter. *Int. J. Remote Sensing*, **11**, 2205–13.
5. Draper, L. (1971). Waves how high? *Motor Boat and Yachting*, **114**, 49–56.
6. Salter, S. (1988). *World progress in wave energy*. Paper delivered to the 10th anniversary conference of the National academy of science and technology of the Philippines, Manila, 12–14 July 1988.

From water wheel to gigawatt 4

How serious is wave energy? Are we discussing a minor option to the ways in which science provides us with an inessential service (and then tries to persuade us that we always needed it)? Or are we discussing a major development in our technological history, comparable with the discovery of steam power, which can provide an answer to the demand for power when the fossil fuels give out or become too expensive, or when environmental concerns make public opinion turn sharply against nuclear power, gas, coal, and oil?

We need to keep a grasp of fundamental values, those which gave birth to the demand for clean, safe electricity. There is no such thing as smoke-free smoke and so burning fossil fuels must cause pollution. And even the supporters of nuclear power accept that it cannot be 100 per cent safe, which means that nuclear accidents are inevitable; and when things go wrong the damage can be appalling. It also produces radioactive waste and society has so far found no acceptable method of disposing of it.

Countries which have to buy and burn increasingly expensive diesel fuel, gas, or coal to make electricity will become desperate to find a better way. That includes many of the Third World countries which want to escape from the poverty of the underdeveloped.

All of this is logical and should be non-contentious. It has an immediate appeal to people concerned with the future of society, particularly the young. But why wave power? Why not some other, perhaps cheaper, simpler way? I chose, and advocate, the appeal of wave power because it does not create environmental problems—its power stations are out at sea, where nobody lives. I do not wish to decry other renewables which may be the appropriate technology in environments where wave power is less suitable. But it is my conviction that, for countries blessed with long coastlines, particularly those in the roaring forties—the stormy areas, between 40° and 50° latitude, north and south of the equator—which happen to be where I live, wave energy is the one with most promise. The most favourable zones include much of western Europe as well as long stretches of the Pacific coasts of the US and Chile, and countries such as New Zealand, Australia, and South Africa. Those are the obvious ones for large-scale wave power generation from full-scale stations with installed capacity of 2000 MW. Indeed, some countries such as Portugal and Ireland will have more wave energy than they can use and will be able to export electricity. But the technology is also easily adapted to countries without such a vast wave power resource; the Norwegians (whose achievements arc discussed in detail in Chapter 9) showed everyone how wave power can be used for small-scale generation, and countries with less fruitful seas to harvest, such as India, Indonesia, Ghana, and Malaysia, or amid less powerful waves in the Sea of Japan, are well placed to build perhaps smaller stations on or off the shore.

But then comes the second question: can the waves supply anything like the amount of electricity that a developed society needs? How large is this resource? It always seemed to me rather silly to be answering this question at a time when there was not a single wave power station at sea. The wave energy teams were trying to get enough money out of mean-minded governments to build an experimental prototype, probably a mere 1 MW device, and were being asked how much renewable energy there was in all the seas all over the world. It was rather like asking the Wright Brothers about the potential capacity of a jumbo jet.

But the question of ultimate potential was and is a question that deserves an answer, however distant the day when we need to worry about the total available to each country and however imprecise the answer must be at this stage of discovery. One of the most respected experts in this area is Dr Johannes Falnes of the University of Trondheim in Norway. In a survey of wave energy[1] he quotes two figures: 1 TW and 10 TW. The first is the power represented by waves hitting all coasts in the world and is, as he says, 'of the same order of magnitude as the world's present *electricity* production'. The second figure is the 'global natural power potential' and includes the harvesting of wave power in the wide open sea, 'energy which is otherwise lost in wave breaking and friction', and is 'of the same order of magnitude as the total present-day *energy* consumption'.

At this stage, like all discussion of this topic, the prospect sounds Utopian. But let us remember that only 30 years ago the idea of giant oil platforms marching out into the North Sea all the way from Scotland to Norway would also have appeared fanciful. But as the demand has grown, the oil prospectors have moved further and further into inhospitable waters and are now considering the prospects for the west coast of Scotland and are moving into the Atlantic. The wave power researchers will do the same.

Here we need to pause to consider the figures given by Dr Falnes. A terawatt is 1000 GW or 1 000 000 MW. For comparison, a large power station usually has a capacity of around 1500 MW. The installed capacity in Britain, driving all the machines and providing all the lighting and much of the heating in a highly industrialised country, is 50 000 MW. So Dr Falnes is talking about a resource which is 200 times larger than the capacity required in, for example, one highly industrialised country to meet the highest demand for half an hour on the coldest day of an exceptionally cold winter. And this is not a stockpile that is going to be used up. The waves go on for ever.

These figures, like all the others in an unknown technology, need to be qualified. How much of it can be brought ashore? And, of course, there is the nagging Treasury question of how much wave electricity will cost.

I resolved when I started work on this edition that I would not allow this issue to dominate the book in the way that it has been allowed to dominate much public debate, because it is nothing but myth-making. I can show you official documents which say that one kilowatt-hour of electricity from one particular device, the HRS Rectifier, will cost 60p and it was discarded early on, on the grounds that it was the most expensive of all. Yet it is a development of that invention, the Norwegian Tapchan, which is the most successful of all commercially and generates for around 5p.

Take another example. Wave power is a form of hydroelectricity which is used for generating on a large scale in Scotland by the two privatised companies, Scottish Hydroelectric and Scottish Power. They produce Britain's cheapest electricity, less than 1p a unit—on condition that it is generated by existing plant. But, the official spokeswoman of Scottish Hydro told me, if they were to build a new hydro plant, it would cost between 8p and 12p for the same unit of electricity. Does this make sense for anyone except an accountant? What has such fanciful costing got to do with energy?

Finally, consider one of the finest achievements of the CEGB, the building of a pumped storage station at Dinorwig in north Wales. Water is pumped up a mountain and released when demand grows for electricity. How much does a unit of Dinorwig electricity cost? The answer is infinity because it actually consumes more energy than it produces. It requires four units of electricity to pump the water up the mountainside, in order to receive three units when it comes down. But it is a wonderful asset for a country which does not want to keep power stations on spinning reserve, burning and polluting and wasting energy through the night when demand is low. They would then have to be brought on stream to meet high demand during the day. Instead, much of what the Grid needs is available for whenever it is wanted, on standby in the mountain pool. But on the basis of costing, the accountants would have said that it should never be built, which is what they are trying to say about wave energy.

The details of costs will be dealt with in later chapters. For the present, let us begin at the beginning, when water power was first used by people.

Wave energy means that we are going back to the water wheel. And we are doing so amid an uncanny echo of the problems that accompanied first the introduction of water power, including the 'religious' turmoil, and then the objections which were raised to steam energy. The closest parallel is with the late eighteenth century when James Watt's steam engines were producing only 11 kW of energy and factories were being built for the textile industry driven by as much as 190 kW of water power. It would have needed considerable vision at that stage to accept that steam would soon be ousting water as the prime source of energy. The watermill had been the earliest form of mechanisation, freeing animals and slaves from the treadmill and peasants from grinding corn by hand. It occupies a prime place in everyone's awareness. It yielded reluctantly to steam and even today, in hydroelectric power, water continues to be a major source of electricity.

At the time of the Domesday Book, in 1086, there were 5 624 mills in operation in Britain, nearly all of them water mills, serving a population of only two million—one mill to every 400 people. Then came progress. Steam was captured and its appeal was irresistible. But *was* it progress?

Mr David Braithwaite, architect and editor, sums up the position in his introduction to *Windmills and Watermills* by John Reynolds.[2] 'If it is true that the discovery of new sources of power has been the basis for the progress of civilisation, and the rate of progress has been determined by the amount of energy available to man, then the superseding of wind and water power must surely be celebrated' he writes. 'But it is an inescapable fact that the harnessing of the chemical forces of fire and steam to drive engines and turbines has proved wasteful and has polluted unimaginably our atmosphere.' Note that Mr Braithwaite did not regard the using up of our fossil fuels as worth a mention. He was writing in 1970, far away in our awareness of the energy crisis.

The great promise of wave energy is that there is, for perhaps the first time since the water wheel was discovered, an opportunity of embracing the concept called progress without needing to lament its undesirable side-effects. The possible environmental consequences are all, so far as we know today, favourable. The problems are: Can the waves ever provide our major source of energy? Which type or types of device should we choose? What will be the social consequences? And, to mention the almost-unmentionable, is it morally acceptable that we could actually use natural resources without penalty? This is the modern adaptation of the ancient Romans' feeling about water power, the 'religious' argument brought up to date with a collective guilt complex added. It is, more simply, the feeling that there must be a snag somewhere.

The first water wheel, known as the Persian wheel, goes back to 200 BC. It worked just as most people nowadays imagine, if they think about water wheels at all. That is to say, a wheel stood in a stream of water and the wheel turned as the water flowed. The wheel had a series of buckets hanging from its circumference, like seats on the Big Wheel in a funfair. The buckets scooped up the water and emptied it just before reaching the top, either on to another higher area which needed irrigation or into an aqueduct. It was another 100 years, in 85 BC, before there was the first reference to wheels being used for a secondary, mechanical purpose.

A poem by Antipater of Thessalonica reads:

Cease your work, ye maids, ye who laboured at the mill . . .
For Ceres has commanded the water nymphs to perform your task.

The mill was where the 'maids' had worked at grinding grain between stones by hand. The first mills were of the pestle and mortar type, gradually evolving into what has come to be known as a saddle quern—the lower stone was ground into the shape of a saddle as the upper stone rubbed against it. A round stone, with a handle, was developed and donkeys were used to drag it. And then man's genius brought together the water wheel, driven by a natural force, and the millstone. Humanity had reached a bread and water economy.

There is no record of how Antipater's 'maids' responded to the prospect of redundancy but when water wheels were next used to replace labour, in Rome, there were considerable perturbations. The wheel is referred to by Vitruvius in *De Architectura* and he mentions a toothed gear, which indicates that the Romans were making considerable advances on the original concept. But they did not use it. One reason is that the slaves employed in the grinding of corn would resist and, with a plentiful supply of slaves, no one was particularly concerned to replace them with machinery. But a further reason is believed to have been the fear of interfering with nature.

John Reynolds, in *Windmills and Watermills*, puts it this way: 'The new machine met with strong official opposition. It was claimed that the state would be endangered if this great labour force were to be thrown out of work.' As to the gears, which must have represented an even more outrageous interference with the natural order, the Romans seem to have reconciled themselves to using them for some purposes where the end sanctified the means—purposes which, as Mr. Reynolds puts it, 'seem strangely frivolous to the modern mind, such as the operation of temple doors or theatrical machinery. The ancients viewed the forces of nature with a deeply ingrained religious awe which tended to inhibit experiments with water power. When every river or waterfall was inhabited by its own *genius loci*, to set up a water wheel was tantamount to harnessing the gods for the menial service of man. But purely practical considerations, allied perhaps to a growing cynicism, ensured the gradual acceptance of the water mill.' But mostly without gears.

Inevitably, the earliest acts of impiety took place far from Rome, in Britain. 'There would have been some difficulty in supporting the large garrison on Hadrian's Wall with a relatively small local population to provide slave labour', says the compiler of *Industrial Archeology of Watermills and Waterpower*.[3] 'Thus, there was an incentive to develop the latest labour-saving machinery before it was used in Rome itself and the sites of two mills have been tentatively identified near Hadrian's Wall.'

When Emperor Constantine introduced Christianity, slavery was abolished and labour for grinding corn became short. In addition, the pagan worship of the water spirits ended. The way was clear for the development of water power.

It was the Romans who realised first the advantage of driving a mill by enabling the water to stream down on to the wheel from above, where it had the advantage of not only a flowing river or stream but also of the weight of falling water. The 'overshot' water wheel, as we now call it, can produce efficiencies of 70–90 per cent, while the original undershot wheel had an efficiency of only 30 per cent. It is worth pausing to appreciate that it took probably 200 years before someone saw the point of this. In retrospect, it is self-evident. Yet even today most people think of water wheels in the way that most of them have survived, on the side of the old mill house with the water flowing placidly, and inefficiently, underneath.

This becomes significant today when many different devices are competing for attention in the race to capture wave energy. The schemes vary enormously and some of them seem so obvious that they naturally arouse scepticism. Why, one wonders, has it taken so long to build something so attractive, simple, obvious? But, as with the water wheel, the obvious is elusive. And we have not got 200 years to spare.

In Britain, the introduction of water power caused considerable social problems. The miller was a central figure in society but, in the Middle Ages, he had to hand over almost his entire produce to the Lord of the Manor who owned the mills, retaining only a small quantity as toll. No one else was allowed to grind corn but, as always happens when the law tries to be all-pervasive, the peasants used quern stones secretly at home. On one occasion, the Abbot of St Albans confiscated them from his tenants and used them to pave a courtyard. During the Peasants' Revolt, the stones were wrenched up and destroyed.

The wheel, so to speak, turned full circle when steam challenged water. For a long time the power of water was greater. As late as 1854, a water wheel was built by the Great Laxey Mining Company on the Isle of Man to pump water from a lead mine. It was 21 m in diameter and weighed 100 tonnes and produced 172 kW. Ten years later another wheel, 190 kW, was erected at Rishworth Mills, near Halifax. In the US, one water wheel developed a power of 7.5 MW. But steam was winning.

Its strength was that it could produce more power than water wheels in most countries. The drainage of land had changed the rivers, which ran at more varied paces and the domestic demand for water was increasing with the population. Looking back, one can see that industry had no real alternative. It would not have been possible to meet the demands of the nineteenth and twentieth centuries without steam, however undesirable many of its consequences have proved.

Which is where we came in, wondering why wave energy should be chosen and how much energy it can provide. Professor Falnes, we have noted, has estimated it as being of the same order of magnitude as the total present-day energy consumption for the whole world. Professor Denis Mollison, mathematician at Heriot–Watt University, who has been closely associated with Professor Stephen Salter, concluded that 'the world's potentially *exploitable* (my italics) wave power resource is of roughly the same magnitude as present world electricity consumption, i.e. around 1000 GW' (which is the same as

Dr Falnes's 1 TW) and urged that it should be considered also for desalination and for chemical production of ammonia or hydrogen from floating factories which could harvest the mid-ocean resource.[4] He made the point that wave power was contained in the top 10–20 metres of the sea while wind power was spread over a height of several kilometres, which meant that wave power could achieve power densities about 10 times as large as the winds.

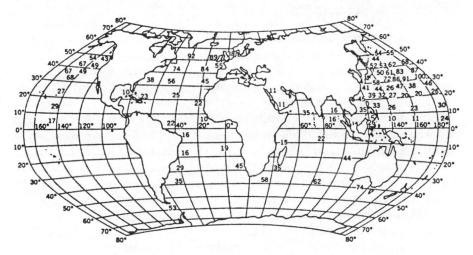

Fig. 4.1 An early map of wave energy around the world, made by a distinguished Scandinavian scientist named Tornquvist.

It is perhaps easier to consider the resource available to Europe. Professor Mollison writes that the mean power available averages over 40 MW/km 'along the best oceanic coasts, such as those of western Europe, of which at least 50 per cent is potentially economically extractable', and he arrives at a figure for Europe 'of the order of 100 GW'.[4] Dr Tony Lewis, oceanographer and maritime civil engineer at Cork University, was asked by the European Commission in Brussels to carry out an evaluation of the wave energy available to the EC (as it then was). His conclusion in 1985 was that 'taking available data, the total is estimated to be 92 GW, which is equal to 70 per cent of the present mainland electricity demand . . . If the Iberian Peninsula were included a further 18 GW would be available.' (Spain and Portugal were not at that time members of the EC.) The new total, 110 GW, reasonably close to Professor Mollison's, is '85 per cent of the European Union's electricity demand'.[5]

Dr Lewis, in a later paper to the Commission in 1993, put the total wave energy arriving around the EC (now EU) coastline at 975 terawatt-hours (TWh). This is an annual total of energy derived from the figure of 110 GW of power. (Energy is power multiplied by time; that is, the amount of power multiplied by 24 hours by 365 days, to give the annual figure. So the 110-odd

GW, which he has identified, is multiplied by 8760 and gives 963 TWh. He has added 12 TWh for the North Sea, which is likely to be part of the second phase of a British programme, after the more fruitful west-facing coasts.)

Now let us narrow the angle of vision still more and consider separately the country about whose wave climate the world knows most: Britain. The sources that I have quoted are all advocates of wave energy and a cynic might say that their judgement is liable to bias in its favour. I would prefer to say that they are all scientists whose research led them to conclude that wave energy is a resource worth developing. But there are those who will assert that, even so, a scientist is only human, and both his attachment to the scientific method, and his objectivity may be influenced just a little by his aspirations. And we are, after all, dealing with estimates of a vast resource which is not amenable to precision at this stage.

So let us turn instead to a hostile source. One of the early estimates—and one which played a major role in changing the official outlook about wave energy in Britain—came from the Central Electricity Generating Board (CEGB) which, in 1977, declared: 'If wave power can be economically harnessed, its development potential along the UK west coast exceeds the present installed capacity of the CEGB . . . There are currently an average of 120 GW of wave power being dissipated on the beaches—nearly five times the average demand on the CEGB.'[6] This was, in the circumstances of that time, and because of the source, a truly sensational announcement.

The CEGB was responsible in law for generating (and delivering through the Grid) all the electricity used in England and Wales, so if it was supporting investment in wave power it needed to be well justified, or the CEGB would have some difficult questions to answer when the lights went out. It was also known to be strongly biased in favour of nuclear power and was behind much of the agitation in favour of spending public money on new nuclear stations. If the CEGB was speaking supportively about wave energy, then this was more significant than the statements made by those who were hoping to become practitioners of the new art and gain government financial support for their own projects.

The CEGB was often criticised by environmentalists but there was widespread agreement and respect for its research centres, and the article quoted above came from one such centre, the Marchwood Engineering Laboratories, which it ran on a site near to Southampton. The author was Ian Glendenning, Leader of Long-Term Studies Projects at Marchwood and a nuclear scientist. He has since returned to his first love and is Technical Strategist for Nuclear Electric. His paper on wave energy came a year after the Department of Energy had launched its study, saying that wave energy was 'intrinsically the most attractive' of the renewable sources.

Let us examine the CEGB's statements in the light of today's knowledge. A gigawatt, as we have noted, is 1000 000 kilowatts—that is, one million one-bar electric fires each of a kilowatt, or 10 million electric lights of 100 watts. And

120 GW is lighting for 1200 million rooms. The CEGB's installed capacity (and that of the generating companies after privatisation) is around 50 GW and average electricity demand is around 30 GW. Hence the calculation that the wave energy of 120 GW is nearly five times the annual average demand for electricity.

At this point, the layman is tempted to start to wonder how we can use this newfound plenitude. Should we not be shutting down the existing power stations, as all of them have undesirable features? And how can we export the surplus? On a call-in radio programme, one person told me that I (sic) had discovered perpetual motion.

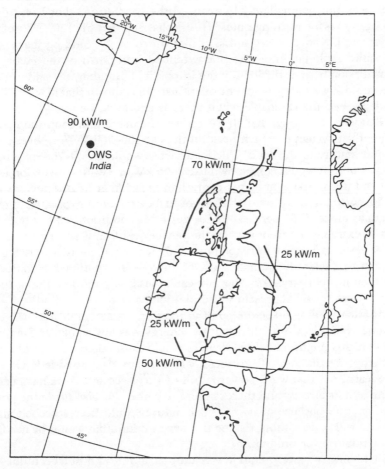

Fig. 4.2 The official British map showing the best areas for gathering wave energy, from 90 kW/m out in the North Atlantic at Ocean Weather Ship India, down to 25 kW/m in the North Sea and off south-west Wales. The accepted estimate is that this is a potential of 120 GW, nearly five times average demand. The west coast of Ireland is ignored.

It is at least partly to counter this reaction from the public and politicians that some people in official positions have tended to emphasise and, I believe, exaggerate the problems. Let us take Mr Glendenning's own cautionary note. He is the type of scientist who was too rare inside the conservative framework of the CEGB. He is mercurial, volatile, and forceful, one of the first to realise that the emperor has no clothes and *the* first to say it. He thinks quickly, challenges everyone he is talking to, and then leapfrogs over their head before they can catch up with his previous argument. He is capable of uttering inconvenient truths.

His papers and lectures had been directed at academic and scientific audiences and, immediately he realised the conclusions that I was drawing, he began to issue warning notes. He emphasised that his 120 GW referred to the whole UK west coast and said that much of it would be inacessible for economic exploitation, as the line extended well north of the Hebrides and transmission became difficult, if not impossible. But that was said in 1977. No one would say it today, when the oil industry has shown that inaccessible areas suddenly become reachable when there is energy to be won.

Glendenning argued that 50 kW/m was the maximum continuous rating of a smoothed system in which peak input is at 150–200 kW/m, 'because of the random nature of the sea'.[6] The load factor would be 60–70 per cent so the average output would come down to 30–35 kW/m. With conversion at 80 per cent and transmission at 90 per cent, then the average *landed* power would be 24–30 kW/m. He added that this could be misleading because one might obtain as much as 60 per cent under desirable conditions and only 1 or 2 per cent in extreme conditions when the devices could not absorb the energy of the waves because they were too powerful, or when the waves were too placid. He said to a scientific audience at Oceanology International, a conference in Brighton in February 1978, that 'we can at least be confident that a 20–30 km long system would represent a useful 1500 MW power station'.

Mr Glendenning made the point to me that as data on inshore wave power became available, it was clear that the energy was lower than at Station India and that this might mean that devices would be smaller; this could reduce or even improve the cost-effectiveness of the system. And he added: 'One thing I have learned is that wave power is full of surprises and there has been much eating of hats already and there is more to come.' He also made the point that wave energy, because of its modular nature, could be researched and even tested at full scale without risking the large amount that would be needed for a major tidal power programme.

Glendenning's interpretation was adopted at the highest level of the CEGB. Its chairman, Glyn England, put the figure into the context of electricity supply, for which he was responsible. On 4 July 1978, he made a major address to the staff of Fawley oil-fired power station, near Southampton, which once generated electricity from cheap oil. England told them that the waves could 'supply the whole of Britain with electricity at the present rate of consumption'. He emphasised that he was talking about what 'could actually be got to the electricity consumer'. I was told from inside the CEGB that a policy announcement of this nature was considered, paragraph by paragraph, by all the experts concerned inside the organisation. It was in no sense an off-the-cuff remark. The text, which was supplied to me by the CEGB, contained evidence in the typescript of cautious, last-minute revision.

He began by reiterating the CEGB view that nuclear energy was safe, reliable, and efficient and appeared to be the most economic. 'However, further upheavals in the energy scene are bound to occur,' meaning that nuclear power might become socially unacceptable.

Mr England continued that if an 'upheaval' occurred, some of the renewable sources would be 'more attractive'.

He said that solar energy could be used for domestic water heating but would be prohibitively expensive for 'electricity production', at least in Britain; apart from the shortage of sunshine, it was most scarce when we most needed it, in winter. In addition, a 2000 MW power station such as Fawley would need an area of 50 square miles covered with solar cells, and the power station itself would still be needed on a dull day.

He dismissed geothermal energy as 'speculative', though perhaps useful for providing hot water for nearby factories, homes, and green-houses.

As to wind power, it would need 4000 aero generators, with a rotor 50 m across, to match the output of a single large power station. It would be possible, because of the lack of sufficiently exposed sites, to meet only about 5 per cent of our electricity demand in this way. He also reminded his listeners that they were not talking about picturesque, old-fashioned windmills but of 'gaunt, massive structures'.

Mr England scouted the possibility of stationing aero generators in the sea and he suggested that this might produce a quarter of the CEGB's output. Since his speech, some work has been done on this suggestion but no one has explained why the problems of building structures able, as he put it, 'to withstand gales and heavy seas' (which are not always in phase) should be undertaken to capture the wind, when the waves are a concentrated form of wind energy.

He dismissed the idea of a Severn tidal barrage on the grounds that it could contribute 'not more than 3 per cent of the country's present total primary energy requirements', that it would be costly and could have a detrimental effect on the environment.

And so to wave energy: 'As we see it at present, wave power is the most promising of the renewable energy sources . . . Averaged over the year, there is about 80 kilowatts of power in each metre of wave-front approaching Britain from the North Atlantic. This implies a total annual availability of 120 000 MW (120 GW) of power along Britain's Atlantic coast. However, not all this power could be harnessed. There would inevitably be substantial losses in conversion, and transmission losses, too, so that probably only about one-third could actually be got to the electricity consumer. Nevertheless, this is still a substantial amount of power—enough, in fact, to supply the whole of Britain with electricity at the present rate of consumption.'

These remarks, coming from the man responsible for supplying the juice, should have galvanised the Department of Energy into an awareness of what is happening in the world of technology. Instead, it allowed events to overtake discovery.

The word 'galvanise' comes from the name of an Italian physiologist, Luigi Galvani, and it is defined as 'a term applied to the method of alleviation of pain and the cure of disease by means of a current of electricity'.

Mr England's statement had come one month after Mr Benn's announcement of the third Government investment in wave energy. But it did not result in any change in the leisurely pace of the British programme. No extra money was produced. It left the country still gripped by what has been called 'the bathtub syndrome'. Tiny models were floated in laboratory tanks. Funds were provided for 1/10th-scale trials on Loch Ness and in the Solent. But all the research in the world will not provide the answers; the open sea always has a trick up its sleeve and it will be only when fullscale prototypes are launched that the answers will become known.

That year, 1978, was the high point of British official enthusiasm for wave energy. I have always suspected that the Glyn England speech was taken by Whitehall as an alarm signal rather than a welcome message. It meant that wave energy could become a contender for government investment and a serious rival to the established sources, particularly nuclear power, if the chairman of the CEGB himself, with the backing of his research departments, was saying that wave power could 'supply the whole of Britain with electricity at the present rate of consumption'.

A cautionary note came from Harwell. Mr Clive Grove-Palmer, the secretary of the Wave Energy Steering Committee, put it this way: 'Divide your 120 GW by two for efficiency and by another two for transmission. Say your average energy is 50 kW/m, then from 1000 km (600 miles) of devices we would get only 12 GW.' Only? Even on this rightly-cautious estimate, we are talking about replacing nearly half our normal consumption of electricity without using fossil fuels. Note that there are experts who will insist that we would lose not 50 per cent but only 10 per cent at each stage, from generation and transmission.

As a footnote to discussion of future prospects, it should not be overlooked that in all the estimates produced under official auspices, it is assumed that the waves stop at Portrush. This is a town in the north of Ulster, close to the frontier with the Republic of Ireland. All the west coast of Ireland comes within the Republic, officially a foreign country. So it was laid down when the wave power programme started that all the wave power to the west of Ireland must be ignored, perhaps for fear that Dublin would think that the UK was laying claim to its seas. The effect was to make the available resource appear smaller than it was.

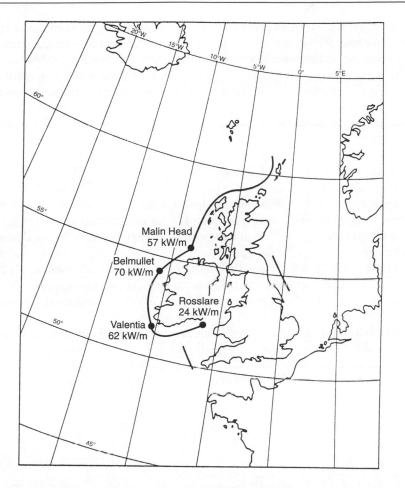

Fig. 4.3 The unofficial map drawn on the basis of information provided for the EU by
Professor Denis Mollison and including Ireland. It shows that a major resource was
ignored by British official planners, possibly to avoid upsetting the Irish.

The great sweep of powerful waves from just to the west of Portrush, all
the way down from Donegal, round the south of Ireland to Bantry, is
ignored in official estimates. The fact that the wave energy generators
could be miles out into the Atlantic, beyond the limits of territorial waters,
was and is brushed aside. But Dr Lewis's version for Brussels is not
confined in this way. He puts the UK resource at 30 GW, and adds on
another 25 GW off the coast of Ireland, most of which will not be needed
for domestic consumption and will be available for export to the UK. So we
are contemplating a figure of 55 GW which, with the energy available from
hydroelectric, tidal, and wind energy, can supply more than all the UK's
needs from renewable sources.

In practice, for various reasons there will undoubtedly be some generation from other sources—no one is suggesting that we should or could shut down every other plant. But what does need to be grasped is that renewable energy, led by wave energy, could supply all the electricity needed by Britain and many other countries. It is an enormous resource, waiting to be enjoyed.

References

1. Falnes, J. and Lovseth, J. (1991). Ocean wave energy. *Energy Policy*, **8**, 768–75.
2. Reynolds, J. (1970). *Windmills and watermills*. Hugh Evelyn, London.
3. Project Technology Handbook No. 11. (1975). *Industrial archeology of watermills and waterpower*. Heinemann Educational Books/Schools Council, London.
4. Mollison, D. (1985). *Wave climate and the wave power resource*. Hydrodynamics of ocean wave energy utilisation, pp. 133–56. Springer, Berlin.
5. Lewis, T. (1985). *Wave energy, evaluation for CEC*. Graham & Trotman, London.
6. Glendenning, I. (1977). Energy from the sea. *Chemistry and Industry*, 588–99.

The letter from the Bionics Department 5

The letter which Stephen Salter sent to Whitehall eventually arrived on the desk of Mr Gordon Goodwin, Principal Scientific Officer at the Department of Energy. My first impression of him was of a man withdrawn and taciturn and the reason for this attitude, presumably acquired in the job rather than inherited, was obvious:

We get a lot of oddball inquiries and schemes into this department, and most of them come my way. We frequently get perpetual motion schemes. Lots of people want to do something about using sawdust. Or painting the moon another colour. And during the oil crisis, there were some very strange suggestions. Salter's letter was from a peculiar address: the School of Artificial Intelligence, Bionics Research Laboratory, Edinburgh University. The letter had been photostatted at some stage on its rounds and the thought crossed my mind that if someone was trying to do a hoax it would be easy to cut up a potato and 'print' a heading and send off a letter like this.

So first I phoned the university and asked if there was someone there called Salter. The switchboard said that there was. I rang off and thought. Then I rang back and spoke to him direct and asked some questions. I asked him did he know what the wave data was like and did he know the difference between winter and summer loading and the best area for wave energy and he came up with the right answers. He *had* covered the ground.

So, it should be mentioned, had Goodwin. He had investigated wave energy more than 12 months before Salter wrote. The Government awakened to the need for alternative sources of energy a year before the Middle East war had brought home the seriousness of the situation. To give credit where it is due, in early 1973 Lord Rothschild and the Central Policy Review Staff, as the Think Tank is known officially, were asked to study energy and Goodwin had been the man who had looked at wave energy. He had only seven weeks to draw up a paper while carrying on with his normal work. He estimates that he had three man-weeks to investigate what was an idea 200 years old and also, in terms of modern technology, brand new. So he was better informed than anyone had a right to expect, as often happens with the Civil Service.

His first discovery was how little was known about the subject. 'People's ideas of a wave were completely wrong. For a start, it is a very flat thing, drawn to scale, hardly a perturbation.' That is, the Atlantic reaches down to 10 000 m; a wave will rarely reach 30 m. A pimple.

Goodwin made the rounds that, since then, have been followed by most people concerned with wave energy—the Institute of Oceanographic

Sciences, the Hydraulics Research Station and the research associations dealing with the Merchant Navy, the Royal Navy and naval construction.

From my work on North Sea gas, with undersea piping, and being not long out of commerical practice, I devised a scheme which could have been built off the shelf. It was based on floats. It was just a constrained float driving a pump into something like a Pelton wheel.

To be confident that the system was not going to be subject to serious criticism, I taught myself a fair bit about the waves. I got a feel of them. I learned things from them. I learned to do a technical assessment of wave energy. The first thing was to do calculations on how much energy was there. It was such an enormous figure that I thought I must have got it wrong by a factor of 10 or something. I tried other ways. And I became certain that there was a significant natural resource. The report was produced and I went on to other things. Then came the Middle East war and the letter from Salter.

What Goodwin did not know at that time was that Salter was imaginative enough to realise how his letter must have been received. He has recorded the facts.

About 10 per cent of the population of this country suffer, at one time or another, from some form of mental disturbance. In a fair number of them, the manifestations involve writing to Cabinet Ministers. In normal times, the mail is evenly distributed among the various branches of government. But at the end of 1973, the trousers-for-dogs and bring-back-the-cat letters faded away and with one mind all the writers switched to helpful proposals for solving the energy crisis: treadmills for fat business men, sewage-driven cars . . . I chipped in with a short letter to Peter Walker who was then responsible for energy. In due course, I received a polite acknowledgment. The fact that my note had come from the School of Artificial Intelligence and some quirk of my literary style suggested that the whole business was a cruel hoax against Peter Walker when he was battling with Joe Gormley and the Arabs. Their initial approach was very tentative. But they were soon in Edinburgh . . .

'They' refers to Goodwin. We met in his large, agreeable office in the Department of Energy, then on Millbank. It was elegant and comfortable apart from one detail. An old tin wastepaper bin kept the door jammed open on to the corridor. He apologised, explaining that he suffered from claustrophobia. This is understandable. The combination of roles as backroom scientist, expert on oddball inquiries, and civil servant is justification for a psychological quirk. He is a chemical engineer and asserts that this is the ideal background because his training embraces every form of engineering and enables him to talk to mechanical, constructional, and electrical engineers on their own subjects. He also has a degree in biology, has worked on computers and spent 12 years in industry, in Britain, Europe, and New York before entering Government service. 'I came to the Ministry of Power (as it was then called) on the basis of my industrial/economic experience', he recalled. 'Yet the first thing they did was to send me off on a course in economics.' Someone, somewhere was determined not to have any outside ideas upsetting the established order.

After satisfying himself that Salter knew something about the waves, Goodwin asked him: 'Have you got a device working in a tank that is absorbing wave energy. I thought he would say No. But he answered Yes, I have. I said I'd better come up and see him.' Goodwin was on the first available train to Edinburgh. He learned how Salter had tried 'various shapes' before arriving at the now-familiar Duck's beak with the rounded bottom which absorbs energy without displacing water and creating new, wasteful waves of its own. And he saw it at work in a tank. Goodwin recalled:

The full importance of what I saw did not sink in until 24 hours later. I was back in London and I realised that I had seen an artificial wave arriving at the beak and calm water on the other side of it. You did not get a strong reflected wave going backwards, as you would with a breakwater. This meant something close to total absorption of the energy. He could measure what was going in and what energy was being absorbed and the result was 90 per cent whereas previously one had thought about capturing perhaps 30 per cent of wave energy. And Salter's figures were borne out by the still water on the leeward side of his device. So here was confirmation of what the instruments showed. You were getting a powered take off. It was the first time that a measured high efficiency wave generator had ever been exhibited. It was a startling thing to see and I was the only person who had seen it, apart from Salter and his colleagues.

Anything like this that could be made to work had to be taken seriously. It completely altered my view of the concept. But at this stage, there was hardly another soul anywhere that I could turn to. Everyone laughed at you—except Don Gore (who, as Deputy Chief Scientific Officer, was Goodwin's senior). He always felt that wave energy did carry credibility. He felt that it was ridiculous that with all our modern technology we could not do something with this. When I was worried that I was getting the energy levels too high, it never came home to him that such a thing was possible.

So, after thinking about it, I rang Salter again. I told him to take a photograph of his device. He said he hadn't got a camera. I said, get one, borrow it from someone. He said he didn't know anyone with a camera. I said I'd seen someone up at the university carrying a camera when I was there. He said he didn't know who it was. And anyway he hadn't any money to buy films. I said steal them or borrow money but I must have some photographs. And then he did it. And it was the first time that anything like this had been seen in the Department of Energy.

Then I said I wanted a cine film. He got me one. We were lucky. We had in the Department a projector which you can stop and play it backwards. And when we did this with the wave hitting the duck we saw some quite astonishing things. It showed us just what was happening, how the wave energy was being absorbed.

The way Salter had arrived at his success was by doing a very clever thing. Before, people had worked *either* on paper *or* in the water. Salter worked on paper and then dipped his paper in water. He went between paper and experiment. He had a tank of water in his laboratory. He looked at how a device worked, tried it experimentally and finally arrived at this profile.

There were a number of institutions aware that we had a crisis but not a dicky bird had come from them on wave energy. A complete outsider like Salter had gone round to Woolworth's, bought sixpen'orth of Balsa and made fools of all of them. This is a way of influencing people but not of making friends' [an oblique reference to Salter's critics in such places as the Central Electricity Generating Board and the National Engineering Laboratory].

All this while Salter was applying for a grant from the Science Research Council, because he was an academic and at university and this was the natural place for him to apply. Very unfortunately, he had only recently been working on a project which had been aimed at producing an artificial engine. In the School of Artificial Intelligence they had built a robot which could assemble a toy steam engine from its component parts. You could put the parts in any configuration and you would end with this toy assembled. Salter had, with his own hands, built the robot part of it. This was the successful part. But there was a hitch. On the instruction, Put all the pieces away, the computer dismantled the engine and put the parts in a box and then went on trying to put the box inside the box! There had just been some laboratory computer software needed to make the experiment a success. But by then the Science Research Council had spent about £2.5 million on it and they just decided to wind the while thing up.

So as soon as you said to the SRC that Salter had been working in the School of Artificial Intelligence, down the shutters went because of this sad experience.

Mr Goodwin, however, took up the battle for Salter with the SRC, saying that the Department of Energy would like to see him funded. He eventually obtained an offer for Salter, for 'a few thousand pounds', which Salter never took up. One understands his feelings.

He had made a staunch ally in Gordon Goodwin, who then tackled another Governmental body, the Mechanical Engineering and Machine Tools Requirements Board of the Department of Trade and Industry which can claim to be the body which has made wave energy possible. Requirements Boards were a useful branch of Government. They were introduced in 1972 by the Heath Government with the purpose of 'identifying requirements' in research and development for both manufacturing industry and research establishments where the Boards considered that there was a likelihood of technical success. They took into account numerous factors, among them reduction of pollution and energy conservation. There were eight of these Boards covering most sectors of industry and they matched the thinking of Benn in one important respect: if they gave help to a project which became profitable, they could ask for a share of the winnings. Yet it was a Conservative Government which introduced the scheme. 'You could regard its main function as priming the pump', said a spokeswoman of the Department of Trade and Industry; it is interesting how many of our well-used phrases come from water power.

The Boards were allowed to award up to £50 000 a year for any project at their own discretion. They gave Salter £64 000 but, by spreading it over two years, were able to pay the money without asking for a Minister's approval. It was difficult at that time to persuade anyone that wave energy was a serious proposition; the tactful accountancy enabled the civil servants to ease the project through without asking permission.

Meanwhile, the National Engineering Laboratory (NEL) at East Kilbride was producing a long survey of wave energy.[2] There are about 50 000 words of text, numerous graphs, charts and illustrations, and an extensive list of sources. Most people regarded it as the standard work.

Mr Goodwin was less enthusiastic. 'We granted them £13 000 to produce this and they had access to Salter's work. It is horrible. It is rubbish. It is paper ideas. I had argued that water would not do what you expected. I thought that we should get our feet wet. I was over-ruled and work went on at the NEL.'

The outburst seemed at first surprising. The NEL enjoys a high reputation and personally I have always found its engineers helpful and, insofar as one can assess the competence of a group of brilliant innovators, of the highest technical quality. Most engineering students, particularly in Scotland, where engineering abilities are so frequently found at their best, regard an appointment to work at NEL as their highest ambition. Why then was Goodwin so critical? It is obviously in part an expression of the competitiveness and tension that were rising throughout the wave energy world as we approached decisions. But there was another aspect to it: the NEL started out as advocates of Salter's Duck and then moved towards favouring the Oscillating Water Column (OWC), which was at that time known as the Masuda concept (see Chapter 6.2). It settled on this scheme 'for further technical and economic assessment'. And today the great resources of the NEL are behind the OWC, while Salter has to rely on considerable but less well-equipped resources.

The NEL would not have been surprised to discover that in the sharpening race for a breakthrough in a new technology, passions were rising. I have been told by its engineers there of some of the opposition that they have encountered when, for instance, they have been called in by manufacturers to help in debugging new machinery which refuses to bed down. No one likes the outsider or believes that he might be able to do something that had proved insoluble to the residents. Yet the NEL, by hooking up machinery to its computer, has often been able to analyse a problem and suggest a solution that had eluded those experts who were most familiar with the particular machinery.

Its reasons for favouring the OWC will be examined in detail later. It is certainly one of the most promising schemes, though it has its drawbacks: for instance, the Salter supporters will emphasise that the Column has to withstand a far heavier battering from the sea than the Ducks which flip up and down in the waves. Against this, the Column has the advantage that it is already working. Masuda, the Japanese inventor, has produced navigation buoys powered entirely by wave energy. They are functioning at sea. And Mr. Goodwin himself mentioned that the discovery that these buoys were working, and working well, 'at a point where credibility mattered', was one of the events that made him interested in wave energy.

The incident helps to illustrate what in industry is called the 'creative tension' which is impelling forward the whole project. It remains 'creative' so long as the project moves forward; it is when backbiting and inward pressures take over that a neurotic atmosphere develops and that is when a new concept is in danger. It happened briefly between the NEL and Salter and happened again, over a lasting period with a bitter, personal edge to it, between Coventry and Edinburgh (see Chapter 6.4). The rivalry between the Duck and the OWC was resolved by an unexpected development. Salter decided that he did not want to put the Duck to sea until he was certain that it would be successful. He was admirably firm, or obstinate, about this, the adjective depending on your point of view. The NEL, however, wanted to go to sea, and with the Japanese example before them could and did argue that their technology was ready. So the two centres could and did pursue their different objectives side by side in harmony, with excellent relations (perhaps better than existed between Glasgow and Edinburgh in most other activities).

Goodwin, for his part, had determined ideas on the future of the project. He had precise ideas about the speed at which it should go and the limitations which should be imposed—or accepted. 'It is a very extensive resource in national energy terms,' he said. 'It is modular and so has an advantage over tidal barrages. You can stop. Or extend it. Or build it up after 10 or 20 years. It peaks with the winter demand and shuts itself off in the summer.' That is the positive side.

And then, prompted by my argument that it could become our basic source of energy, he gave the other point of view.

He did not accept, as the CEGB was starting to do, that by stationing your generators off different coasts, you could be certain that there would almost always be wave energy pumping ashore. 'It must be off the Hebrides', he insisted. 'Nowhere else is significant.' I put it to him that even if one achieved a smaller number of kilowatts per metre of device, it would make sense to use the energy of, say, the North Sea or the calmer waters off the Scily Islands as alternatives. He disagreed.

Why should it not be a basic source of energy? 'You cannot make an unfirm source into a firm source,' he insisted. 'Forget it.' I have since spoken to other engineers, including Salter and a very senior figure inside the CEGB, who contest this argument. With storage and the Grid, the sea can be regarded as a 'firm' source.

Why not build a full-scale prototype now? Here he was particularly insistent. 'We are talking about what is probably the most awful engineering job that anyone has ever taken on. There is no device that has not got real and intense problems. If and when all systems are fully engineered, you will find that each has its strengths and weaknesses. It is far, far too early at the moment to start saying what is the obvious line of approach. I am fairly certain that if and when wave energy devices get deployed, the first generation will be expensive, unreliable, and inefficient. And if they are not, by some miracle, they will be different from every other engineering development we are used to.'

Another scientist, Ian Glendenning of the CEGB (see Chapter 4), was also firing warning shots at me. He was an advocate of the Oscillating Water Column which, as the Japanese had already shown, was a practical proposition, but he was scathing about the Duck. I had met Glendenning by happy chance on an appalling day in mid-winter, when the press officer assigned to accompany me was stricken with 'flu, which, five years earlier, had attacked Salter and given his wife the occasion to spur him into action. This time the bug prevented the press officer from accompanying me to Marchwood, and as the boat crept through freezing fog across Southampton Water, I admired his judgement. But the 'flu bug was working well for wave energy once more: the press officer would certainly have hushed up Glendenning when he started being indiscreet (and honest). As it was, the two of us could talk freely.

Glendenning had a lively and fertile brain which had not been crushed by the institutional conformity which weighed on the CEGB and prevented many of its better minds from exercising their potential. His remarks were certainly not the boring, anodyne placebos which were on the usual CEGB prescriptions for awkward journalists, and soon after the meeting I received an anguished appeal from the organisation.

It agreed that Glendenning had made a number of critical remarks but asked me to withold them. The grounds given were that publication would make it impossible for Glendenning to continue as a member of the Technical Advisory Groups of ETSU and that it would damage the wave energy programme. I doubted that this was the case but, as a compromise, retained the remarks in the first two editions of this book but attributed them to an unnamed scientist 'close to the centre of the wave energy programme'. Now that the official programme has been suspended for the second time by the British government, I feel free to identify him.

Of the OWC, he said that it could prove expensive in construction and less fruitful in its productivity but it should be cheaper to maintain and less demanding in any novel technology—everything about it was standard engineering.

Glendenning put another device, the Cockerell Raft (see Chapter 6.3) a close second and the other two devices on the official programme far behind.

The Hydraulics Research Station Rectifier demanded an enormously strong building, standing on the seabed, with non-return valves the size of a shopfront window. Glendenning told me with animation about his objections to the Duck. 'Salter does not deserve even a tick,' he said, as he chalked away furiously on a blackboard with coloured diagrams to explain his views. 'The Duck is complicated to build, while the Raft could be constructed on any slipway in the country. How do you manufacture the gears, the power take-off and the drive that Salter would need? Imagine the problems when a Duck goes wrong. The repair work would be below water on a device as big as that'— pointing at a large laboratory. 'You have a mechanism moving up and down, mostly below sea level, and you would need divers to work on it beneath the surface while it rolled.'

I put it to him that the more ardent supporters of the Duck argued that there would be little need for maintenance. He retorted: 'Show me a ship that goes to sea without someone going around all the time with an oil can.' Well then, it had been argued, notably by Dr Norman Bellamy, then head of the Electrical and Electronics Department at Lanchester Polytechnic (now Coventry University) that the 'float' or nose section of the Duck, which does the bobbing up and down, could be unclipped from the spine in ten minutes and towed away. Glendenning swooped.

We were lunching in a large restaurant and he leaped out of his chair and marched from one end of the room to the other, counting loudly as he did so. 'One, two, three . . . fourteen steps.' Then: 'You see, this restaurant is 14 metres from one end to the other. The diameter of the spine alone holding the Duck is 15 metres. Then you have the outer structure. Do you realise now the size of the operation that we are talking about?' I got his point, though some of the other diners appeared puzzled.

In defence of the Duck it must be said that the part which has to stay fairly stable, the spine, is smaller than the bobbing cone. In this it is different from all the others which need stability for their biggest components: the outer casing of the Oscillating Water Column, the whole 'block of flats' of the Rectifier and the rearmost pontoon of the Raft. So the problem of holding them steady will be that much greater than for the spine.

But let us return to Mr Goodwin who was the best ally of wave energy inside the Civil Service. He did make one statement that worried me. He is a gifted engineer who deserves most of the credit for winkling the first money out of a Government body to help Salter. But he said to me: 'It is the judgment of the people concerned that the project is expanding as fast as prudent. *We would be negligent if we did not establish whether it was possible.*'

Here, I fear, is an unfortunate echo of some of the thinking behind Government policy, as inspired by the Civil Service. The Government dared not turn its back on wave energy when the project was presented with insistence by Salter, Goodwin, Cockerell, and the rest, and when the energy crisis was ringing alarm bells in quiet corridors where chaps prefer not to make a fuss. The government did not wish to be accused of indifference to our futures. Nor did it wish to arouse public anxiety and opposition with a nuclear-based energy policy. So it assigned what seemed to be a reasonable sum of money in order, it may have hoped, to deflect criticisms of negligence or indifference.

It launched itself, with a tolerable show of goodwill, into programmes designed to save fuel: double-glazing and insulation and solar panels and windmills on top of every cowshed. But it shied away from the really big decision, the development on a major scale of the energy that surrounds us, the waves which pound against our beaches and cliffs and are available for the taking—provided that we are prepared to invest the money needed to capture and transmit their power.

I did not believe that the Government's attitude was adequate for the next stage of development of a new source of power and in this I was encouraged by a scientist of eminence who was aware of the political significance of the issue. He was engaged in energy research and I had to choose between using only formal sources of information and going behind the scenes to obtain unofficial guidance, with an assurance of confidentiality. I chose the second course because it yielded the information that I needed in this instance.

He was convinced that two strands of thinking were intertwining in order to encourage a cautious creep forward. 'The people experimenting with devices,' he said, 'were very insistent that the Government should help when they were getting little or no money. But now they have a comfortable arrangement. And the last thing that some of them want is for the Government to move in, in a really big way, with perhaps £1000 million and say "Right, let's get some of these things into the sea and find out how they function." That would mean Government control because the Government is not going to hand over that sort of money to private consortiums. And then there are the civil servants who are naturally reluctant to take a big jump ahead. But what we need is to get something into the sea on a full-scale project and find out just what it can do.'

My source was one of those people who believed that the need to provide productive employment should be a major consideration in our future policy on wave energy. I put this to Mr Goodwin. 'Ah', he said, 'now you are talking about a Public Works Programme. That is not really my subject.'

Agreed. But it is ours, along with our future energy.

References

1. Salter. S.H. (1974). Light from the face of the deep? *Univ. of Edinburgh Bulletin*, **11**, 1–3.
2. Leishman, J.M. and Scobie, G. (1976). *The development of wave power, a techno-economic study*. National Engineering Laboratory.

6 The catalyst

The conference at the Heathrow Hotel, on 22 and 23 November 1978, was the catalyst. For two years wave energy had been existing in an ideal world. The injunction from government was to find a clean energy source that would save Britain and many other countries from running out of electricity. But at the Heathrow Hotel we were suddenly presented with the unacceptable face of Mammon. We were told that wave energy must be not only clean, not only renewable, not only environmentally acceptable, but also cheap. The wave energy family was presented with cost estimates and it was made plain that for many people money was the first consideration.

The acceptable face of the energy establishment was expressed in the opening remarks by Alex Eadie, the Energy Under-Secretary. 'It is hard to realise that it is only five years ago that the fuel crises caused by the Yom Kippur War burst into everybody's lives. To a country cushioned as we were by the abundant supply of cheap imported energy, oil at $2.50 a barrel, cheap gas, and an inexhaustible supply of coal, the thought of cutbacks in consumption, widespread conservation, forced self-denial, and much higher fuel bills seemed light-years away. And suddenly it was all gone. Many of you, like myself, must have woken up on one of those cold, unlit mornings in January 1974 and wondered just what in the world had happened . . . The price of oil had gone up four times overnight. All of which was being imported. Overnight it cost £2 billion more on our balance of payments. It taught us a lesson . . . And I am determined that however quickly the deprivation of the fuel emergency fades from people's memory, however easily North Sea oil enables us to look at the future through more rose-coloured spectacles, that this complacency will not return.'

Eadie surely meant what he said. But behind him there was the Civil Service machine working away. It was not concerned with the long term. 'The medium term' is the Treasury's favourite goal. It realised that the immediate crisis had passed and wondered why anyone was proposing to build 2000 MW power stations in the sea. It did not see the justification. And, in the words of Rabelais, 'when the devil is sick, the devil a saint would be. When the devil was well, the devil a saint was he.'

To look back through the record of that conference is revealing.[1] It is only 17 years ago but it was still possible for Sir Hermann Bondi, the Chief Scientist, to tell the conference: 'I would like to express a straight irritation that we know so little about the sea and the waves of the sea. Windmills have been there for hundreds of years; the waves of the sea have been there for very much longer and it is very irritating that at this stage, after oceanography has existed for a long time, we should still have such large margins on the power, on directional data, on (wave) periods.' He would not say that today.

The conference was opened by Dr F.J.P. Clarke, Research Director at the Atomic Energy Research Establishment, Harwell, and chairman of the Wave Energy Steering Committee. He was bullish. He listed the difficulties but concluded with praise for the quality of the work done by many teams in industry, universities, and government laboratories, saying, 'the natural resource is there, and if anyone can learn how to capture it, this team will'.

Dr Clarke emphasised some of the problems that had arisen during the first two years of the programme: directionality, meaning that some of the waves would come from an unexpected angle; the need to convert the slow and irregular motion of the waves into the fast and regular movement needed to produce electricity; anchoring and mooring; environmental problems and 'the high costs of the early designs'.

And then came the presentations from the different teams: Cockerell and his Raft, Salter and his Duck, Bellamy on the Loch Ness trials, National Engineering Laboratory on the Oscillating Water Column, ETSU reporting on what the Japanese had achieved, the Hydraulics Research Station on its 'Rectifier', Vickers on its submerged OWC, Queen's University on the Belfast Buoy, David Evans on the Bristol Cylinder, and Michael French on his Airbag.

The Cockerell team, who had an array of three Rafts at 1/10 th scale functioning in the Solent, were practical. Their chief engineer, Jim Platts, made the case for using concrete rather than steel. Little experience existed of mass production of large concrete structures but they had studied the problem in some depth. Reinforced concrete ships built in the 1914–18 war had demonstrated hull lives of 50 years compared with the 'rather pessimistic life of 30 years' assumed by the wave energy programme.

Their research indicated that a Raft could be built, under cover, in 24 working days—that is, four weeks. So that would produce 12 Rafts a year. Best use could be made of manpower and plant by grouping berths in pairs and phasing activity between them. A two-berth module would have an output of 24 Rafts a year. A mooring barge would lay moorings at the rate of one a week through a 24-week summer weather window. With tugs delivering one Raft per week during that time, a total capacity of 600 Rafts with a total hourly rating of 1.5 GW would be reached after 25 years. 'After that time the factory, mooring barge, and tugs would continue to be totally occupied producing replacement Rafts, removing old moorings and Rafts, and installing new ones.' He wanted a 10-year period at sea with a prototype and looked forward to 'a fully developed production and maintenance technology available by 1990'. As it could have been.

Stephen Salter contributed in his strongly individual style: 'Ducks evolved from simple, vertical flaps. What we wanted was a flap which had a front but no back. The idea is that the front surface should move in a way which matches the orbital motion of water particles in any approaching wave while the displacements astern are very small. No new waves are generated astern until the Duck moves through large angles but then the incident waves are so large that we do not mind losing some of the energy.'

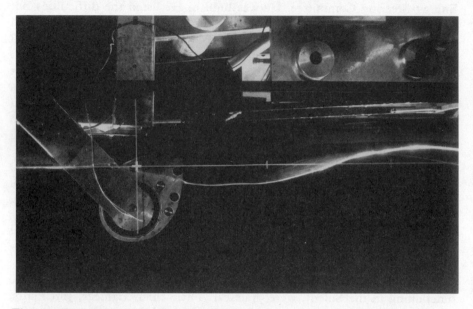

Fig. 6.1 The picture that changed official thinking: a wave hits a model Duck in a narrow laboratory tank. The water emerges at the other side completely flat, with its energy removed by the Duck.

He explained his plan (much of it changed later) for power take-off: 'Inside the Duck we build two large gyros arranged to spin in opposite directions . . . I am sure that you will all instantly know exactly what will happen to the gyro gimbals when the Duck nods! They will precess about the axis which is perpendicular to both the axes of spin and nod. [Precession is the slow movement of the axis of a spinning body, gyroscope, etc, around another axis. See Chapter 6.4.] You will remember the equations . . . We need gyro discs weighing about 50 tonnes spinning at 1000 revolutions per minute (rpm) with a diameter as big as can be fitted inside the Duck. . . .' For an irreverent moment, it made me admire the prescience of Lewis Carroll when he wrote: 'Twas brillig and the slithy toves did gyre and gimble in the wabe.' What had he known? But Salter continued: 'In case anyone thinks that this scheme is far-fetched and that we could not work gyros of this size at sea, perhaps some of the marine engineers present remember the Italian liner, *Conte di Savoia*, which used gyros for stabilisation in the 1930s. Three gyros, each weighing 100 tonnes (double the weight I have mentioned) were run at 950 rpm. I understand the method was quite successful . . . The most attractive feature is that we have a completely opaque barrier between ourselves and the salt water. The gyros do not know that they are at sea. I do not need to know about marine biology and corrosion to make them work.'

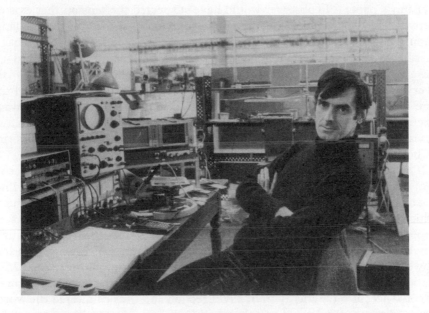

Fig. 6.2 An early picture of S. Salter in his laboratory.

Then came Dr Norman Bellamy, then of Lanchester Polytechnic, now head of Coventry University, who described what he had done on being, as he put it, 'inspired by Stephen Salter's work'. His group had experimented on Draycote reservoir at 1/50th scale and then moved to Loch Ness, 'the largest natural wave-tank in the country. It is orientated towards the south-west where the prevailing wind is supposed to come from. We investigated the wave climate and found it to be about 1/10th scale of the North Atlantic.' They set out to build a spine four times bigger than the Draycote model but 'the volume and weight at four times cubed is rather a large figure. The spine was nearly 1 m in diameter, 50 m long.' They added on a string of 20 Ducks and the whole device weighed 25 tonnes.

What did they learn? He looked ahead to the time when full-scale Ducks were built and Bellamy said it 'certainly gives cause for worry when one thinks of increasing the scale by a factor of 10. Tackling engineering problems at 1/10th scale is difficult; to go 10 times bigger when the strength of materials does not increase proportionally is a formidable problem. Even so, the device does work, it does produce power and it demonstrates that you can gain energy at relatively high efficiency. It also demonstrates that survival is the main problem and that reliability is all-important. We regard this device and the Loch Ness trials as a major evolutionary step in wave power.'

It was all very civilised. Salter, who must have been embarrassed as he heard this discussion of his invention, did participate in the exchanges about Bellamy's paper. No observer would have suspected the tension that existed between the two. My view as a bystander, for what it is worth, is that Bellamy should not have borrowed Salter's Duck and used it, and that Salter has a justifiable complaint in saying that it was not his design and that it should not have been presented in that way. Against that, I believe that Bellamy did everyone a service by making wave energy visible; the television film of the line of Ducks, whether or not they were faithful reproductions, made wave energy alive for millions of people who could not be reached by laboratory research. But I do appreciate Salter's annoyance. So I find myself a supporter of both sides of the argument.

The rest of the conference contained fascinating material. From Queen's University, Belfast, which has played an increasingly significant role, Professor Adrian Long and Dr Trevor Whittaker explained the Belfast Buoy, which sounded like the title of an Irish folk song. It was one of the earliest to exploit the usefulness of what became known as point absorbers, a single device instead of the line of dozens of energy collectors which were the usual power stations designed to meet the government's proposal for a 2000 MW station. In the audience was Alan Hidden who had done the initial work on it. It could accept wave energy from any direction and thus countered the worry about 'directionality'.

Long and Whittaker explained that their Buoy had the essential feature that 'it prevents vertical heave motion at the wavelengths which you would want to derive energy from, but when storm waves come on the scene it allows the device to ride them out . . . An out-of-phase movement of the water surface inside the pressure chamber is induced. This change in inside water level relative to the buoy has the same effect as a piston in a cylinder.' This was in effect an answer to the NEL argument, put by George Moody in Chapter 6.2, that an OWC stationary on the seabed gives you the major efficiency. The scientists from Belfast were arguing that flexible moorings which allowed the Buoy to rise and fall were not necessarily a disadvantage because the Buoy would rise and fall out of phase with the waves in the sea. This meant that the water inside the device would be going up when the device was going down, and vice versa.

There were reports of progress with other devices which have never gained the attention given to the main contenders, and the conclusions of highly qualified observers, led by Ian Glendenning of the CEGB.

This was the culmination of the first two years of the government programme. The first four devices—the Duck, the Raft, the OWC, and the Rectifier—had dominated the first stage of the programme and they became the wave energy classics. They were joined by the Airbag, which was different from all of them and which gave birth to the Clam; the Belfast Buoy which was to have counterparts in Norway and Denmark; the Vickers submerged OWC; and the Bristol Cylinder. All of this was positive, new, and encouraging. It provided signposts towards a future which would be free of the need to consume fossil fuels and uranium.

But what the Heathrow Hotel conference came to be noted for was the first official set of costings for wave energy. Those figures broke over the conference like a thunderclap. Peter Clark of Rendel, Palmer, & Tritton (RPT) presented the major overview of the scene. His company had been employed as the government consultants and it had done its work impressively. Its survey of wave energy was, for that time, comprehensive and invaluable. Reading it with the advantage of hindsight, one can see what a useful contribution it made. It focussed on essential issues: feasibility, reliability, efficiency, and output. If it had stopped there, it would have received widespread acclaim. But then it responded to the government's demand to assess cost. RPT should have told the government not to be silly, not to imagine that any sensible statement could be made about the cost of one unit of electricity from a 2000 MW power station, using a new technology, at a stage when there was nothing bigger than experimental 1/10th scale models in the water.

Instead, it said that wave electricity from the main devices would cost 20–40p in three cases and 30–60p in the case of the HRS Rectifier. (Grid electricity in 1978 cost 2p a unit.) The only device to receive a nod of approval was the Airbag, which was costed at 5–10p, with a question mark against both figures. It had been entered into the programme at a late stage and it gained from what Grove-Palmer called 'the new device syndrome: the problems look easy because you don't know what they are.'

Peter Clark almost apologised for the vast range in the pricing or 'very broad limits', as he called the 100 per cent leap from 20 to 40p. 'The reason why we don't want to be more exact is that . . . the designs are changing and improving so fast that costs which were produced last July wouldn't apply to some of the devices which you have seen today.' It would have been better if he had said that it was not possible at that stage to make any sensible estimate.

As events worked out, RPT had scored a double zero. It had praised the Airbag and this was the first device to be abandoned, by its own inventor, Professor Michael French, who himself decided that it was unreliable; and it had said that the HRS Rectifier was the most expensive. In fact, it was this device which, in the form of the Norwegian Tapchan, was the first to succeed and to gain commercial backing and orders. So the one 'winner' chosen was the first to be discarded; and the one written off most fiercely was the first to succeed.

On that day at the Heathrow Hotel, the bleak cost estimates did enormous damage. Journalists and overseas buyers lost interest and left the conference, not bothering to return for the second day. Worse still, the costings were repeated in an official energy paper a year later,[2] and they have continued to darken the image of wave energy. They were misleading because they were based on preliminary plans for prototypes and gave little allowance for the benefits to come later from mass production of identical modules. There was no allowance for competitive tendering which would bring down the absurdly high costs attached to many components. To touch on two typical examples, which are examined in detail in Chapter 8, the cables which bring the electricity ashore were held to be many times more faulty than similar cables anywhere else in the world. (The leader of the Norwegian wave energy team, Knut Bønke, wrote to Salter: 'If failure rates on sea cables in the UK would be as predicted, the UK faces no energy crisis, only a cable crisis.') The main structures were given a 25-year lifetime when many of them were similar to harbour walls which can last for a century and more.

I had resolved to prevent this book from becoming too concerned with costings, which I insist are an irrelevance at this stage. But there is one aspect of the Heathrow Hotel conference estimates which needs to be examined: they were based on premises which were far more favourable than those which have since been imposed by Whitehall. The Heathrow figures assumed an interest rate of 5 per cent, which was standard for the Treasury at that time. But since then Whitehall thinking has changed: today, everything is based on *discount* rates and with a capital-intensive technology such as wave power, in which most of the expenditure is at the start of the project, this can make the energy appear more expensive than that of its competitors, which are cheap to build but likely to be increasingly expensive to run.

Worse still, the Treasury discount rate was increased in 1989 from 5 to 8 per cent. If that basis had been used in 1978 at the Heathrow Hotel, then the figure of 40p (which was anyway 20 times the standard rate for electricity and absurd enough) would have been even higher. The obverse of this argument is that the present official estimates of around 8p, based on an 8 per cent discount rate, would have been much lower if based on a 5 per cent interest rate and would have made wave energy appear wonderfully cheap.

This needs a little expansion. A discount rate is weighted against investing in the future. It is a method of calculating costs which is biased against capital-intensive projects such as wave energy, which have heavy expenditure at the onset when construction takes place but become profitable later on when the running costs fall because the 'fuel' is free. Hydroelectric schemes like those in Scotland, Norway, Switzerland, Italy, and many other countries, which produce some of the world's cheapest electricity, would never have been sanctioned if present-day methods had been applied. Yet hydroelectric power is generated by Scottish Hydro for less than a penny per unit, though the electricity consumers were not happy when they had to produce the capital in the 1930s and 1950s to build the huge stations in the mountains.

By contrast, a Combined Cycle Gas Turbine is cheap to manufacture and so appears a good buy, although in the future it can be expected that the price of the gas which it uses will rise steeply as demand increases, with the growing popularity of gas as a fuel, and as gasfields are depleted. But wave (and wind and tidal) power can anticipate a wonderfully favourable future because their fuel comes free, and their running costs will be relatively small items once the value of the capital has been reduced by the passage of time. It is, in real life, similar to a mortgage on a house, in which the householder pays the same amount throughout, with the sum dwindling in real terms. This counts for little with calculations based on discounting, where the argument is that cash now is more important than tomorrow's balance sheet. It is the formula to use if you wish to have gold bars lying idle in the vaults of the Bank of England and in the coffers of local authorities which are not allowed to spend their own money. For anyone seeking a better environment, the opposite applies.

Discounting is based on the theory that costs which arise at the start of construction are of greater significance than costs (or benefits) in the future. So future expenditure and gains are 'discounted'. Then comes the question of what discount rate is chosen. For many years in Britain it was around 3–5 per cent per year. That encouraged growth. But in 1989 the Treasury was dominated by monetarists who wanted to accumulate money, not invest it, and they persuaded the then Chief Secretary, John Major, to raise the government rate from 5 to 8 per cent. The argument used to justify this was that it needed to match the rate of return in the private sector.

Since then, the economy has slumped and returns have declined to below zero as companies have gone into liquidation; interest rates have also been brought down and with them the returns on deposits in building societies and other savings accounts. But the discount rate has stayed high.

If the rate had been 8 per cent in the past, many major projects would have been forbidden. There is nothing sacred about 8 per cent. OFGAS, the Office of Gas Regulation, has suggested that 2.5–5 per cent is adequate. The Director General of OFWAT, the office of Water Regulation, Ian Byatt, himself a former Deputy Chief Economic Adviser at the Treasury, recommends 5 per cent. Tim Eggar, the Energy Minister, disclosed in the House of Commons that the case for going ahead with THORP (the Thermal Oxide Reprocessing Plant at Sellafield) was based on 6 per cent. And in his report on the Sizewell inquiry in 1986, Sir Frank Layfield made it plain that his recommendation that the nuclear power station should be built rested on a discount rate of 5 per cent; had it been 8 per cent, he said, a coal-fired station would have been cheaper.

Yet not only has a discount rate been used by the government and ETSU, not only has it been set at 8 per cent, but in the latest official calculations a commercial rate of 15 per cent has been added on. Thus, in 1993 the

Department of Energy published an important report by Tom Thorpe[3] which gave costings based on these two discount rates, and it should surprise no one to discover that it yielded high costings. For instance, a unit of electricity from the Duck would be 16p at 8 per cent and 26p at 15 per cent. But Thorpe's report includes graphs which enable the reader to discover the cost of a unit if the discount rate is removed, and at that point the Duck would come down to 6p. A shoreline Oscillating Water Column such as the one at Islay would generate for 3, 6, or 9p, depending on discount rates of 0, 8, and 15 per cent. The figures for the Clam are 5, 8, and 12p. And for the OSPREY, the newest device planned for the open sea off Dounreay, the figures are 4, 7, and 10p.

But, an accountant might say, how can you possibly justify charging a zero discount rate? That is, happily, explained by the Energy Minister himself, Tim Eggar. He was asked in Parliament by Llew Smith what assessment had been made of the effect of the 8 per cent discount rate on public sector invesment in energy technology projects. Eggar, who is a merchant banker, replied: 'My Department's investment in energy technology projects is for research or regulatory purposes, for which assessment on a discounting basis is not appropriate.'[4] A splendid reply—if only Eggar would be consistent and use it for wave energy!

How should a true cost be calculated? The best answer to the Treasury has come from an unexpected source: ETSU. In its 'obituary' of wave energy, R26, it wrote: 'The simplest way of calculating the cost of wave energy is to divide the total cost of a wave power station (capital and interest cost plus the costs of operating and maintaining it) by the energy the station delivers to the Grid.'[5] Excellent! The most radical critic of government could not say it better. If only ETSU had stood by this, we might now be gaining benefit from the ceaseless, free activity of the waves which has, ever since the Heathrow conference, been allowed to roar across the world, usually unseen and mostly unharvested. But ETSU went on to say: 'In practice . . . calculations of cost and energy are . . . discounted back to an initial or base year with a discount rate chosen to relate to the rate of interest possible from alternative uses of the capital employed. Discounting these calculations enables the preference for benefits now or later to be quantified.' Except that the benefits of free fuel are ignored and the Treasury game of playing up and down the scale, applying whatever number seems convenient to the monetarists, reduces the world's energy future to a game of chance.

That, I hope, should be sufficient background about the wild card which was thrown into play. I have divided the rest of this chapter into five sections, to recapitulate the stories of the five classic devices, which dominated the first stage of the programme, and resume at Chapter 7 with the story of how wave energy survived.

References

1. Bondi, Sir Hermann (1979). In *Proceedings, wave energy conference, Heathrow Hotel, London, November 22–23 1978*. pp 15. HMSO, London.
2. Clarke, F.J.P. (1979). *Wave energy*. Energy paper No. 42, iv.
3. Thorpe, T.W. (1993). *A review of wave energy*, vols. 1 and 2. ETSU R-72. Department of Trade and Industry, London
4. Eggar, T. Feb. 17 1993. *Official report*. (Hansard) column 209. HMSO, London. vol. 219.
5. Davies, P.G., Cloke, M.S., Major, K.A., Page, D.I., and Taylor, R.J. (1985). *Wave energy*. ETSU R26. pp 87.

6.1. The first big scheme

The pioneer, this century, of wave energy on a large scale is a civil/electrical engineer who learned about the power of water while working on hydro-electric schemes in Scotland in the 1930s. There had been several small schemes for the use of wave energy, including one in Monte Carlo. But in the 1950s Walton Bott came within reach of launching a scheme which could have produced all the power needed for the 800 000 people who live on the 2000 km^2 Indian Ocean island of Mauritius, one of the most densely populated areas in the world (roughly twice the density of the United Kingdom). It has no fuel of its own and could have led the world in producing benign power from the sea when, in 1966, the decision was taken to abandon work because the world price of oil was falling, and it was cheaper to bring the oil almost 5000 km from the Persian Gulf and burn it to make electricity than to build a wave energy plant on the beach.

Twenty years later, in December 1986, Bott stood beside me on a Norwegian island. It was bitterly cold and we were being showered with water from the man-made fountain produced by the wave power station. Rocks, too, were slamming down around us, picked up from the seabed by the waves and lifted up and thrown out of the water. Bott, then aged 79, was impervious to the cold, the wet, and the danger. He was simply delighted. 'It's Mauritius, it's Mauritius!' he kept shouting. It was a slight, excusable over-simplification. The Norwegians (see Chapter 9) had had to build and substitute their own way of capturing the waves to replace what nature had given to Mauritius. But Bott was entitled to his cry of triumph.

The Bott plan was based on a natural advantage enjoyed by Mauritius. The island is surrounded not only by water; it has a fringing reef which offers, literally, a stepping stone, saving the cost of underwater foundation work.

Bott went to Mauritius in 1953 to set up an electricity board after having spent many years in Scotland working on hydroelectric schemes which are still producing cheap power. He set out to plan the island's future energy resources and was given financial support by the Crown Agents.

Fig. 6.3 Bott, at the age of 79, flew to the Norwegian site near Bergen and stood, impervious to the cold, the water, and the rocks which were being lifted up by the waves and were landing all around him. The splash in the background shows water landing in the reservoir after being carried uphill in a tapering channel called a Tapchan. It was a development of the idea that he had pioneered in Mauritius.

Mauritius has a small tidal range and its problem of capturing sea power might well prove significant to many countries which could build their devices on or close to the beach. Bott set out methodically, reading all the literature available on waves and tides, which goes back to 1848 when Sir George Airy pioneered the study in his book *Theory of Water Waves*. Information on wave *energy* was effectively non-existent. Bott also approached the Hydraulics Research Station at Wallingford, Oxfordshire, which produced a scheme that is a development of his ideas.

He decided that, at least in the Indian Ocean, the waves that must be used were those breaking on the beach because there was no way of building structures that could survive the force of the open sea. In semi-retirement at home in Winchester, he told me: 'I came to the conclusion that you could not put anything mechanical or electrical in the open sea. In Mauritius, we experienced cyclones which could bend 25 cm girders double. In Scotland, a 7000-ton breakwater was rolled over. It was replaced by a 14 000-ton one, which was also destroyed. An American heavy cruiser lost 30 m of bow from wave action.'

He is also sceptical of the prospect of capturing energy in deep water off Britain. 'You could have two 30 m waves meeting in phase. That is a force that could move St Paul's Cathedral. The only way to protect your structure would be to submerge it in time, if that is indeed possible. You cannot compare it with an oil platform which is solidly based on four legs and which is designed to let the waves through. It is not there to collect and process them.

'Then you have the problem of transmitting the power to land by cables not only resistant to sea water and sea animals but also presumably capable of dealing with violently-moving cable connections at the sea end.' He is not seeking to belittle alternative schemes which come from people with a different engineering background. They believe that the problems he and others have listed can be overcome.

The Raft is an obvious candidate for survival—Kon Tiki demonstrated that. The Duck has the advantage that its biggest part, the beak, is designed to flip up and down in the waves. It would also be part of a line of perhaps 50 Ducks, so that if one were damaged it could be taken out of the generating system: the electrical connections are being arranged 'like the lights on a Xmas tree', as one expert has put it, so that one can go out without shorting the whole system. It is also thought possible that a Duck could do a complete somersault and still function. And there are also systems being devised which would enable a beak to be unclipped from its bearings and towed away as soon as there was a 'weather window'. The OWC may present more problems because it is estimated that one unit—a Masuda 'ship'—would need to be about 220 m long and 33 m in beam to be comparable with one Raft. This will be a problem for the National Engineering Laboratory, who are perhaps the world's leading experts on mooring; they are not sanguine about the size of the problem.

As to the cable, this is less of a problem today than it was at the time of Bott's early experiments. Pirelli have devised a method of manufacturing cables in lengths of 80 km—an important development because joints are always a weak point. They have experience of laying submarine cables going back many years. As long ago as 1965, they laid a cable of 119 km from the Italian mainland at Piombino to Corsica and Sardinia, able to carry 300 MW.

By coincidence, they have been working on a cable that will answer many of the new problems and it is, ironically, nuclear energy which has led them to it.

An American company, Power Service Electric and Gas Co., asked them to produce 345 kV a.c. submarine cables from floating offshore nuclear power stations. The distance would be only 7 km and the cables would be embedded in the sea bed.

There is no problem about manufacturing it for that distance without joints, but the final cable section to the floating power station provides exactly the problems that will have to be solved if we choose floating wave energy generators. The cables must be able to follow the platform as it moves in the waves and tides. The solution chosen by Pirelli is a flexible cable with a corrugated aluminium sheath, instead of the normal reinforced lead sheath of the submarine cable. Full-scale tests have been carried out on prototypes, including fatigue-bending tests intended to reproduce the maximum mechanical stresses anticipated. The answers were judged satisfactory. So technology, designed for nuclear power, is moving towards solving one of the problems associated with wave energy which would have been judged insuperable only a few years before.

To return to Bott: in March, 1975, he gave the first major address on wave energy to the Royal Society of Arts.[1] Indeed, it was probably the first time that a scientific audience of that eminence had been made aware of the subject in detail. He began by explaining how the waves convey energy and it is interesting to note that the basic facts that he spelt out would have been new at that stage to a large number of our most distinguished scientists who had never before had occasion to pay much attention to what Bott rightly called 'a neglected corner of natural science'. Had he been talking in this way of, say, steam power, it would have been regarded as insulting to explain how that fellow Watt managed to do it; but on the waves, in 1975 we were nearly all at fifth form level.

Bott produced a table to demonstrate a fact which we have already encountered: that the height of the wave is the most significant measurement. Thus, a wave 1.5 m high with a wavelength of 15 m will produce 4.33 kW while a wave of the same length but double the height (3 m) will produce 17.9 kW, more than four times as much energy, because the height is squared in the equation accepted by scientists as depicting wave energy. But a wave of 1.5 m in height with a wavelength of 30 m will produce 8.9 kW, while a wave of the same height and double the length (60 m) will produce only twice as much power—17.8 kW. And when we move into the realm of higher waves, the difference is even more startling. A wave 6 m high will contain energy equivalent to 220 kW while one of 12 m will be 880 kW. That is why the highest waves are the most attractive, although they create the greatest design and construction problems.

This is the area in which hard decisions are soon going to be demanded: how much do you spend on building a device which can withstand, absorb and process giant waves and, if successful, will produce more electricity than a cheaper device in calmer water? At what point is it sensible to concentrate

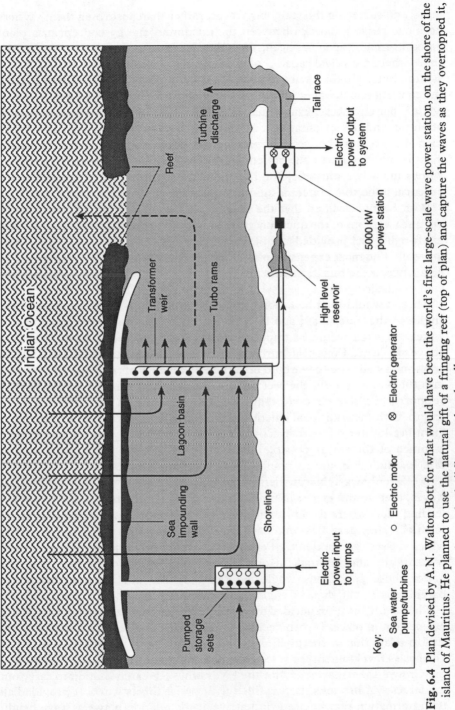

Fig. 6.4 Plan devised by A.N. Walton Bott for what would have been the world's first large-scale wave power station, on the shore of the island of Mauritius. He planned to use the natural gift of a fringing reef (top of plan) and capture the waves as they overtopped it, turning the coastline into a lagoon by building crossbund walls.

merely on surviving the really big waves, rather than absorbing them? Where does one strike a balance between the maximum energy concept of a plant based in rough, open sea against a rather less energy-intensive plant on the shore where a survival capacity of virtually 100 per cent can be achieved? For Walton Bott, with his civil engineering background and knowledge of the sea, the constructional, operational, and survival problem is naturally uppermost, while other engineers, from other disciplines, will emphasise the significance of output and the advantages of a floating structure. It is like the battle at the turn of the century between the protagonists of alternating and direct current. That is one reason why the present stage is so exciting: we are privileged to be witnessing what must be, for the moment, a theoretical discussion on a practical issue that concerns all our futures.

Bott, having decided that the idea of placing an operational plant in the open sea was 'out of the question', turned instead to the shore. He realised that the fringing reef provided a stable foundation on which to build an impounding wall. The most expensive part of any sea barrier is the foundation and in Mauritius, as he put it, 'nature has done it for us', thus greatly reducing the civil engineering cost.

All that would then be needed would be to build two crossbunds, at right angles to the outer wall, and turn the shore into an enclosed lagoon inside which the water would be trapped at a top water level of between 2 and 3 m above sea level. Low-head turbines and generators would be built into the crossbund walls and they would be turned by the flow of sea water rolling back into the ocean. Would the reef be able to take the strain? It would have to support a massive concrete ramp weighing many tons per foot run of its length, with the additional kinetic pressure provided by the sea. It would be a giant breakwater but with exactly the opposite function—instead of repelling as much of the sea as possible, it would have to allow waves over the top offering the minimum resistance above a certain height.

Bott's reply was: 'Nature herself has built the reefs in the very teeth of the waves, even to the extent of providing an extra tough species of coral at the leading edge, where the impact is greatest. This species (*Madrepora*) is in the form of a steel hard boss and has proved itself capable of resisting anything which the sea can hand out.' (Personally, I would prefer to put that point less romantically and say that the only type of coral which could have survived under those conditions would be the toughest; this is a philosophical parenthesis rather than an engineering quibble.)

The Mauritius team decided to experiment with small ramps but they could not be kept in place. It then decided to use wave recorders anchored offshore and to relate this to energy in tank experiments. So it asked the Ministry of Overseas Development for research funds and then, with the collaboration of the Crown Agents, arranged for the Hydraulics Research Station to carry out model tests in its tanks. Bott is filled with praise for its work. It provided all the information that he needed to arrive at the relation between wave height and period and retained energy after overspill. It varied the wave periods from 6 to 10 seconds, which are the normal limits off Mauritius. The period is significant because the arrival of each new wave tops up the level of the reservoir and changes the pattern of overspill back into the sea. Then the experimenters varied the wave heights and lengths, the wall heights, the depth of water immediately outside the wall and even the type of surface of the mock seabed.

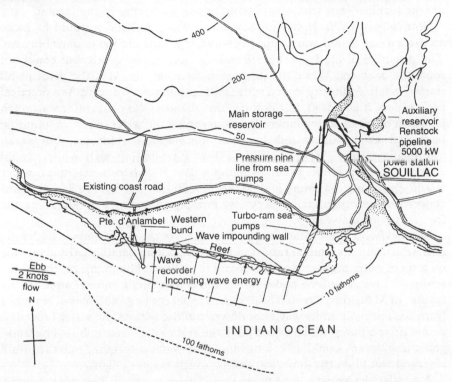

Fig. 6.5 The Bott plan to receive sea water into a low-level reservoir, pump it up to a high-level reservoir with turbo-ram pumps, and let it run down into a 5000 kW power station.

A wall that was too high would provide a deep reservoir part of the time but would admit little water at other times and this could make wave energy a non-firm source of power. Bott wanted his scheme to be a basic, steady provider and that had to mean a lower height than a wall that would provide the deepest reservoir on favourable occasions.

Yet the lower the height of the wall, the smaller the reservoir would be and this would also mean a low turbine head as the water ran back into the sea. The cost would be greater—a head of 10 m for a turbine is about one-third the cost for a head of two metres. Instead of being able to provide two 2500 kW sets, they would have had to think in terms of five 1000 kW sets with all their auxiliary gear. Bott calculated that a shallow reservoir meant that the water power would be able to provide less than one hour's running at full load of 5000 kW. Even this would need a dredged channel to enable the water to run out freely and that would cost more money. The power would be non-firm and there would have to be a thermal generating plant as insurance. So everything indicated a higher wall, a deeper basin, and a more economic head for the turbine—but with less potential energy arriving in the lagoon.

Bott calls it a Charybdis and Scylla situation; perhaps it would be more accurate to say that he was trapped between the devil and the shallow blue sea. The resources of the Hydraulics Research Station could help but could not solve the problem. While the discussion went on, in 1966, the price of oil started to fall. Authority looked at the scheme and said: forget it. As a practical proposition, it was dead, but Bott did not abandon the plan and it was much later that he hit upon a solution. It was to regard the water in the impounding basin not as the direct link between the sea and a turbine, but as an intermediate store. It would have a low surrounding wall which would enable it to receive energy for 24 hours a day. But then the captured water would be converted from low grade (so far as the hydraulic head was concerned) into high grade energy by pumping the water uphill, using the free energy of the sea to do it.

Bott devised a pump which was a rotary form of the old-fashioned hydraulic ram, which with its familiar thud-thud has been a long-established and reliable method of pumping water on farms and in villages. His pump combines the action of a water turbine and a water pump in a single rotor housed in one casing. In Mauritius, it would be designed to accept large volumes of sea water from the reservoir on its way back down into the sea. As the water flowed, it would drive a pump which would push the rest of the water uphill. The water going into the sea would drive a turbine. The water returning from the uphill reservoir would do the same, but from a much greater height.

A similar device was used more than 50 years ago in Germany when a 'transformer pump' with a double runner was built on a weir on the River Izar near Munich. It was given its name because it 'transformed' low pressure water into high pressure water. The mechanical efficiency is estimated at only 60 per cent but this is of only academic interest when the energy driving the pump is free. It should be noted that the CEGB and many other authorities use pumped storage by feeding the upper reservoirs from power stations driven by fossil fuels, providing four units of electricity to push the water uphill for every three units produced by the water coming back. Gravity absorbs 25 per cent.

Bott points out that the storage required would be much smaller than is normally needed for a conventional river hydro project, where water flow can be insufficient for six months of the year. In Mauritius, it would be as little as six weeks in total, spaced out at different periods of the year.

As we know, it did not happen for the ludicrous reason that oil was then cheaper. But the plan remained and it was not forgotten at the HRS, where the director, Robert Russell, acknowledges his indebtedness to Bott. 'Our system goes on from the Mauritius scheme', he told me.

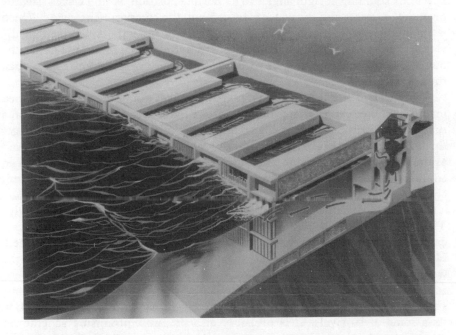

Fig. 6.6 The HRS Rectifier. Gates (which are non-return valves, like letter boxes at right angles) open and close as the water pressure changes and the waves roll in. The crest of the waves, and the increased hydrostatic pressure below the surface as the depth (and therefore the pressure) increases, force the valves to open. The water enters high-level reservoirs and finds its way out through the only exit, into a low-level reservoir, driving a turbine as it goes. It is sucked back into the sea as the waves fall, the pressure is reduced, and the alternative set of gates opens.

The scheme has been the least-publicised for two reasons: it is not photogenic and it has an unfriendly-sounding name, the HRS Rectifier. It was originally the Russell Rectifier but Russell, for reasons of modesty, preferred to keep his own name out of it. So, apart from the lack of attraction of a series of initials which need to be explained, the layman needs to be told what a rectifier means to an engineer. It sounds vaguely like a course of remedial physiotherapy. In reality, it is a method to rectify, or change, a movement. In the HRS Rectifier, the movement of the waves is changed from up and down into a stream of water which drives a turbine.

A better name would be the Russell Lock because it does resemble a lock gate dividing a high-level reservoir from one lower down. The plan is to have a rectangular box standing on the seabed in some 15–20 m of water, possibly 5–10 km from the shore. It will be the size of a giant tanker. One half of it is divided into a column of gates made from concrete, with hinges of reinforced rubber. These gates open only inwards and the easiest comparison is with a letter box standing at right angles to its normal position. As the waves rise, the pressure increases and the water is forced into the compartment inside, which is the high-level reservoir. The pressure comes from the movement of the wave energy at the crest; lower down, it is a hydrostatic pressure. That is, the increased depth as the waves rise produces increased pressure and forces open the gates.

The gates are, like the letter box, non-return valves and the water is trapped inside a tall box. As the water mounts, it is driven to the only available exit, a turbine which leads into the lower-level reservoir. And as the water surges through, the turbine turns, driving a generator and producing electricity. And as the water builds up inside the low-level reservoir, pressure increases on an adjoining series of gates, this time designed to allow water out but not to admit any.

Can such a structure stand on the seabed without being smashed to pulp? Those who were sceptical of its chances tended to say, 'Well, if Russell says it can, then it can'. His reputation in the wave industry was very high indeed. His team were unrivalled in their experience of making things stand up in the water.

It was a scheme which, as Russell put it to me, 'has the virtue of extreme simplicity'. That may also be one reason that it has attracted less attention than some of its rivals. It is probably also the most promising scheme for countries with a low tidal range, such as Mauritius itself and the Mediterranean countries. It has a major advantage over the original Bott plan, in that it uses the trough of the wave to suck water out of the low-level reservoir; his plan depended on potential energy responding to gravity.

The full-scale model would be designed to produce 10 MW on the basis of 70 kW/m. A 1/30th scale model was built at the HRS at Wallingford. Russell wanted to build a set of flap gates full-scale, mount them on a 'rig'—which means any test device that can stand in the sea—and test them in real-life conditions. This would have made good sense because the only part of the structure which involved new technology was the gates.

Russell was confident that they could withstand the pressure and was unusual among the experimenters in that he put great store by that natural, old-fashioned material: rubber. 'We would use stiffened rubber, incorporating something like tyre fabric,' he said. 'Rubber is infinitely long-living in salt water if you keep it out of the sun. Keep it wet and keep it cool. You can find tyres on the beach 20 or 30 years old.'

The thinking was typical of Russell's style. He is a tall, thin, aloof man with a rather sad manner. The mansion in the Oxfordshire countryside where his headquarters were based seemed a generation away from the brasher laboratories at Marchwood and East Kilbride. One felt that Russell, though he was too polite to say it, had a slight disdain for the newer arrivals on the scene. His Hydraulics Research Station had been advising chaps about building things in the sea for a long time now . . . He also made a natural ally for Bott, who is a kindly, elderly engineer; both are very far from the whizz-kid atmosphere that surrounded the Salter project.

The Mauritius and HRS projects had one asset that was enjoyed by none of the others: both were designed to form artificial lakes of huge area in the sea. They would be ideal for fish farming. There would be a continuous throughput of sea water, excellent oxygenation because of the wave and spray action, continuous throughput of plankton and other small fish organisms, and a fully-enclosed sea area which could be sub-divided for the separation of fish varieties and sizes by means of floating sea cages, without the danger for the fishermen of working in the open sea.

There was another advantage, which could apply also to some of the other devices, which must not be overlooked: electrolysis. By passing a direct current through a liquid, it can be separated into its constituents. With water, it can be turned back into hydrogen and oxygen. The hydrogen can be used as a gas for cooking and other purposes or it can be combined with limestone and made into methanol, a liquid fuel on which cars and aeroplanes can run. The difficulty until now has been that the energy needed to produce the electric current was greater than the energy produced by the hydrogen. It was, therefore, wasteful. There is no sense in using up more fossil fuel to produce energy than the substitute fossil fuel will produce. But this ceases to be a factor when, in Salter's words, 'the gods pay for the waves'. We could be on the eve of a development when we can produce not only electricity from the sea but also the motor car fuel which we are consuming at a frightening rate by eating into our oil stocks. We may, in fact, have more than one tiger in our tank. We could also run desalination plants on the 'free' energy provided by the waves. Bott's conclusion is that world interest is mounting into the desirability of creating nucleus communities, virtually self-sufficient in energy, food, water, and other essentials (and petrol has become one of them). A Mauritius-type project would, in his opinion, be 'an almost perfect catalyst for such development'.

Fish farming, desalination, and electrolysis are not the main purposes of wave energy. They are the possible spin-offs. All of them give an advantage to the Mauritius-type project which Norway has developed successfully.

References

1. Bott, A.N. Walton. (1975). Power plus proteins from the sea. *The Royal Society of Arts Journal*, **CXXIII**, 486–503.

6.2 Changing water into air

The catalogue that came through my letterbox from Japan made it all real: for the first time, I was looking at graphs showing not what the various wave energy devices would or should be able to do, but at what they had actually done. I understood just what Mr Goodwin of the Department of Energy had meant when he talked of his discovery, 'at a point where credibility mattered', that wave energy was working, in that case in Salter's laboratory. In this case, the power point was no bigger than the dynamo on the rim of a bicycle tyre, compared with a power station needed to fuel a factory or a city. But it worked: it provided a navigation buoy which burnt neither gas nor oil and would never need refuelling, and it demonstrated that wave energy could function in real life.

It was the product of Professor Yoshio Masuda, a former Japanese naval commander. His inspiration was to turn water power into a stream of air. It was to be used by nearly everyone in the first generation of working devices. It was a key feature of one of the Norwegian stations at Bergen, of the Gully station on Islay, and of the OSPREY. In fact, the only device which did not use it was the Tapchan, which used water directly.

Without the Masuda invention, wave energy would have appeared even more daunting. The problem for the early research workers was (in the words of the Thorpe report[1]) to turn 'the low velocities and high forces associated with sea waves into the high speeds and lower forces required by conventional electrical generators'. In non-technical terms, the waves arrive every seven or eight seconds and they land at times with enough force to smash down a concrete sea wall or a steel pier. This huge force had to be made gentler but also faster, so that it could make a turbo-generator revolve at 1000 rpm or more.

The simple brilliance of Masuda's solution has been so completely absorbed by wave energy that it is sometimes forgotten what an inspiration of genius it was. He trapped the waves inside a hollow cylinder which was open to the sea at its base. As the waves rose and fell in the sea outside, the column of water inside the cylinder mimicked the movement (because water finds its own level). So you had a column of water inside the cylinder oscillating—that is, going up and down every seven or so seconds. It was originally called the Masuda Device but then acquired the unattractive name of Oscillating Water Column. As the Column rose, it forced the pocket of air above it to rise. The air went out through the only exit, at the top of the cylinder, which was occupied by an air turbine which revolved as the stream of air rushed through. Then, as the wave fell in a trough, the column of water desended, and air was sucked in from the atmosphere to fill the vacuum, spinning the air turbine again.

On such a small scale, and for the purpose of lighting a 60-watt bulb and driving a flasher unit, it would obviously have been possible to use other sources—for instance, solar panels, or wind turbines. But the significance of Masuda's invention was that it was showing that the waves themselves could be made to serve the needs of an electricity consumer (in this case, the ships which were sailing across those waves) instead of drawing on some other source. Three hundred OWCs are functioning in the Pacific. And obviously they could be, and have proved to be, the forerunner of a power station using this completely new source.

Any engineer will tell you that when you have a device which works at small scale, the problems that arise when you move upscale can rarely be anticipated in advance; but press your engineer and he will admit that the unforeseeable problems are invariably capable of solution. For months I had been looking at documents showing what could be done with devices in laboratory tanks and with scaled-down models on fairly open water; it is now difficult to convey how illuminating it was, at that point, to see what had happened when the wave energy generators had been functioning in the open sea, in real life, for a purpose, to guide shipping. It was the first step from the theoretical to the practical.

How efficient was it? In the early days, the answer was: who cares? As Salter said in a light-hearted moment, 'efficiency itself is of no concern when the gods pay for the waves'. I think that that was the right attitude. The wave energy people allowed themselves to be harried and nagged by ETSU into thinking that cost was the most important issue. In fact, none of the renewables had been promoted as a way of saving money. They were intended to save the earth. It was nuclear power that claimed to be dirt cheap.

But for those to whom efficiency does matter, the more precise answer was that, when fuelling navigation buoys, wave power was actually too efficient. Trinity House found in tests that the six 2-volt batteries (divided into six units deliberately, to guard against failure) which received the electricity were 'on charge all the time' and designed so that when they reached a fully-charged state they had to shut themselves off from the battery so that the water did not boil away. A motorist will appreciate this. The batteries were the same capacity as a 12-volt car battery which has to drive a starter motor, boost the heater, and power the windscreen wipers as well as all the lights and the flasher unit, and do it with a charge which, in many cases, is supplied only during short journeys; the Masuda Buoy had to light only a 60-watt bulb and a flasher supported by a 24-hour charging process.

What happened to them? Trinity House tried them out but found that they were rarely suitable to its needs. Its practice is to keep its fossil-fuel buoys at sea for four years before servicing them but with wave energy buoys, using a fast-spinning turbine and generator, it needed to change the bearings after two years. That meant sending out a ship (at a cost of £900 an hour) every two years instead of every four, so that, even with free fuel, it did not pay. It has now settled for solar photovoltaic power for the simpler buoys. But for the more elaborate ones, which send out fog signals and employ radar transponders as well as light, solar power is insufficient, and here Trinity House is conducting experiments with wave power, which is more bountiful. Irish Lights, which services its units every two years, found that they were excellent for what they described as a good number of years but then they needed new generators which were expensive. So they, too, converted to solar photovoltaic power except for those which needed a fog signal as well as a light; here they used the waves to blow air through a warning whistle.

These experiences indicate how important is the practical application. Could these unsuspected problems have been detected by computers in the laboratory? I doubt it.

The Japanese brochure took the reader into a world very different from the 2000 MW power stations which we had been discussing in Britain. It talked of producing 30 W in waves of 40 cm with a 3-second period. This is a very small sea compared with the waves of perhaps 15 m which we have become accustomed to thinking about in the North Sea and the Atlantic. The Sea of Japan does not have the waves which we enjoy in the North Atlantic. The Japanese also wished to emphasise that their buoys could function in a placid sea. They are moored on a long chain so that, inshore, they can rise and fall with the tides as well as the waves and still generate.

In all these activities the Japanese have gone storming ahead, just as they did during the last war, and in their post-war industrialisation, in what was once thought of as the British style: the pragmatic approach. They have used the waves for lighthouses, ocean survey instruments, and observation towers as well as the *Kaimei*, a ship with holes drilled in its stern. They were given a seven-year programme backed by $39.5 million (then about £22 million) while the British Government allocated first £1 million in 1976, followed by £2.5 million in 1977, and £2.9 million in 1978—'drops in the ocean', as one commentator called them. We carried out research; Japan acted.

The original NEL feasibility study,[5] in February 1975, described the Masuda device as 'the most promising scheme' on the grounds that it had no large moving parts, high efficiency, a valved air turbine generator system which had already been demonstrated as effective and reliable in small units, that the devices could be built using existing shipbuilding and construction technology, and that it had a higher credibility rating than most of its rivals. Note the high priority given to efficiency.

Just over a year later, when the Department of Energy began to distribute money for further research, the NEL was assigned the Masuda project to work on. The engineers there remain strong advocates of its virtues.

One leading engineer from another organisation made the point that it would be able to respond to the rate of irregularities in the sea more easily than the Duck and the Raft. He put it this way: 'The Raft and the Duck have the bad thing that they transmit with high torque and low speed. But wave energy can rotate an air turbine at 1200 rpm. So with the Duck and the Raft you have a slow movement at first. The device has to accommodate its speed to the

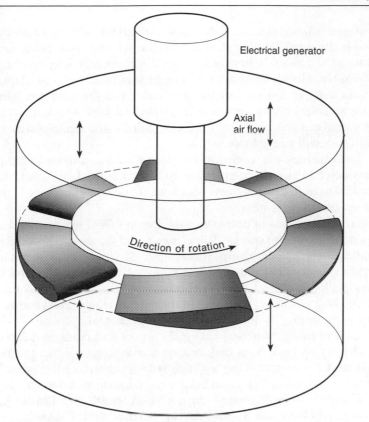

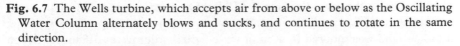

Fig. 6.7 The Wells turbine, which accepts air from above or below as the Oscillating Water Column alternately blows and sucks, and continues to rotate in the same direction.

particular type of waves which are hitting it. If something is slow to respond, it won't be able to react quickly. And the higher the torque and the slower the speed, the bigger the machine and therefore the more expensive it is. It would be easier to smooth out the erratic output of an OWC.'

In all the early OWCs, the air was 'rectified' by valves and pipes which rerouted it so that it entered the turbine from one direction only. This had the disadvantage of valves which needed to be pushed open, with a loss of energy, and which are bound to stick and leak from time to time. To solve this problem, Queen's University, Belfast introduced a revolutionary turbine which revolved in the same direction whether the air came from above or below. There had never before been a turbine like it.

It is called the Wells Turbine,[2] after its inventor, Professor Alan Wells, FRS. It has been adopted by nearly everyone in wave energy, including the Japanese. It was described by one of the team working on it at Queen's as resembling an aeroplane propeller producing no forward thrust. Its inventor, now semi-retired, is also the designer of the OSPREY (**O**cean **S**well-**P**owered **R**enewable **E**nergy), which at the time of writing was being built for launching as the world's first wave power station standing on the seabed in the open sea. His turbine has also been incorporated into the Clam, which uses an enclosed air system but has the same need for a turbine which can accept the air from either direction as it is squeezed forward and aft. It has also been challenged, particularly by Professor Salter, who believes that variable pitch turbines will prove more efficient.

The Wells turbine was a refinement—that is, it was intended to improve a system which had already been shown to be workable. Until then, the main purpose had been to devise a plant which would deliver electricity. The Wells turbine set out to do it better.

Another 'luxury' was to devise a shape for an OWC which would capture the maximum amount of energy. It was, again, the Japanese who led the world by building a wave energy ship, the *Kaimei*. It was a brave sortie into the (largely) unknown. They did what many of us in Britain would have liked to see: they drilled a row of holes in the bottom of a ship-shaped barge and pushed the boat out to see what would happen. It taught everyone a lot. Not all of it was promising. It demonstrated that a great deal of energy was lost in a power station which, itself, was riding the waves and rising and falling with them. That could have been deduced by many scientists but the Japanese showed that it was correct. They also learned a lot about conversion efficiency from wave power to air power and the best places to position the openings.

The *Kaimei* was an 820-tonne ship, 80m in length and 12m in breadth, launched in 1977 by the Japan Marine Science and Technology Center (JAMSTEC), the world's first 1 MW wave power station. It had eight openings to the sea along its hull, with turbines on top, each rated at 125 kW, and was moored in 40m of water, three kilometres off shore. Seven of the turbines were Japanese and the eighth was contributed by Britain.

The *Kaimei's* movement means that she is losing much of the energy which is represented by the difference between the movement of the ship and the movement of the water column. It is true that the two will be moving in different phases and the ship could be moving down as the column was rising and there would be an advantage in this. But the consensus is that there is nothing better than a firm base on the seabed for an OWC. The Japanese worked closely with the British, used the Wells Turbine, and publicly credited the contribution of George Moody, a mechanical engineer specialising in fluid dynamics at the NEL.[3] He was one of the early team at the NEL dealing with wave energy.

I met him in his NEL office in East Kilbride outside Glasgow in 1976, when wave energy was young. The *Kaimei* had not been launched but the NEL had been conducting its own experiments on OWCs, which it envisaged as shaped like a floating arch, or an upside-down U-shape, in the water.[4] Moody put it this way: 'If you could fix it on the seabed, you would be on to a great thing.

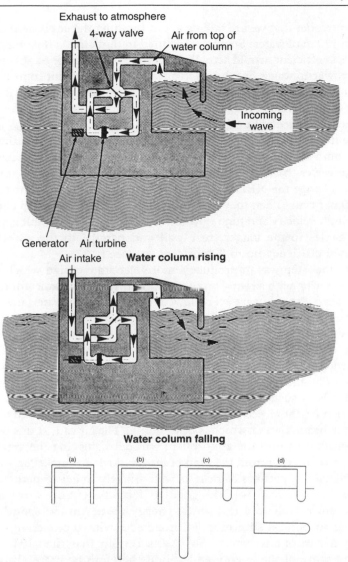

Fig. 6.8 Schematic operation of NEL Oscillating Water Column. This design shows how the flow of air had to be directed along a tortuous path in order to strike the turbine from the same direction, whether the wave was rising or falling, before the invention of the Wells turbine. Its progress depended on a four-way valve (centre) which had to change the direction of the powerful stream of air as the waves rose and fell. The operation would have to be halted whenever the valve jammed or leaked.

The second bank of drawings shows how the NEL design evolved. (a) shows the original idea of an upturned canister; (b) shows the first improvement that gave it an asymmetric design with the shorter side facing the waves; (c) shows the elimination of the sharp corners which cause high velocities and high flow losses; and (d) shows the addition of a base plate, resulting in the most efficient design.

But remember that we are talking about building the equivalent of a harbour wall in 120 m of water. So we are inclined to think that a floating device, even if it is less efficient, would actually be better. It would not be able to accept the most powerful waves but the mechanical energy could not cope, anyway. You have a finite structure so it is just as well if these devastating forces are filtered out. You are actually better off with a less efficient device. There is a sharper decline in efficiency but the output is still high.'

The first improvement suggested by the NEL had been to make one side of the column shorter than the other, to provide a gap at the side facing the most fruitful waves (b). This would help the waves to enter and go 'up the spout'. By this change the NEL increased efficiency from 30 per cent to something like 70 per cent. Then they improved again to eliminate sharp corners which cause high velocity and high flow losses (c). Finally, they built a base plate, at right angles to the longer, rear wall and parallel to the seabed, and this increased efficiency up to 90 per cent (d) (see p. 77).

The final step was to produce a more elaborate design which showed the water entering with a rising wave, meeting the air at an isolated, high point of the system (if the air were ever allowed to get below the water, it would bubble upwards through the water, destroying the scheme). The air then pushed shut a valve so that it could circulate, travelling down through an air turbine, before rising and blowing along a horizontal channel from where it was directed (by the closed valve) down, along, and up and out into the atmosphere. The final illustration shows what happens when the wave falls in a trough: air is sucked in from outside and it races round the twisted track, pushing open the closed valve, blowing through the turbine, and then rising to meet the head of water which is descending. The air can, at this point, escape through the sea into the atmosphere without damaging the system because fresh air is entering from the high point (marked 'air intake' on the diagram). It is ingenious, perhaps as near as we are likely to get to perpetual motion.

The Masuda ship was designed to face the waves, with holes in the bottom of its hull, and less of the energy going 'up the spout'. The NEL planned to build a ship moored broadside, with the openings in the side facing the incoming waves. So it was certain that the NEL ship would capture more of the energy and would therefore be more efficient. But it presented problems as well as promise. Colin Greeves, an engineer who had been my patient guide on visits to the NEL, put it this way: 'The water particles will be going through a motion of 20–30 m diameter and the device would try to follow it.' They had to find a means of mooring it so that it was sufficiently stable to resist this torque, without being smashed by it. It was to have been only a 1/10th scale model, taking to the water a year after the Japanese had launched the full-scale prototype. If it had happened, we would have had a superior but smaller device to display to the world. In the event, we were left with nothing but a better plan (on paper) because the government ended funding.

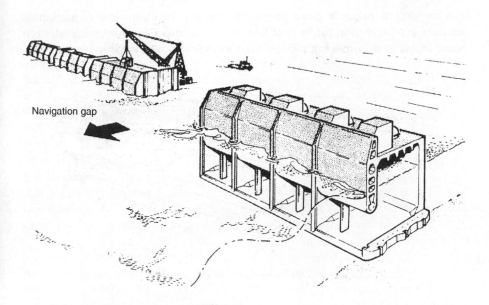

Navigation gap

Fig. 6.9 The design of the NEL 'breakwater' OWC. It stands on the seabed and, like a breakwater or a harbour wall, receives the full force of the waves broadside-on.

What was particularly annoying for students of sea power was that the NEL had set themselves a greater problem than the Japanese had faced over mooring, because the NEL 'ship' would have had to absorb a greater surge of energy. It would have taught everyone many lessons. The NEL were not ones to underestimate the task because they had done a great deal of work with North Sea oil platforms. Unlike Salter and Cockerell, they did not want the major part of their structure moving with the waves. The NEL was proved right in one of its forecasts—that the *Kaimei* would prove less efficient than planned.

The NEL had produced the first major study of wave energy in February, 1975. It is a classic, the basic survey of information which propelled the British Government into the brave step of identifying wave energy as the country's most promising renewable source of energy and investing in it. The study[5] is now nearly 20 years old which makes it, in this field, almost archaic but certainly not obsolescent. It gives a measure of the talent available at the NEL, which was the most elaborate centre of engineering technology in Britain, with a staff of 850 able to cope with any of the problems facing industry. It has 67 acres of laboratories with everything available, from anechoic chambers for studying noise pollution to teams of scientists and engineers able to visit factories to diagnose gremlins in new machinery that failed to bed down by seismic testing, using computers which are more powerful than those available to most companies. The staff level has been cut to 300, to make it more profitable for privatisation; the reduction in services available to industry is of less consequence to a government which is more interested in making money than in making quality products.

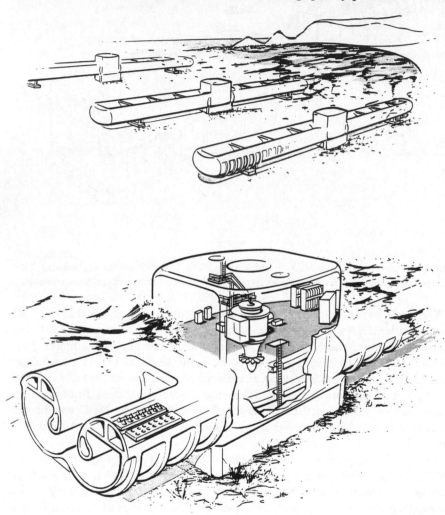

Fig. 6.10 The Vickers OWC which lies on the seabed, away from the surface turbulence, and is 'driven' by changes in depth as the waves pass over it.

After being defeated in its effort to float a wave energy ship, the NEL very nearly succeeded in 1982 in building a Column rated at 4 MW off Barvas, on the west coast of the island of Lewis in the Outer Hebrides. It was to have been a bottom-standing, breakwater type, 65 m by 32 m, a kilometre off shore in water 20m deep. It was backed by the North of Scotland Hydro-Electric

Board (later privatised as Scottish Hydro-Electric). The cost was put at £12 million, with a replica costing only £6 million. Lewis at the time had a 30 MW grid served mainly by imported diesel fuel which was costing 7–8p a unit. The wave energy prototype would cost more like 9p, with later models bringing it down to 4.5p. The Hydro Board, in its annual report that year, said: 'A study of wave energy devices undertaken by the Board has shown that a design proposed by NEL is practical, has economic potential, and should prove to be worth developing further. The Board has made a proposal to the Department of Energy . . .'

And then what happened? The plan went to the Department of Industry's Mechanical and Electrical Engineering Requirements Board for a grant of £650 000 towards the cost of a feasibility study. The Board met on 7 September 1982 and reached no decision; the Department of Energy was quibbling. It was demanding to know why the most suitable device was the NEL breakwater and not one of the others. Two months later, on November 8, the Requirements Board decided to go ahead with the funding. But then word emerged that a decision was being delayed by objections from the Department of Energy.

The matter was raised at what was described as the 'top level' and articles by me formed part of the interdepartmental brief. The decision, I was told, was 'with Thatcher'. One informant told me: 'The PM stuck her nose in because the Secretary of State for Scotland had written to her, giving it his blessing. The Department of Energy came off the fence. They said ours was the only device ready for exploitation. The CEGB also came out in favour.' A spokesman for the Hydro Board was quoted as saying: 'We are very keen to encourage the development of alternative sources of energy. We are always looking for ways to reduce our dependence on diesel.'

And how did the story end? A representative of ETSU appeared at an Open University conference in March 1986 and said that the reason that the Lewis plan had fallen down was that British industry, unlike Norwegian industry, had failed to provide adequate support. The facts are that the NEL had assembled a commercial consortium which was ready to back the scheme. The DTI said it was prepared to pay 25 per cent, if the commercial backers put up 75 per cent. The consortium said that this was too high (in Norway the split was 50:50).

This excuse about industry's lack of support is one of two regularly offered by ETSU and the British Government for their own unhelpful attitudes. The first excuse is: 'Ha, why does no other country invest in wave energy?' That died when first Norway, then Portugal, India, and Denmark did so. The second excuse was, 'Ha, why doesn't industry invest in it?' That was killed off in 1993 when the OSPREY was offered support by some of the government's favourite companies: GEC (chief executive, Lord Prior, former Tory Party chairman); privatised British Steel and Scottish Hydro-Electric; the Atomic Energy Authority, aka AEA Technology, which is the parent body of ETSU itself, and which decided to invest in a technology which its own subordinate described as unlikely ever to be commercial. Did the British Government then move in, to back up industry's judgment by offering investment? On the contrary, the response of the British Government was to refuse any support and by its action risk cutting off the 550 000 ECUS (£425 000) which had been offered by the European Union.

The truth is that it is difficult to persuade industry to invest in a high-risk project with a long-term timetable; it should be the role of enlightened government to 'prime the pump', as the DTI and its predecessors have always talked about doing. Industry looks for short-term profits for shareholders.

The Oscillating Water Column principle produced a number of devices, and a tragic loss was the Vickers model.[6] This really did have industrial backing because it was invented by Vickers, a company which had the money, the skills, the workforce, and the need for jobs. The company was one of those involved in the original British programme, which was ended in 1982 when the Department of Energy withdrew funding. Vickers could have gone ahead alone but it preferred to concentrate on products with a more immediate market, such as Trident submarines. When that work was petering out, Vickers was divided into two companies; Design and Projects Division was no longer attached to the Cumbrian branch, and attempts to interest the Cumbrian branch came to nothing.

The beauty of the Vickers invention is that it is, as might be expected, mainly submarine, so that it sits in calm water on the seabed and reaps the benefit of the turbulence of the waves on the surface, without being buffeted by them. It is the only OWC which does not pump air to and from the atmosphere. The entire system is enclosed under the water, with only a conning tower breaking the surface for access purposes. It is, however, different from the other enclosed systems, such as the Clam, because it has a hard skin, which does not expand and contract.

The submerged power station, 196 metres long, receives the wave energy in the form of fluctuating pressure as the depth increases and decreases. When the wave is at its peak, the sea at that point is deeper and the increased pressure forces the pocket of air inside the submarine from what has become a high pressure zone into a low pressure zone. Then, as the crest of the wave on the surface changes into a trough, the pressure falls and the air flows back.

Each station is rated at 3 MW and a full-scale power station of 1000 MW would require 350 units stretching over about 30 miles on the seabed. It would have provided a lifeline for VSEL (Vickers Shipbuilding and Engineering Ltd) which is usually in the news only with announcements of wholesale reductions of staff because defence orders have disappeared, a plight which could have been avoided if its management had recognised the need for diversification into wave energy.

References

1. Thorpe, T.W. (1992). *A review of wave energy*, vols 1 and 2, ETSU R-72. Department of Trade and Industry, London.
2. Whittaker, T.J.T. (1988). *Energy from ocean waves*. Euromechanics Colloquium 243, Programme and Extended Abstracts,, University of Bristol.
3. Masuda, Y., Shinichi, I., Takeaki M., and Gentaro, K. (1982). Reports and Future Plans for the Kaimei Project, Wave Energy Utilisation. In *Proceedings*, pp 305–21, Norwegian Institute of Technology, Trondheim.
4. Elliot, G. and Roxburgh, G. (1980). *Wave energy studies at the UK National Engineering Laboratory*. NEL, Glasgow.
5. Leishman, J.M. and Scobie, G. (1975). *The development of wave power*. NEL, Glasgow.
6. Vickers Design and Projects Division (1983). *The development of Vickers' Oscillating Water Column*. Presented at Marintec China 83, Vickers plc, Eastleigh, Hants.

6.3 The ship with the broken back

Sir Christopher Cockerell has already contributed a word to the language: he was the inventor of the Hovercraft. He brought to wave energy an understanding of the frustrations that engineers must expect when dealing with government and the prestige of one who had overcome it. His presence helped to give credibility to the new concept. He also produced a device, the Raft, which had great attraction. It was easy to understand, it was visually attractive and it could be, and was, built at 1/10th scale and demonstrated (in the Solent). The Raft floated on the surface and followed the rise and fall of the waves. It was one of the earliest devices to be abandoned by the official programme.

But consider first the case made for wave energy by Sir Christopher. He gave the appearance of being the archetypal country gentleman who raged against the Civil Service and adored private enterprise. Yet he was also the person who first put forward the social case for wave energy. It was he who first suggested that there should be 'a crash programme' which would provide employment for the depressed shipbuilding industry from public funds.

He made the suggestion in a letter to *The Times* which practically nobody noticed; certainly none of the major figures in wave energy saw it. It appeared on 21 December, 1976, a time when even engineers and scientists were too busy thinking about Christmas to read the papers properly.

He wrote:

We have a small, leisurely, safe programme for the development of some of the renewable sources of energy, with a 30-year target; meanwhile, each day we hear that the shipbuilding industry, or the oil rig builders, or the builders of conventional power stations are without enough work. Is there not a case for mounting a crash programme for the quick development of solar, wind and wave devices so that we can the sooner get work back into these valuable industries and save some of the misery and unproductive expense of further lasting unemployment? Consider the amazing crash programme for the Spitfire. It could be done again if we have the will to do it. 'There is a tide in the affairs of men which, taken at the flood, leads on to fortune.'[1]

Sir Christopher, lacking Salter's talent as a publicist, may have himself missed the tide with the timing of his suggestion, but he did win the race to launch a fair-sized wave energy device. On 19 April 1978 he unveiled his Raft on 1/10th scale in the Solent and it produced an average of 1 kW of electricity from waves roughly one-tenth the size of those expected in the open sea. The full-scale generator, roughly 100 m long, would produce a steady 2 MW and a series of rafts stretching over 15 miles would be the equivalent of a 500 MW power station.

Sir Christopher received me in his home overlooking Southampton Water and explained his involvement in wave energy as a series of reverse operations. The waves had proved a problem for the Hovercraft and in seeking to overcome the damage that they could do he had realised their strength. He had thought about throwing a stone in the water and watching the ripples run out in growing circles and had contemplated the power that one stone produced and had wondered about the opposite configuration when the waves were rolling in towards a single object. And then he had developed a device which, he said, 'is like a ship that has broken its back. The naval architect goes to school to find out how to design a ship that won't do that. Now we have to reverse the drawings.'

The Cockerell Raft is actually a series of Rafts, or pontoons, linked by hinges. For convenience, everyone is calling it 'a' Raft. The first idea was that a string of seven pontoons, linked by six hinges, would make one unit. Brian Count, a physicist at the CEGB's Marchwood Laboratories, close to Cockerell's headquarters, was able to show by theoretical work that fewer Rafts would be more fruitful. The unit was brought down to a line of three. The units would be multiplied again and again, making a line of anything up to 1000 km.

The Raft followed the contours of the waves. The front pontoon bobbed up and down pretty freely as it was hit by the violence of the sea. The second one moved less, because the water had been flattened by its impact with the first and much of its energy had been absorbed. The third in the series was twice the length of the other two and relatively stable. So you had a trio of pontoons moving in different phases and the difference was the motive force.

Fig. 6.11 The Raft floating at one-tenth scale in the Solent, bending as it falls into a trough (a) and bucking as it rides a peak (b).

On top of each hinge there were two hydraulic jacks—long pistons inside cylinders. The movement of the sea drove the pistons up and down, and sent hydraulic fluid moving inside a sealed system. The fluid was driven through a non-return valve into a manifold. There is low-pressure fluid which flows out of a reservoir and high-pressure fluid from the business end of the pistons. It is mixed in the manifold and directed out of a single exit into a hydraulic motor. This is the opposite of a hydraulic pump, which is more familiar to most of us and which throws up a stream of fluid. The hydraulic motor is hit by the fluid which drives it around. The motor drives a generator and the electricity sparks.

Fig. 6.12 Sir Christopher Cockerell (left) on board with the then junior energy minister, Alex Eadie (centre), and Jim Platts, Chief Engineer at Wavepower Ltd, which built the Raft.

Sir Christopher is not enthusiastic about hydraulic power. 'The kind of chaps you send out to maintain this won't be highly qualified hydraulic engineers in white coats,' he told me. 'So we want to get a system with the same advantages as the old steam engines—easy to maintain, whether it's sitting off Brazil or Scotland. You go aboard with a bloody great spanner and that is all you need. With hydraulics, the tiniest bit of grit puts them out. It is for me the practical things that matter. So you use the lowest form of technology that you can get away with.'

He was touching on a point which has still to be decided. His own instinct is for a mechanical system and, like many of us, he thinks that the fashion for hydraulic power systems is being overdone. In old-fashioned motor cars, it was certainly easier to deal with a bent brake rod than it is to bleed a hydraulic system nowadays. Against this, there is the problem of over-heating. With the enormous electricity generators that we are considering, a mechanical engine would create problems.

It would require something like a row of cooling towers on top of the Rafts to keep down the engine temperature, and this would add to the structural difficulties. A possible solution would be to use sea water as the fluid, dumping it over the side when it became hot and replacing it with cold water.

One of Sir Christopher's engineers, Michael Urwin, elaborated. 'Hydraulic fluid is much stiffer, like brake fluid, than water and that is why we are using it on the model. But in the real-sea situation, with full-scale generators, a small loss of efficiency doesn't matter. In fact, by going for a very efficient system, we would get more power in a rough sea than we could cope with, so a less efficient system is in some ways an advantage.'

Sir Christopher kept an open mind on what form of power station he would settle for. 'We have been looking hard at pumps on top', he said, 'and there are pros and cons. You have got to take into account maintenance. Can you do it better right inside the device, in a sort of ship's engine room? Or could you just put a chicken house over the pump?'

On the model, the working parts were on top. This was inevitable for one practical reason: the Rafts were too small for a man to get inside an 'engine room'. The likelihood was that the full-scale Raft would have an enclosed room, partly beneath the surface, where maintenance and repairs could be done in comfort, apart from the rolling motion created by the sea. It would be necessary to have helicopters available, either on a nearby shore or perhaps on the deck of the Raft, ready to pull off the engineers, fast, when a storm was approaching.

One problem which seemed for a time to be a major one proved less worrying. This was the fear that in a strong sea the front Raft would be thrown right over and would cease to function. Tests showed that the hydraulic system served to dampen the motion of the front pontoon, acting rather like a shock absorber.

For the Raft, as for all the devices, mooring was a major problem. The Solent model had been held down with four flexible ropes. They need greater elasticity than in the deep sea because there was a rise and fall of three metres in the tide, in water only 8–10 m deep. This problem would be less in the deep sea. The ropes, 50 m long, would go down to a block of concrete weighing 136 kg in the air, which itself would rise and fall with the tide. The block would be linked by 10 m of chain to a 180 kg anchor. The main purpose of the mooring was to hold the Raft on station; its own weight, and particularly the weight of the third and largest pontoon in the series, would hold it down on the surface and provide the difference in movement of the three pontoons, thereby producing the energy.

Mr Urwin said that their plan was to go about 50 km out from the shore where the long, rolling waves would suit the Raft. In shallow water, he noted, the height of the waves increases and the length decreases. The Raft is most efficient when the wavelength is the same as the length of the Raft. So they would most like waves of 100 m—those with a period of roughly eight seconds, and a height of 10–12 m. With such waves, the Raft would be, although 100 per cent efficient there would still be a loss in generation and transmission—possibly 10 per cent for each.

With most longer waves, efficiency would decrease but output would remain the same. However, with very long waves, the whole unit of two or three would tend to ride in one section, instead of moving at different paces and for different distances. In that (rare) case, no energy at all would be extracted because the three pontoons would be just one bobbing Raft with the hinges open.

The problem for this, as for all wave energy generators, would be survival in a really big sea. Mr Jim Platts, one of the senior engineers on the project, put it this way: 'The average sea gives you the value. The extreme sea gives you the cost. If you can find a sea where the average is low but the extreme is even lower, it might prove cheaper.' He estimated that when the sea was producing more than 50 kW/m, the main interest was in survival, because it was not going to be possible to absorb and process the really gigantic waves. Off the Hebrides, it is possible to have waves producing 1000 kW for a day and 10 000 kW for a minute. No one has even contemplated designing a device that could handle such enormous waves.

One advantage of the Raft is that it is designed to allow the big waves to 'slop over the top', as Mr Grove-Palmer, then secretary of the Wave Energy Steering Committee, put it. He compared it with the Kon Tiki, which had no freeboard—the part of a ship's hull reaching up from the waterline. None of the other devices had this advantage, although the Duck came close to it. The exact opposite was the HRS Rectifier which would cope best with local seas— the sort of excited condition that you find closer to shore where the device would sit on the bottom and enjoy the benefit of waves which were being compressed by the rise in the seabed as they approached the land. These waves have a shorter length but a greater height. The Cockerell team compared the HRS Rectifier to a high-rise block of flats standing in the water. Their own lines of Rafts would be more like a sprawling estate of semi-detached, two-storey houses.

It was perhaps not an accident that Sir Christopher was the first to get electricity out of the (fairly) open sea around Britain. He had a streak of the old buccaneering engineer. He first went to see Goodwin at the Department of Energy, but that was 'before the Arabs upped the price of oil and it didn't look as though the thing was viable'. But he pressed on, using his own money, and still expresses a little indignation over the fact that Salter had the facilities of a university and Government backing before the official grant was made. Sir Christopher went to see the British Hovercraft Corporation and they, 'out of the kindness of their heart', agreed to make some models and put them in a tank. Then he interested some friends: E.W.H. Gifford and Partners, civil and structural engineers based nearby

Fig. 6.13 Portrait of Sir Christopher Cockerell.

in Southampton. From this informal start, the company called Wavepower was set up.

He talked staccato: 'What is the replacement value of the present CEGB? £30 000 million, or add another nought on that. The money is so vast that we should press ahead to a realistic stage on more than one of these gadgets. We don't limit ourselves to buying one motor car or one TV. Never is it one individual. You could not have a school of painters with only one painter' (Sir Christopher, as a trustee of the National Portrait Gallery, worried that Britain was not doing sufficient to preserve paintings).

With wave energy, there is an extraordinary advantage: we don't have to standardise at any time. With the railway system, you have to decide a gauge and whatever forever. With wave energy, you could have a fleet of devices which could be one design, and you could have a Mark 2 next to it and a Mark 3 next to that. Because design can improve, you can change again and again. Eventually, you chuck out the early ones and replace them with Mark 7. That is one of the delightful things about it.

We know we would produce energy. The question is: will it survive? Will it break away? How much maintenance will it need? You are dealing with a probability. This is not static. It is living in a filthy environment. Not enough is known about it. Look at aeroplanes or washing machines. Designers have to have at least four shots before they have got a chance to have ironed out the worst of the trouble. The designers have got to have a chance of making mistakes. Think of corrosion and metal fatigue and storms and maintenance and cable connections and so on. We will make some errors. Everyone makes them. They built the M1 and now you have to repair the thing. You must allow the engineer to have these shots.

It would be fatal to reduce the scheme to one team and one device. That is what the accountant would say, rationalise the thing. It is wrong. Not all of the good ideas will come out of one of these schemes. But civil servants are so naive. And this is what enables the accountant to muck it. The Civil Service chap must not blot his copybook. It is safer not to put your nose out too far. It is not the people I quarrel with. It is the set-up which produces a certain result which is not favourable to new projects.'

He excluded the Wave Energy Steering Committee at Harwell, and its Technical Advisory Groups, from his attack:

One feels at home with Harwell. They want the job done well and as cheaply as possible. They have taken on a good bit of the attitude of private enterprise. They know that hanging around costs money. That is so much better than my previous experience with the more orthodox bodies. In the development of anything, if it is done well it must show a waste of money. The Civil Service can't justify it. It has not got a column which justifies it.

While the world still has fossil fuels, it is the equivalent of Mrs Thatcher having a lot of groceries in her larder which she can call on when she needs them. When you are right out of fossil fuels, you cannot call on supplies you have not got. To use our oil to produce electricity is just terrible. We are using up the capital of the country. Anyone who lives by using up his capital is a mug. It does not matter whether the predictions about the length of time we have are wrong. When you run out, you have lost your money in the bank.

A splendid, charming old gentleman with the mind of a young radical.

Why was the Raft then scuttled? The explanation from official circles was that it was too expensive and that there were problems with the power take-off. A bystander might think that, given its suitability for mass production and its lack of engineering design problems, these difficulties could be overcome.

Another explanation was given by Grove-Palmer in his paper to the Trondheim Symposium. He said that the devices were divided into three basic types for presentation at the ACORD meeting of June 1980: the open OWC, the closed water column, and the mechanical power system. The ones selected for further study were the seabed breakwater type of OWC (open to the sea), the Lancaster Flexible Bag (a soft-skinned blow-up), and the Bristol Cylinder. He commented drily: 'It did not escape notice that the last two were also the most recent designs, thereby reinforcing the second law of wave energy that "the device you last thought of is the most attractive." '[2]

He meant that they had not been subjected to sufficient scrutiny to show up their problems. The Raft, however, had been. It had floated in the water and people had walked on it and there had been enough time to carry out 'costings' which are heavily biased against capital-intensive projects. Being hard-skinned, it stands a good chance of long-term survival. Being designed to float, it stands a good chance of surviving the heaviest storms which always threaten an OWC standing rigid on the seabed. (The OWC also must have a weak point: the opening which lets in the sea). In addition, the Raft can be manufactured by a fairly primitive Third World economy. But it was dropped from the programme.

The designs exist. The concept is straightfoward. It is waiting for a country, or an entrepreneur with vision, to pick it up and make it as successful as Cockerell's other great invention, the Hovercraft, which was also snubbed by government.

References

1. Cockerell, Sir C. (21 December 1976). Letter in *The Times*, London.
2. Grove-Palmer, C.O.J. (1982). Wave energy in the United Kingdom. In *Wave energy utilisation* (ed. H. Berge), pp. 23–54. Tapir, Trondheim.

6.4 The Duck that won't lie down

The hero of this story is Stephen Salter. He is a good man and, in the words of the Blues classic, 'a good man nowadays is hard to find'. He is also a difficult man. He has insisted, with iron determination or, if you prefer it, with obstinacy, that his creation, the Duck, which has come to symbolise wave energy for much of the public, will not go into the water until he is satisfied that it is absolutely ready. His admirers say that this is a decision founded on engineering judgement, a refusal to be tempted, even after so many years of preparation, before he is absolutely certain that the time is right. They point out that the Duck has undergone considerable changes since it was first devised, arising out of problems that were identified, and that launching it too soon could have been expensive and damaging. Other wave energy researchers have chosen the path of seeking a simple design and have suffered his scorn for 'simplicity' which, as he puts it, has a strong appeal 'for simple and conventional people'. They tend to wonder whether Salter's reluctance to try out a Duck at sea is due to apprehension that it will not perform well. Is the Duck really chicken? Is he being over-cautious?

Having observed him for nearly 20 years, I have mixed feelings. I have been in favour, ever since the start of the programme, of getting something into the water as fast as possible. I believe that, with such a new technology, informed professionals and members of the public will understand if problems arise. The OWC has not been written off because one of them was swept off a cliff face in Norway. The idea of a jet airliner was not abandoned when the early Comets crashed. Space exploration survived, despite disasters.

Indeed, the Duck itself has gained in the public imagination because of the line of small-scale models of 'Ducks' which were tested on Loch Ness in the 1970s. They duly sank. They had been disowned from the start, *before* they failed, by Salter. They were different from his own design and would have had poor capture efficiencies. Lanchester Polytechnic (now Coventry University) hijacked his idea and used his invention. Coventry should never have done it. Yet the film of the event did make a favourable impact on the public. People still recall seeing on television that line of generators nodding in the waves; most of the viewers were probably people who will never be bothered by the load factor and mean annual output or even the design-life of the Duck.

Salter trained first as a physicist with an MA from Cambridge, then he went on to become an engineer. He prefers to be described as an engineer and is a professor in the Department of Mechanical Engineering at Edinburgh University. But inevitably his critics tend to think that this is a case of the scientist who prefers working with models in the laboratory. It is sometimes said that engineers do what scientists think about. Could this be an instance of the scientist in him taking precedence over the engineer? That would be to misunderstand our role, say the engineers, because we are the ones who take the greatest pains to ensure that no failure occurs; our errors have consequences greater than those of a scientist. We are not the sort to take avoidable risks.

However, I do recall vividly the shock many of us felt at a conference in the European Commission in Brussels on 25 April 1991, when there was for the first time a likelihood that EC money would be available to launch a wave power station. Salter responded: 'I don't want to be the first wave power device at sea. I want to be the last one. I want to make all the mistakes in private, with instruments to tell me what mistakes I have made so that I don't do it again. I want to do all the difficult things in the laboratory.'[1]

An enormous amount of work had been done, with Salter in the lead, to argue the case for wave energy, to refute the calculations made by its enemies, and to expose their figures. Now at last we were within reach of at least some funding and here was Salter saying that he did not intend to use it to go to sea. Professor Norman Bellamy from Coventry came up to me afterwards and said: 'Now do you see what I mean?' He had argued for years that he had been right to build a line of Ducks and launch them on Loch Ness, and he was (and is) campaigning for the money to build a full-scale Clam and launch it in the open sea. He knew that I admired Salter and the Duck but that I wanted to see wave energy working at sea. This was his moment and I could not deny that he had a point.

The future of wave energy will provide part of the answer, though we shall never know if development might have been faster if the real Duck had taken to the water sooner. What is certain is that Salter will not be persuaded against his convictions; and wave energy exists today in Britain because he came out of academia and conducted a fighting campaign, in the House of Lords and the House of Commons, and as an objector at a public inquiry into the building of Hinkley Point nuclear power station, to express his outrage at the way in which wave energy had been treated and to ensure that it would not be sidelined into oblivion. He prepared dossiers of irrefutable evidence and presented them brilliantly (they are reported in some detail in Chapter 8). He took great risks with his prestige and with his chance of gaining official funding at a time when others were keeping their heads down. He had attractive personal alternatives, for instance in electronics, hydraulics, and artificial intelligence, where he could have pursued a more peaceful, and probably better-paid, career. He did work in those fields, but only as a stop-gap. He believes in wave energy and will not be deflected.

The first time I visited him in his laboratory at Edinburgh University, in 1976, I had just encountered the idea of wave energy and it took him about one minute to realise that he was dealing with an ignoramus. He rattled off a few mathematical formulae, stared at me scathingly, handed me a bundle of documents and left me to his assistant, David Jeffrey. Salter is a tall, lean, intense engineer suffering from what Louis Aragon called the passion for the absolute; Sigmund Freud defined the condition as fanaticism. Salter needs to be that way. No one without that mixture of imagination and determination could have persevered as he has done. In one of the documents that he gave me back in April 1976, he illuminated the whole subject with a marvellous phrase whose significance has still not been grasped by some of the people engaged in quantifying the project: 'Efficiency itself is of no concern when the gods pay for the waves.'

He also maintains a sense of humour. Describing his early attempts to win wave energy, he remarks that 'the obvious extraction mechanism was something like a lavatory ball-cock bobbing up and down.' That captured about 15 per cent of the available energy. Then, with the hinge below the surface, he captured 60 per cent. He moved on to a vertical flap but this yielded only 40 per cent because it was creating reflected waves by its own movement to the rear. He tried something shaped like the British Standards kite-mark, and 'its round rump' displaced no water as it moved and captured 70 per cent. Finally, he devised the duck, which can win 90 per cent. And so it began.

His critics are numerous. As Mr Goodwin said (see Chapter 5), Salter is inclined to make fools of people who had greater facilities than he enjoyed and 'this is a way of influencing people but not of making friends'. Salter has made enemies.

For instance, I have been told that he poses as 'Dr' Salter, while lacking a doctorate. The explanation is that he was once referred to in a newspaper as Dr Salter, and newspapers and other sources have repeated the error. It is infuriating for many journalists to discover that when they describe him rightly as Mr Salter, some helpful ass looks up the cuttings in the library, sees that he is called Dr Salter and 'corrects' the text in order to avoid downgrading and offending him. That's newspapers. Nothing is more difficult to erase than an error. But Salter is not responsible and he is now Professor.

Again, I was told that he was nothing but an amateur with oily fingers and no academic qualifications. 'He started as an apprentice and just got Edinburgh University to give him facilities,' said one of his critics. Another remarked that he enjoyed an unfair advantage because he had the university's laboratories and youngsters who came in to help, unpaid, in their lunch breaks. The way to discover the facts, plainly, was to return to Edinburgh.

I rang Mr Salter and this time the reception was different. 'Ah,' he said, 'you wrote an article in the *Sunday Express*. It was a pleasure to see something in a newspaper that was accurate.' From then on, we could talk.

He did, in fact, start as an apprentice—with British Hovercraft, Cockerell's firm on the Isle of Wight. 'I did start at the very bottom,' he said, 'learning how to use a file, and they eventually taught me as much as Cambridge.' Which is where he went on to, to take a physics degree. He had the essential qualification of A-level maths which enabled him to become a professional engineer. (This, in passing, is the hurdle which everyone has to surmount. We are producing school-leavers who have given up maths at O-level and can never return to any branch of technology with a hope of a useful degree).

Some of the sniping at Salter's qualifications may arise from a misunderstanding: Cambridge awards its science degrees as BA and Salter went on to take an MA, but a superficial reading of his qualifications might suggest that he was just another English Literature fellow.

He surrounded himself with a team of enthusiasts ranging in age from 17 to 34. One of them, Glen Keller, was an American who was studying ocean engineering at the Massachusetts Institute of Technology when Salter gave a visiting lecture. He asked if he could join the Edinburgh project after graduating, wrote to Salter a year later and was accepted. Salter insists on this form of approach. He does not *seek* recruits because he wants people who want to work with him. He once said that his ideal collaborator should be an expert in physics, electronics, naval architecture, stress analysis, biology (because of the barnacles), computer programming, meteorology, economics—and public relations. In the event, the public relations were handled with natural talent by Salter himself. His recruiting method and his own personality have created a team with striking enthusiasm. The secretary, Miss Jean Richmond, is as immersed in the waves as any engineer, and when they move in a group to the canteen for lunch the work is not interrupted. They talk shop.

They built a testing tank, 30 m by 12 m, made of concrete and glass with miles of Dexion on top. It was completed on Christmas Day 1977 with Salter (and his wife) present as the final nuts were tightened. It cost £100 000 and holds 100 000 gallons of water.

It was the most advanced testing tank in the world for the waves. They were told that it would be impossible to build. Along one side are 89 wave makers—yellow paddles, each with its own control panel, designed by Mr Jeffrey. The controls push the paddles forward at varying strengths. The control panels are stationed up above each paddle and each one contains 14 integrated circuits, all of which had to be wired and soldered by hand, together with resistors and capacitors. Each panel looks like—and indeed is—a delicate electronic printed circuit board such as are mass-produced for transistor radios, stereo amplifiers and TV sets. But the wave controls each needed individual assembly. This meant 1246 integrated circuits put together with delicate fingers and sharp eyesight by a man and a boy: Mr Jeffrey and Ian Young, a student of 17. It took them two months of non-stop dedication.

The effect was fascinating to watch. The operator pressed a series of numbers on a keyboard, or fed in a length of tape which had been cut in advance with a pattern of holes, for the more complicated operations.

Now imagine this huge swimming pool slowly being crossed by a majestic swell, a long line of rolling waves maybe eight seconds apart as though they had travelled across a fetch of 160 km with a wind speed of 30 knots behind them. But in a normal swimming pool they would hit the opposite side and bounce back as reflected waves (or like echoes if they were sound waves). In real life, the waves end up on a beach, which absorbs their energy in a wasted froth of breakers. To avoid the reflected waves, it is obviously necessary in a wave tank to create an artificial beach and this has been done with weld mesh. It looks like a series of pillars of steel wool, such as one uses for scouring dishes. They are about 2 m high and they soak up the energy to ensure that the waves go forwards but not back. The beach takes a tremendous pounding and it is startling to realise that once a line of ducks, at only 1/150th scale, are sitting in that storm sea, the water will be a dead flat calm behind them—as Salter has already demonstrated in narrower tanks.

But the real sea never performs in such a regular way. Waves come from different directions, with different periods, overtaking one another and crossing one another's path, as Draper explained in Chapter 3. The question then that has to be answered is what will happen to real-life wave energy generators when they encounter a turbulent sea with, literally, an infinite variety of pressures that must be absorbed and processed? It is here that the controls begin to show their worth. They receive different instructions from the computer and operate the paddles at varying pressures and speeds. Within seconds, the sea can be turned from a gentle swell into a fury of turbulence. Waves criss-cross, form humps which glide across the surface in a diagonal pattern, and crash into the 'beach'. The Salter team claim that they can emulate any wave spectrum in any sea.

This gives them two separate results: they can see how the energy varies with frequency, and they can see how the Ducks will perform in a sea which can produce the equivalent of 500 kW/m—'the sort of sea in which we want to survive', as Keller put it. They have built a spine of PVC with ping-pong balls in clusters at each joint. They put between 20 and 30 Ducks at 1/150th scale on the spine to see how they manage.

I have laboured what may seem like a secondary aspect of laboratory testing for one reason above all: the tank, the size of a large swimming pool, with waves raging across it and rising above 'sea' level in just the way that waves do at sea, is intended for testing a string of Ducks of only 1/150th scale. That is to say, the diameter of the spine on which they pivot will be a mere 10 cm. The larger models which were tested on Loch Ness were 1/15th scale and their diameter was one metre. The real Ducks out at sea will be about 15 m in diameter. That, remember, is the diameter of the spine. Then you have to add the Duck's beak, made out of concrete, which bobs up and down in the waves and you get a device measuring from the Duck's beak to the Duck's arse probably more than 30 m—that is, a building the size of an eight-storey block of flats.

And if it is to operate well, it will have to be one of a string of about 20–30 Ducks on one spine, with spaces between each Duck. So one wave energy device would probably be about 1200 m in length, nearly a mile. And that should produce on average between 30 and 50 MW. Think back to the swimming pool, multiply by 150 to get the diameter of the spine, add the beak, then multiply by 30 to get the length of 30 Ducks that you will probably need, and you have some idea of the size of the beast we are talking about. And then you will start to understand why it needed someone close to the frontiers of genius and lunacy to persevere and to persuade the Civil Service that he was talking sense.

Stephen Salter has retained his confidence and his coolness through an extraordinary odyssey. He does not try to brush aside the difficulties. But Salter's team believe that their device will be able to cope with the worst forces of the sea. It has the most ambitious design and is consequently the most difficult to build and possibly to maintain. But it is designed to be hit by furious waves and survive because its design limits the forces that each part of the structure experiences by yielding, and the biggest part of it will be the moving part. It is the spine which has to stay fairly stable, while the Ducks will bounce up and down. With the Raft, exactly the opposite applies: one pontoon is twice the size of each of the others, and it is the big one which has to stay steady. And with the OWC, the whole pillar of concrete needs to be steady in order to create the maximum relative motion of the air bubble. So one can contemplate a situation in which the Ducks could survive off the Outer Hebrides and, although they would present problems in construction and servicing, would be very fruitful sources of power, while other devices would survive more happily in calmer seas, producing less electricity but costing less to build and maintain.

The second advantage is that the Duck would be more easily mass-produced than any other because it comes in smaller, more numerous units. One of Salter's team put it in a striking way. At that time, a conventional power station, he argued, could be regarded as costing £400–500 per kW. A motor car engine, if used in combination with a generator, could easily produce 20 kW. The engine would cost only about £50 because of mass production. So the cost per kW would be £2.50. He was satirising the problem and the prices have since changed. But, as with all good satire, it contains a nucleus of truth.

How will the Duck work? Mark 1 consisted of a spine with a diameter of 15 m, and a length of roughly a mile. Most of the structure was to be built of sections of reinforced concrete, joined together. There would be hydraulic rotary pumps based inside the spine, and the aim was to make the spine as stable as possible while the Ducks flopped up and down. The power is the relative motion between the Ducks and the spine. If the spine yields too much, you lose power. If it does not yield at all, it will break. As Glen Keller put it, 'all the Ducks are trying to make the spine move as the waves hit them. You want to make the spine long enough, and with sufficient number of Ducks, so that when you average all the Duck torques on the spine, it should come close to zero.' Rather like two chaps of equal strength clasping hands, putting their elbows on the bar counter and pushing against one another, so that their hands are immobile, except that each individual Duck would be driving a pump. That pump, the front end of the system, would be pushing out fluid, either water or oil, inside an enclosed system. The fluid would drive a generator installed in a black box, probably stationed between the Ducks and certainly above the surface because, as Keller put it, it would be 'very painful' to have to service it inside the spine under the surface of the water. Or the fluid might be pumped ashore to a land-based generator. They needed, he said, a system like the electric lights on a Christmas tree, to ensure that when one light (or Duck) went out, the others continued to function.

They had contemplated direct drive of a generator from the Ducks but decided that it would be too slow. It could be geared up, but this would need 15 m gears which would depend on close tolerance, something that one did not wish to rely on.

The spine remained one of the key issues to be solved. In addition to the torques on the spine from the power take-off, there would be bending movements caused by the waves themselves and these would push the spine sideways and up and down. If the spine were entirely rigid, it would break, so it must have joints between sections. It would obviously be easier to build if it could be rigid. 'Once it is flexible, it gets more subtle. We have to reach a compromise.'

Fig. 6.14 A line of Ducks.

Richard Jefferys, an expert on hydrodynamics, was particularly concerned with the problem of efficiency in different wave conditions, something which is of even more concern to the group experimenting at the
National Engineering Laboratory on the Oscillating Water Column. From
their standpoint, it is probably more 'efficient' to take a smaller amount of
energy from a wider range of waves than to be '100 per cent efficient' in
absorbing the energy of fewer waves. Indeed, with the OWC it is possible
actually to have more than 100 per cent efficiency by absorbing energy
from different directions. But what is needed for all the devices is a means
of accepting and transmitting as continuous a stream of energy as possible,
even with lower 'efficiency'.

The way Jefferys regarded it, so far as the Duck was concerned, was: 'You
could make a Duck that was very efficient for one particular period, but for
other periods it would drop off' (period referring to waves, arriving at
anything between 5 and 15 second periods). 'You can tune it so that it is
better over a wider band of frequencies but is not quite so good at its peak. We
are thinking of 100 kW/m as the maximum amount of power the Duck can
handle. But if you got 2 MW/m hitting it, and it is 5 per cent efficient in these
conditions, you would still get 100 kW/m.'

David Jeffrey, one of Salter's earliest collaborators, wanted to see full-scale
work on parts of the Duck. He wanted to simulate the motion of the sea by
'driving' a Duck with a hydraulic ram, so that they could see how the power

fluctuated as the Duck wobbled. He also wanted to try out drive mechanisms, to see how to communicate the force of the Duck's movement to the hydraulic pumps. He was impatient of the step-by-step progress that had been the fashion.

The only reason for the 1/10th or 1/15th scale work is to prove that the 1/150th scale models' forecasts are correct. There is no reason to say that you can't say precisely what will happen to full scale. On 1/150th, our predictions were still accurate for 1/15th, and there is no reason to assume that they would not be correct at full scale. Once we have the 1/150th working on a spine, we could go up the scale without difficulty. We would like to test certain parts at full-scale. At 1/15th scale you could not model the power take-off. The reason is that you want to try to design as far as possible using things easily available off the shelf and small hydraulic systems are not in that category. They *are* available for hundreds of kilowatts, but there are not enough diverse systems for dealing with hundreds of watts. We are talking about power, and the power of the 1/15th scale model is going to be 3/10 000th of the full power. Three watts from 1/15th scale would mean 10 kW full-scale.

I had better butt in here with an explanation. Scale does not go up in a straight arithmetical progression. For instance, it is obvious that if you take a three-dimensional model and multiply it from 1/10 th scale to full-scale, you do not simply come up with something 10 times as big. As every dimension is multiplied by 10, then a model of 2 m by 2 m by 2 m becomes 20 m by 20 m by 20 m; the difference is between 8 m^3 and 8000 m^3. In the same way, the power output is greatly increased. Jeffrey was hinting at something that aroused a great deal of backstage fury in wave energy circles.

The project for a trial on Loch Ness came not from Edinburgh but from Lanchester Polytechnic in Coventry, now Coventry University. There was little love between the two scholarly establishments. And the poly was critical of the National Engineering Laboratory, which provided the power pack for the trials. Somewhere, someone blundered, as Tennyson would have said. And, as President Kennedy did say, defeat is an orphan. Edinburgh would say that Lanchester should never have boasted that it would put out a string of Ducks by the autumn of 1977. Lanchester would retort that it would have succeeded in doing so, before the weather broke and the Loch froze over, had it not been for the NEL, which failed to provide the power pack in time. And the NEL says that it received a request only on September 29 to produce a special generator which was delivered on November 1 and was produced in the usual NEL style—which meant that, as one of their spokesmen put it to me, 'we put much more effort into these things than we charge.' This I can confirm from my own knowledge of NEL. Its competence is unquestioned. Yet the poly then decided that the generator needed modification.

A lot of people will be arguing about who was to blame. I am not going to jump into that whirlpool. I merely report that in Edinburgh it is being said with bitterness that the poly jumped on to a bandwagon by a side door.

Edinburgh received a friendly communication offering to put the proposed design of the Duck through an analogue hybrid computer, to see if it was the most efficient design. The next thing that Edinburgh knew was that the design had been modified by Lanchester and models of 1/10th scale (as Lanchester saw it) or 1/15th scale (as Edinburgh saw it) were being built to the Lanchester design. It was different from the Salter Duck, and Salter felt keenly about this. He said that he had never given it his sanction and yet stood to be blamed for any faults. He told me this *before* the spine had broken.

Yet Lanchester Poly's Electrical and Electronic Engineering Department, then headed by Bellamy, was convinced that it was making a great contribution. Dr Bellamy, who comes from a mining family and started his working life as an underground miner, is highly enthusiastic about wave energy and is convinced that his department can make a great contribution. 'I started out very sceptical,' he said. 'Then I realised that the energy was there. And it is there forever.' He was hoping to move on from Loch Ness, once it was functioning properly, to 1/4th scale, analysing the data as he went. He said that there were many months of analysis to be done on a computer.

The Salter team were cool to the whole concept of going up the scale in this way. They believed that what could be done at 1/150th scale, in their extraordinary tank, would prove accurate for the full-scale prototype. 'The only reason for 1/10th scale work is to prove that the forecasts from 1/150th scale are correct' said one of them, commenting bitterly on Lanchester's contribution.

Apart from continuing in the laboratory, Salter did on just one occasion contemplate going to sea. He told me that he would like to build a full-scale power take-off and one joint from the spine ('a slice of Duck', he called it) and test it. He wanted to attach it to an obsolescent, laid-up oil tanker in the days when we had a surplus of carrying capacity (the price of Middle East oil had shot up and we were using more coal to make electricity). It would have been an ideal way of proving or disproving the Duck; but the government was not interested and nothing came of it.

Salter was thus forced to confine himself to his tank. His main problem at that stage was the power take-off. The Duck would nod slowly, and this movement had to be converted into the high angular velocity needed to produce electricity. There were critics who doubted if it could be done at all, and if a method were found of converting the slow motion into fast motion, by gears, levers and chains, then it would not last for long. Salter recognised the force of this argument. He has admitted that no seal had been devised that could keep out the water indefinitely. The motion had to be taken from the Duck to the spine, and sooner or later the sea would get in and corrode the workings.

Salter was, as he put it, 'getting nowhere' and 'beating my head against a wall trying to think of a way to make very low speed electrical generators'. He decided to discuss the problem with Professor Eric Laithwaite of the Department of Heavy Electrical Engineering at Imperial College, London. Salter told the Heathrow Hotel conference:

Professor Laithwaite said immediately that it was impossible. But then he suggested a particularly intriguing way of getting power off a Duck. Inside the Duck we build two large gyros arranged to spin in opposite directions. Their axes are perpendicular to the Duck's axis of nod. I am sure that you will all instantly know exactly what will happen to the gyro gimbals when the Duck nods. . . . You will also remember the equations relating output torque to spin speed, disc inertia, and input angular velocity, and will have no difficulty in working out the way to load pumps acting between the gyro Duck frame and the Duck casing so that the Duck feels the right damping coefficient . . .[2]

This statement was, I am certain, intended as a good-natured nudge. But it is an excellent example of the way in which Salter does not realise how sharp his elbow is. One could sense many of the distinguished audience bristling. The gyroscope, that neglected invention of the French scientist Foucault, is the sort of item that many students tend to put on one side soon after starting their university courses. Salter had irritated his listeners, and their rather superior comments could be heard as they chatted after the session. I heard some of them; so did Salter. But it is interesting to note that not one delegate challenged him in open combat in the formal question-and-answer period. Those who might deplore his manner will just have to accept that genius can be difficult, but is more stimulating than the thinking of people with smoother graces.

Salter had gone to see Laithwaite in search of a solution to one problem—to convert a slow movement into electricity. But later, as Salter thought about it, he realised that he had within reach the answers to not one but three of his difficulties. In addition to solving the problem of power take-off, the gyroscope would provide a new 'frame of reference'. He had until then needed the spine to remain relatively stationary. It would stay mainly upright, while the individual Ducks nodded at different moments and evened out the tendency of the waves to set the spine spinning. But with the gyroscopes inside the Ducks, they would serve as an independent entity, and there would be no need to transmit the nodding motion from the Ducks to the spine. This would also reduce the torque on the spine.

The third advantage was that the gyroscope could serve as a flywheel. At that moment, as Laithwaite has explained to me, it ceases to be a gyroscope because it is no longer free to turn about a different axis. But it does become a power converter. It drives a fluid into a hydraulic motor, which in turn drives an alternator. Or it can be diverted to another hydraulic motor/generator, which makes the flywheel go faster, providing the flywheel storage which is needed.

Perhaps a crude comparison can be drawn between the way in which an alternator charges a car battery when the demand is low; when the engine is idling or switched off (or when the fan belt is too slack!), and the lights, windscreen wipers and booster fan are all on, the battery feeds back some of the power it has accumulated. As always, it is Grove-Palmer who sums up the process most succinctly: 'The nodding motion gives you power out *or* an increase in the speed of the gyro.' Salter put it in greater detail in an address to an energy conference at Gothenburg in October, 1979:

The hydraulic fluid, almost certainly oil, will drive a swash plate motor at each end of a gyro shaft in parallel with another driving an electric generator. If the pressure tends to rise as a result of a burst of wave energy, the angular deflection of the swash plates will increase so as to allow the extra energy to speed up the gyro flywheel. If the flow of energy is at exactly its mean value, the gyro swash plate motors will move to their zero displacement angle and all the oil will flow to the motors driving the electrical generator. If, during a lull, there is less oil from the ring cam pump than is necessary for the generator drive, then the swash plates on the gyro motors will swing over so that they pump and draw the energy deficit from the gyro disc.[3]

Some other quotations from Salter's account (at the Heathrow Hotel, at Gothenburg, and at a London conference of the Institution of Electrical Engineers on 30 January 1979) help to illuminate just what he has achieved:

We can use the gyro spin for energy storage. At full speed each gyro stores about three-quarters of a megawatt hour, so that very little speed variation can provide the few minutes of storage necessary for wave power. We have a completely opaque barrier between ourselves and the salt water. The gyros do not know that they are at sea.

(Heathrow Hotel)[2]

The gyros can store prodigious amounts of energy, enough to provide a completely smooth output. The energy stored in each gyro spin is about the same as the kinetic energy of a 747 airliner in flight and is enough to run a megawatt for three-quarters of an hour. . . . If any readers think that this proposal is far-fetched, I draw their attention to the method of ship stabilisation developed by Sperry and used successfully in the Italian liner Conte di Savoia of 41,000 tons. Sperry used three gyros of 100 tons weight spinning at the high speed which we are suggesting and solved the high bearing load with pre-war technology.

(I.E.E. conference)[4]

The reserves of energy instantly available from the flywheels make for better control characteristics than any land-based system, whether steam or hydro. The entire Duck string constitutes a spinning reserve capable of stabilising the grid rather than causing it problems. Whenever a pumped storage scheme is proposed, the generating boards emphasise the value of spinning reserve which is said to be worth hundreds of millions of pounds a year, even if never used. The Ducks are claiming those millions for being a short-term but instantaneously responsive storage scheme. They will leave pumped storage to do its proper job of overnight working.

The vast amount of flywheel storage means that every piece of electrical equipment from the shaft of the generator to the land connector can now be rated at its mean rather than its peak rating. We can deliver some of the electricity when the consumer wants it, rather than when the waves provide it.

(Gothenburg)[3]

His plan was to use four gyros of 17 tons—one-sixth the size of those used for an ocean liner.

How, exactly, does a gyroscope function? A scientist will usually start to explain by pointing an index finger upwards and a thumb at right angles to it, and trying to make revolving movements. Laithwaite uses a bicycle wheel. A distinguished mathematician says that whenever he tries to describe it, he is driven eventually to tell his students to go back to equations. Malcolm Cloke, who was on the staff of ETSU, produced a brilliantly compressed explanation and devoted great patience to explaining it to me. He also referred inquirers to the *Encyclopaedia Britannica*, which has a four-page explanation. Salter lamented at Gothenburg: 'Our only problem has been that physical arguments and mathematics are not sufficient to persuade critics. The feel of a working model is necessary.' So Salter ('he is a superb craftsman,' as one of his admirers noted), got to work in his laboratory and produced a beautifully-engineered model of the power take-off. He took it to a conference of NATTA (the Network for Alternative Technology and Technology Assessment) at the Open University, Milton Keynes, in August 1979, and said most flatteringly that he had brought it specially to show me. It is 75 cm long and plugs into the National Grid. You can hold it and try to turn it and feel the gyroscopes inside resisting your pressure.

The gyroscope is used nowadays on ships to activate stabiliser fins. The gyros control the fins, which would otherwise lack guidance. As Sperry, the manufacturers put it: 'The ship rolls. The gyroscope tends to remain stationary.' You can perhaps most simply visualise it as a wall in space, with a stream of hydraulic fluid coming at it from different directions and being bounced back into a pump.

The key word is precession. It means that the gyro cage reacts against being moved, so long as the disc is spinning. High pressure oil is driven into the generator and any surplus goes into the flywheel, where it is stored. It will give, in Salter's view, a 45-minute warning to the Grid when the sea is turning calm, far longer than it enjoys when, for instance, a much-advertised television programme disappoints the viewers, who move in their millions to the kitchen and switch on electric kettles and lights. The Grid is good at responding to a sudden peak in demand—we don't often have power cuts these days—and the Ducks, 'a varying and partly unpredictable supply of electricity', to quote the original official view, would actually help to lessen the very problem which they were said to represent.

It was at the Gothenburg conference that Salter suddenly rounded on his critics. He did it in a style that Swift would have appreciated. He noted that Glendenning had said that a reliable system 'is one which is simple' and that Bellamy had said that 'simplicity should be the over-riding design principle'. Then Salter said:

There are no recognised units for the measurement of simplicity and the various national standards institutions have not suggested approved levels for the engineering profession. But we can turn to the *Oxford English Dictionary* for a clue. There are 12 columns devoted to the concept. They begin harmlessly enough with:
'Free from duplicity, dissimulation or guile, innocent and harmless, undesigning, honest, open, straightforward (so far so good) . . . Small, insignificant, slight, of little account or value, also weak or feeble (this is all a bit much but we have only covered two columns so far) . . . Deficient in knowledge or learning, characterised by a certain lack of acuteness or quick apprehension, lacking in ordinary sense or intelligence, half-witted . . . unlearned, ignorant, easily misled. . . .'
It seems to me that 'simple' is not a simple word. While I do not argue that simplicity is for simpletons, I believe that it is an irrelevant factor. I want to get things right, whether rightness comes from simplicity or complexity. The history of technology has many examples of designs which were 'right'. Very often, these 'right' designs are elegant.[3]

And so, of course, is the Duck and the literary style of its defender.

But this was only the beginning of the story. Salter does not believe in stagnation, and he was soon considering how to combat the criticism of his revolutionary power take-off based on gyroscopes. He also met the government's obvious reluctance to build a full-scale wave energy station by reducing his target from a spine of 20–30 Ducks to a more modest objective: the solo Duck. In doing so, he also abandoned his argument that a seal would be a liability, because the sea would always find a way through it, into the machinery, and decided that on balance it was less of a disadvantage than some aspects of his earlier plan.

At this point, one can understand the irritation of his critics. Salter exists in the esoteric region where one needs to be both a scientist and a professional engineer, as he is. He throws out ideas and then applies them to detailed mechanical engineering, He produces conference papers, beautifully written and with witticisms which are often barbed. By the time his readers are catching up with his latest proposal, this modern Renaissance man has abandoned it and moved ahead to a new one.

The gyroscope, for instance, contained a flywheel which, produced in association with Peter Williams of Laing, would have contained 45 minutes' storage when the sea turned calm. It had, and still has, great potential in many other areas. But, says Salter, it was difficult to design high-speed bearings which did not absorb a lot of the energy. He also found it difficult to convince everybody of the achievability of the sealed vacuum in which it worked. It was also heavy and expensive. 'It was also impossible to obtain any cash benefit from the generating boards for the ultra-smooth output and the rapid-response, medium-term energy storage.'[4]

Fig. 6.15 Stephen Salter at the site of the Norwegian wave power station near Bergen. The waves behind him are surging up a concrete channel, gathering force as they are squeezed between its tapering walls.

In response to the Thorpe report in 1992, he attacked the potentially 'weak' aspects of his design. He devised a means of pumping high-pressure oil from a pump based in the middle of each Duck, with 'a peak instantaneous power rating of 23 MW and costing £300 000 . . . twice the torque at a quarter of the weight of the gyro design'. All the working parts were small enough to pass through a manhole and 'it may even be possible for a brave and well-paid engineer to service some parts while the pump is on line . . . The railway pioneers would have had no hesitation and the working conditions would be much better than in a coal pit. Losing the gyros means that we lose the incidental power smoothing of the flywheels. We can replace this with pressurised gas accumulators but their present cost seems to be excessive—about the same by weight as mass-production tools. Cheaper accumulators are urgently needed.'[5]

A 'generous amount of power take-off' could be provided by a ring-cam pump in the middle of each Duck. A 45-Mega-Newton pump with a peak instantaneous power rating of 23 MW would cost £300 000 and would weigh 70 tonnes. 'This is twice the torque at a quarter of the weight of the gyro design.' This is a major improvement which 'conventional' engineers would find more acceptable.

Then came the problem of controlling the motion of the spine. The position had 'changed dramatically over the last 11 years' (since his 1981 design) with the advances of computer technology. An all-digital hydraulic machine known as the wedding cake completely changed the way in which multiple sources and sinks of hydraulic energy could be combined, Salter explained. Its shaft rotated at a constant 1500 rpm. Oil flow was controlled by electronic poppet valves in each of many pumping modules which could be latched at rotation speed and connect each chamber to the high-pressure or low-pressure manifolds. Valves could operate in less than 2 milliseconds. According to the way in which the valves are operated, the machine can act as a pump or a motor, and some modules could be pumping while others were motoring and yet others were idling. 'Variable displacement in the pumping mode is achieved by holding open a selected fractional set of the inlet poppet valves so that unwanted oil is returned to the inlet manifold.' These multiple sources of hydraulic oil are then fed to hydraulic rams at the ends of each section of the spine to control their relative motion. The power to supply oil to the 'wedding cake' comes from the new design of hydraulic oil pump.

It is necessary to pause here. The description given by Salter is of a line of Ducks nodding in different phases and thus preventing the spine from spinning. Instead of the gyroscopes, which would have acted independently, he is proposing to use a computer-controlled manifold which would prevent all the Ducks responding to a stream of hydraulic fluid at the same time, in the same way. The precise method needs close study of his full text and the mechanical drawings which accompany it; it is not for the general reader. 'Latching' is a term used increasingly in wave energy and it comes from the Norwegians, Budal and Falnes, who were trying to improve the performance of their heaving buoy, which had a natural frequency higher than desirable—that is, it bounced up and down faster than the waves. They found that this could be remedied by 'latching' the buoy, or holding back the valves, so as to delay any movement until the wave force had built up to a sufficient level. The buoy would then be released so that its movement would be more nearly in phase with the force of the wave. Salter will do this with the oil flow from the 'wedding cake,' with the valves responding in less than 2 milliseconds.

Salter visualises the scene: 'Maintenance personnel will be able to walk from spine to spine through the U-bridges and across the link, even if waves are beating over them . . . There is now no need for even a single sub-surface penetration at the spine end.' As to leaks from the seals, he reduces the risk by designing his Ducks so that the oil pipes do not enter from the wet side; the entry point is for electric cables only.

The latest development has been the Solo Duck. This is, I believe, an innovation with great appeal. It is a return to the first Duck which Salter floated in a narrow tank at Edinburgh University. Its attraction was explained by Dr David Pizer, a Ph D student who was attached to Salter:

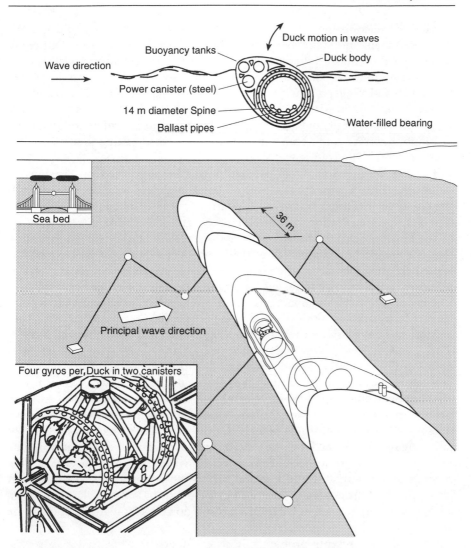

Fig. 6.16 The Duck, inside and outside. It has undergone numerous changes as its inventor improves on its design.

'A disadvantage of the spine-based system is that the reaction torque between a Duck and the spine is provided by the other Ducks on the spine. Consequently even a prototype system will require many Ducks. The solo Duck reacts against the seabed and so a prototype may consist of a single device. Being a point absorber, the solo Duck may absorb more power than is incident in the width of sea it occupies. An array of solo Ducks may therefore prove to be more cost-effective than a spine-based system.'[6]

In addition, a single, full-sized prototype of the solo Duck could be built at a fraction of the cost of the minimum length of spine-based Duck.

The reference to the 'reaction torque' on a spine means that the spine is prevented from spinning when a wave hits a Duck because other Ducks are moving in the opposite direction or are idling and providing counterpoise. The concept of the 'point absorber', much favoured by Falnes and developed by French and Wells, is that a single unit can absorb energy from a wavefront greater than its own—in this case, twice its own width. This is an appealing way of visualising the Duck, particularly for any country which does not need or cannot finance a large-scale power station, or which wants to make a more cautious start. The solo model would be of 2 MW capacity.

The key to the Solo Duck is that it will be supported on tension leg moorings. This enables it to control horizontal and vertical movements, thanks to an invention by the oil industry. In 1984 Conoco introduced the first Tension Leg Platform in the North Sea. It stands in 148 metres of water, in the Hutton field, 90 miles north-east of the Shetlands. It is an invention that has enabled oil companies to drill into deeper water at less expense. I visited the first one soon after it came on stream. Standing on its deck is uncanny. It is floating but, instead of pitching up and down like a normal ship, it seems at first to be stationary, and then you perceive an uncanny movement from side to side but not up and down.

Most normal platforms rest on steel legs which are piled into the seabed. The Tension Leg Platform is connected to the seabed by tubular steel mooring lines and the natural buoyancy of the platform pushes upwards, keeping the legs under tension as they strive to hold it down. Conoco used elastomeric technology first developed for the space programme to form rubber-and-steel flexible joints. The system is similar to mooring, but it does not allow the platform to bounce in the waves. This is exactly the form of tethering needed. If the Duck were held rigid on normal steel legs, it would be unable to benefit from the movement of the waves at the surface; if it were moored on a chain, it would rise and fall in the waves and drift on station, losing much of the energy. Tension Legs enable it to float and slide sideways, without turning into a Duck bobbing up and down like a real-life duck in the water.

Naturally, it presents problems. The worst one is what Salter calls 'the snatch load'. He put it to me: 'We did a lot of work on the worst combination of freak waves, and what happens is that you can make a tension leg that would take the biggest tensions that would arise when the biggest wave is trying to pull it out of the ground, but what you can't do is to design for the case when you have had a trough of a wave and the lines go slack and the next wave comes along and the wires go taut again when the Duck has built up a lot of kinetic energy. It really is a very unpleasant design problem.' So for the moment the Solo Duck is on hold. Salter is investigating a Swedish design for a wave energy buoy (see Chapter 7) which could benefit from many of his innovations concerning hydraulic power take-off and working for the European Union on variable-pitch turbines which should increase the output of OWCs.

What needs to be grasped is that, despite all the rebuffs from government and the deliberate obstacles erected, Salter has never given up: the Duck lives on. At the present stage, he is temporarily dependent to some extent on the success of those with less ambitious projects than his own. If the OSPREY or other versions of the OWC can succeed in the water, it will be natural for wave energy backers to turn to the Duck for a device that is intended to face, and to survive in, the roughest seas in the world. But he is not idling. He is constantly redesigning and improving his concept in answer to his critics and to his own restless search for improvement. He is also an indefatigable writer. He has produced numerous papers in a style that is compulsively readable, presenting brilliant summaries of the essential facts about wave energy. They are mostly typescripts, issued by him and available to people concerned with wave energy, or articles in learned journals. He produced an 'Assessment' of wave energy in 1985, a survey of the world wave energy scene in 1988,[7] a long study of the changes he had made to the design of the Duck in 1992, a study of power take-off systems for the Brussels Commission in June 1993, and a summary of the Edinburgh conference in July 1993; he has maintained a continuing presence on the Parliamentary field, ensuring that MPs are aware of the facts. His latest was a response to the Public Accounts Committee which in September 1994 complained that much of the UK spending on renewable energy had been wasted:

'You may be surprised to hear that I agree entirely with your conclusion that much of the UK spending of £340 million has been wasted. I would put the fraction at well over half. Much of this has gone on very high fees to consultants for some rather mixed quality work. From the wave programme I can give you an example of the same text appearing twice, and presumably being paid for twice, in different reports . . . I could show you many totally absurd cost estimates. The heavy spending on the wind programme began only *after* officials from Harwell and the old Department of Energy had visited California and concluded that a similar environmental impact would be unacceptable here. They then pushed hardest at the large machines which had shown the shortest fatigue lives in America, Sweden, and Germany. Most of the money is now going to subsidise imported machines which I fear may last only as long as the subsidy.'

And then he gave a summing-up of how those who are insiders have always tried to preserve their pre-eminence by excluding the outsiders who might otherwise join them: 'The problem is that established industries will always try to suppress challenges. The canal owners tried to stop railways. The railways tried to stop road transport. The makers of piston-driven aircraft engines tried to stop jets. Makers of electronic valves ignored transistors. Similarly, the existing energy industries, and in particular the nuclear people, try to stop renewables.'

References.

1. Ross, D. (1991). Sea-change for wave power. *Safe Energy*, Edinburgh.
2. Salter, S.H. (1978). In *Proceedings, wave energy conference, Heathrow Hotel, London November 22–23 1978* p. 20. HMSO, London.
3. Salter, S.H. (1979). *Proceedings*. First symposium on wave energy utilisation, pp. 36–76. Gothenburg, Sweden.
4. Salter, S.H. (1979). *Future energy concepts*. Power conversion systems for Ducks. Conference of Institution of Electrical Engineers London. pp. 100–8. IEE, London.
5. Salter, S.H. (1993). *European wave energy symposium*, pp. 295–309. NEL, East Kilbride, Scotland.
6. Pizer, D. (1993). *European wave energy symposium*, p. 129. NEL, East Kilbride, Scotland.
7. Salter, S.H. (1989). World progress in wave energy—1988. *Int. Journal of Ambient Energy*, **10**, pp. 3–24.

6.5. Blow-ups

The arrival of the Air Bag was the surprise, and in one sense the high point, of the Heathrow conference in 1978, at which Rendel Palmer & Tritton (RPT) introduced their estimates for wave-electricity. The one device which was given a hint of approval was the French Air Bag, which was costed at 5–10p. It was not one of the four devices in the original ETSU programme and so was relatively unknown. It was brought to London by an engaging individualist, Professor Michael French of Lancaster University, who has a habit of saying disobliging things. He looks like the popular image of an eccentric scientist: fluffy tufts of hair around his head and a beaming smile for almost everyone.

He is a mechanical engineer who has worked on nuclear energy and has never wavered in his insistence that wave energy is no more than 'insurance technology' in case the price of fossil fuels rises considerably or the development of nuclear power is restricted by public opinion. I may have annoyed him by pointing out in *New Civil Engineer*[1] that both of these things were happening—it was the year of Three Mile Island. The following year he wrote to the editor of *The Guardian* to complain about an article of mine and marked his own letter 'not for publication'. I would not have known of its existence or been able to defend myself if the paper's Science Editor, Anthony Tucker, had not sent a copy of the letter to me. However, it is difficult to dislike Michael French and we are now, I believe, on excellent terms again.

He came to wave energy after working on harbour defences. He had devised a scheme for positioning flexible air bags on the seabed at the entrance to

Fig. 6.17 The Lancaster flexible bag, invention of Professor Michael French of Lancaster University, which gave birth to the Clam.

harbours to provide what he called 'bubble breakwaters' to take the energy out of the waves and calm down the water—which is what wave energy devices do, but for the opposite purpose. They want to use the energy; the damping is a secondary bonus. He wanted to damp down the force and the energy was of no significance. Then in 1974 he read a paper by Salter and drew from it exactly the opposite message to the one intended (a typical Michael French reaction). He became convinced that 'there was not enough energy in the waves to make it worthwhile and I still think it is possibly true.' He wrote to me: 'The "first generation" of wave power devices were dinosaurs—enormous and unwieldy. My first device I regard as a wombat, say, a very primitive mammal. What I am looking forward to is the first placental—then wave power will be verging on the practical.' (Note: a wombat is a marsupial and does not have a placenta.)

But this has not prevented him from carrying on exploring wave energy, popping up like a jack-in-the-box at conferences, with comments that could come only from him. One of his inventions is called PS Frog, and he explained how it was named to a conference of the Institution of Mechanical Engineers:

'This paper . . . is presented with hindsight as a rational process, whereas in fact our approach has been tortuous . . . We substitute hindsight for insight as if we had known all along which way to go and had proceeded directly to the device we call PS Frog. Frog is just a name that appealed, but for anyone who likes acronyms it stands for

French's Reactionless Oceanic Generator. The P.S. stands for Pitching and Surging or, if you prefer, for PostScript, since it was an afterthought.'[2]

This is his style, mixing serious contributions to wave energy with self-mocking whimsy. This may have been a cause of the lack of attention paid to his contributions; but his ideas cannot be ignored. They are highly original, and his first incursion on the wave energy scene with the Air Bag was extremely important at a time when official thinking was writing off all the other inventions.

It is obvious to even the least cost-conscious of observers that there is strong appeal in a device which uses a rubber bag as the outer casing instead of steel or concrete; it is almost certain to be cheaper to build than its hard-skinned rivals. The question mark over the Air Bag is whether it is possible to find a material which is flexible enough to be squeezed and expanded 15 times a minute, 900 times an hour, 21 000 times a day, non-stop for 365 days a year, without the material splitting or being punctured by the detritus floating in the sea. It is sometimes compared with a car tyre which is put under a greater strain by the weight of a loaded vehicle and uneven road surfaces. But cars do not travel all the time without a break, and even then they puncture frequently or valves burst.

Nevertheless, it must be said that the concept did appeal to chemists concerned with polymers such as rubber. Among them was Dr Anthony Challis, who became Chief Scientist in 1980 after working for ICI. He was also director of polymer engineering at the Science and Engineering Research Council and is now Professor at Brunel. He was a strong supporter of the French concept, confident that such people as Avon Tyres could produce a Bag of reinforced rubber that would survive at sea.

The first French design consisted of a concrete beam 190 m long, lying head-on out to sea. The main part of the hull was submerged 13 m below the mean sea level. It was kept afloat by flexible Air Bags forming a sausage balloon, divided into cells, which French calls bags, attached on top. As a wave crest squeezed a bag, the air inside was forced out, through a non-return valve into a high pressure duct and through a turbine into a low pressure duct. It re-entered the first bag when the water level fell into a trough and the bag inflated. French said: 'Each bag (that is, cell) works more or less independently as a simple bellows, pumping air from 'low' to 'high' pressure. The air circuit is completed via two single-stage air turbines through which air returns from the 'high' to the 'low' pressure side. It is sometimes useful to think of the bags as collapsing in a crest and expanding in a trough.'[3]

It was a departure from the Japanese idea of a column of water, open at the base to the sea and at the top to the atmosphere. The French device contained the air it was using in an enclosed system and kept the sea, and the air from the outside world out of the system. Many engineers believe that the weakness of the OWC is the opening at which it admits the sea and this is avoided by French. Another plus point was that there was no chance of flotsam being swept into the blades of the turbine, as could happen with the OWC. But the Bag's obvious weakness was that it would be liable to punctures, and then the air would vanish in a puff. French defended his invention. He told me: 'There is a lot of experience of this kind of rubber in sea water. Unlike with car tyres, you are not rolling it down on sharp objects. It is like the side wall of a tyre, which is flexible, and the sharpness of flexing is less than on the side walls of a tyre.' Preliminary tests had been made on suitable reinforced rubber materials 'which can easily meet the high strength requirements and are relatively cheap (in pounds per kilowatt). Questions of Bag design and durability constitute the most critical area of uncertainty with this device and may possibly make it impractical.' This was an approach that appealed because of its frankness.

French changed the design, putting the bags underneath and the valves above the water level, and devised protective devices to isolate any bags which were punctured. He concentrated on bringing down what he (and most people) saw as 'the really expensive thing in wave power—the structure', and he brought it down, leap-frogging other, longer-established schemes. It is about one-quarter the size of the Raft or Duck for the same power, in his view. It has a big piston area compared with the total device area. A generator 200 m long would have an installed capacity of 8 MW and a mean output of 3–4 MW. It was tested at 1/100th scale in the Cockerell wave tank. It used non-return valves to ensure that the air moved in the right direction and returned to the deflated area by the designated route; in those early days, French had not considered using the recently-invented Wells turbine which could take air from two directions.

RPT said of the device: 'It has turned out to have significantly lower structure costs than other devices and a lower total cost and simpler mooring: we think he has actually achieved the objectives which he was aiming for. The crucial question is whether it will survive (in the sea) or not; this is something which only further work will determine.'[4] The opportunity of testing it at full-scale in the sea was not to be granted by the British Government, but its importance for wave energy at that time was that it made it appear economically possible, even by the gloomy RPT standard. Later, when the wave energy family had grown older and wiser, it became accepted wisdom that there was, in the words of Grove-Palmer, 'the new device syndrome: the problems you get look easy because you don't know what they are.'[5]

French set off back to Lancaster and was awarded a grant of £175 000 on 7 June 1979. He immediately put his questioning and irreverent brain to work. It was then that he told *New Civil Engineer*, with a typically disobliging remark, that his Bags 'will not become competitive with major energy sources unless the price of fossil fuels rises considerably or the development of nuclear power is restricted by public opinion.'[6] It was particularly unfortunate just after he had been given government funding. Wave energy teams recalled that French had been a keen nuclear supporter. He wrote to me in March 1979: 'I first looked at wave energy in 1960 and decided that it was not practical as yet, a view I still hold.' But he was not going to be deflected from saying what he believed. He continued working on the Bag for four years and then stopped at the end of 1982, not because of government policy and not because of worries about finding the right material; it was, as he wrote to me, because 'the cost of the device was simply too high'—this despite the fact that he had achieved 'nearly double' the reference design figures for the power level. But Professor French, independent as always, decided to move on to other inventions, called Flounder and PS Frog.

The idea of an enclosed air system was taken over by Coventry Polytechnic, which did a very clever thing. Recognising that the Bag, exposed to the sea,

Fig. 6.18 Cutaway section of the Clam showing protective flap outside the flexible bag and turbine inside the main structure.

Fig. 6.19 A circular Clam under test. This has become the favoured design, which can accept wave energy from all directions.

was liable to be damaged by detritus floating in the water or by stones thrown up by the waves, it provided a line of steel flaps, hinged at the base, which would move forwards and backwards in the waves. The Air Bag, renamed the Clam, would be placed between the flap and the main structure, squeezed by the flap as the waves rose and fell. The flap would protect the rubber and the Air Bag, moving like the bellows of a concertina, would force the air through a self-rectifying Wells turbine.

But then a second consideration came into the picture. To cut costs, the steel flaps were abolished and the unit was redesigned with, once again, the rubber Bag exposed to the waves directly. Coventry said that this eliminated 'the engineering liability of large moving components', which was true; and it reduced the displacement from 48 000 to 44 000 tonnes. But it had the disadvantage of exposing the rubber to the sea without a protective steel shield. A third version of the Air Bag was tried by Coventry when it redesigned the power station as a circular structure—12 interconnected air bags built around an inner steel ring 60 metres in diameter, with an air duct linking them all. As the waves rise to a crest, the air is forced out, along the duct, through a Wells turbine on its way to another which is expanding as it rides a trough. As the peak of the wave moves on, the air is forced back, again through the turbine. The estimated cost came down to around 5p/kWh, and Coventry had support from Dr Challis and from RPT, who remained faithful to the concept, as their spokesman made clear at the Edinburgh conference of 1993 and afterwards. But it did not succeed in saving Coventry's efforts. The device had funding from a company called

Sea Energy Associates who stayed with the project as long as it appeared to have any chance of government support. They were entitled to feel that they had been robbed when the government walked away from wave energy.

Coventry was particularly active in arranging trials of models of its version of the Duck and of the Clam in Draycott Water at 1/50th scale, and then at 1/10th scale on Loch Ness, which it called 'the finest natural wave tank in Britain' because of the funnelling effect of the prevailing south-westerly winds. It wanted to launch a two-thirds scale Clam in the Western Approaches, using Milford Haven as base, in 1982. It was to have been built by Howard Doris at Loch Kishorn in Scotland and would have been 180 m long, with a capacity of 2 MW. (Full-scale would be 270 m and about 10 MW). It would have cost about £10 million, chicken feed by government standards, and would have provided a model that could be replicated easily and moored off almost any island with a good wave climate. It was probably the device nearest to gaining official support. The hope was destroyed by the government.

Coventry had a lively team working under its director, Dr Norman Bellamy, and whatever views may be held of his action in borrowing the Duck, that trial did make an enormous contribution in public relations terms: the television film of it on Loch Ness won over millions of people who would never have known about laboratory experiments.

Coventry received substantial backing in the places inside the energy establishment where it mattered. At one point, in April 1981, it was actually told by Rendel Palmer & Tritton, the government consultants, that its own cost estimate for its own device was too *high*, and it was brought down from 6.3 to 5.7p. We know that Dr Challis favoured rubber as a containment material. And we have discovered since the official programme was ended, at the 1993 Edinburgh conference, that Peter Clark of RPT was a close associate and adviser, even after the official programme ended, of Dr Bellamy. But none of this was sufficient. The British government had lost interest. It wanted wave energy out of the way so that it could pursue its illusory goal of building 10 Pressurised Water Reactors in 10 years.

References.

1. Ross, D. (12 July 1979). Challenge of wave power (Letters page). *New Civil Engineer*. Thomas Telford Ltd.
2. French, M. (1991). *Wave energy*, pp. 13–18. Mechanical Engineering Publications Ltd., for the Institution of Mechanical Engineers.
3. French, M. (1979). In *Proceedings, wave energy conference, Heathrow Hotel, London, November 22–23 1978, pp. 59–63. ETSU*.

4.   Clark, P.J. (1979). In *Proceedings, wave energy conference, Heathrow Hotel, London, November 22–23 1978*, pp. 59–60. ETSU.

5.   Grove-Palmer, C.O.J. (1979). In *Proceedings, wave energy conference, Heathrow Hotel, London, November 22–23 1978*, pp. 143–6. ETSU.

6.   French, M. (14 June 1979). In *New Civil Engineer*. p. 28. Thomas Telford Ltd.

7 Ideas proliferate

Michael French once said that anyone could invent two wave energy devices before breakfast, and there was some truth in this, once Commander Masuda had launched the *Kaimei* and Stephen Salter had turned turbulence into a calm stretch of water in his laboratory tank. But to build power stations at sea would need money.

Apart from the classics described in Chapter 6, there were several devices being developed in different countries. They often had strange names: the Lilypad, the Backward Bent Duck Buoy, the Mighty Whale, the Hose Pump, the Bristol Cylinder, the Tapchan. They were presented regularly at wave energy conferences and have been discussed at great length; any of them might provide the breakthrough into regular generation, if it can gain the right financial support.

The first, chronologically, came from Norway, whose major incursion on the international scene is discussed more fully in Chapter 9. But the earlier theoretical work was an important factor. As early as 1975 Dr Johannes Falnes of Trondheim University and his late colleague Kjell Budal proposed a heaving buoy as a point absorber—the phrase means a unit which accepts energy from all directions, unlike the line of devices facing the direction of the prevailing winds and wavefronts. Dr Falnes puts it more precisely (in a letter to me): 'A point absorber is a wave energy converter whose largest linear extension is very small compared to the wavelength.' And he added, at the Cork conference organised by the EC: 'Such devices, well suited for the offshore deployment of wave power, have a rather narrow resonance bandwith. For this reason, it is essential that they are equipped with means to achieve controlled optimum oscillatory motion. The aim of the control is to approach a maximum of converted power in relation to the structure invested.'[1] The shape of a buoy naturally suggests itself. It bounces in the waves, like an ordinary navigation buoy, but with the difference that it is attached to a static, rigid object, such as a pole standing on the seabed. This provides the frame of reference, while the buoy, oscillating up and down, provides the energy, which is then usually converted into a stream of air in an OWC.

The point absorber can actually have an input of energy greater than its nominal installed capacity. It is this which enables Thorpe[2] to write that the OSPREY (which is also a point absorber) has an average capture efficiency of 115 per cent—that is 15 per cent greater than the energy in the oncoming waves along the 40 m facing out to sea. The extra 15 per cent comes from the waves at each side, and in the short distance between the land and the device. In a power station further out at sea, waves coming from the 'wrong' direction can be almost as ferocious and fruitful as those from the best direction, though less frequent.

But a point absorber, as Dr Falnes indicated, needs a control mechanism to enable it to work efficiently in waves with which it is out of phase—that is, the buoy is bouncing faster than the waves are arriving. So this led the Norwegians to experiment with what has come to be known as phase control. The Japanese have shown that it can increase OWC output by as much as 10 times.

Dr Nancy Nichols, a mathematician from Reading University who became involved in wave energy via a project for the CEGB, gave an excellent description of the problem at the same Cork conference:

At certain "resonant" frequencies the device achieves maximum energy capture and the force acting on the device is then in phase with the device velocity. Losses in energy capture occur at other frequencies due to the relative phase difference between the device motion and the wave-exciting force and the device may be much less efficient at non-resonant frequencies . . . By adding a control mechanism to the power conversion system, the average energy generated over a broad band of the sea wave spectrum can be increased and the delivered cost of the energy can be reduced.[3]

I asked her for a non-technical way of presenting it. She put it this way: 'If you push a child on a swing at the wrong time, the swing pushes you.' And then instead of the swing moving more, it moves less.

That is the problem. What is the solution? Your device needs to know every few seconds what size wave is about to hit it. Dr Nichols told me:

You can get some reasonable amount of information if you station a waverider buoy ahead of the device, and combine it with a predictor based on past information about the shape of the curve (of wave height and length), and you predict what the future shape will be on the basis of it. But my feeling is that this is not very practical, and it is more likely that the operation will be done with some kind of feedback which does something automatic. It does not try to predict change. It just changes automatically.

What could that be? An automatic operation can be observed at first hand by a do-it-yourself experiment in a lavatory. Unscrew the top of the cistern, pull the chain to empty the water and then wait as fresh water flows in to refill it. The floating ball is attached to an arm leading to the inlet valve. The arm rises gradually to close the valve and stop the water entering. If it rises too soon, before the cistern is full, you will not get all the water you need for efficient flushing; if it rises too late, the water will overflow the cistern and you will have to mop up the spilt water. It is easy to adjust the moment when the valve shuts off the inward flow of water, by turning a screw at the end of the arm close to the valve. This changes the moment when the water is turned off. Can something like that be done automatically on a buoy floating in the waves? The technical term in wave energy language is 'latching', defined by Salter in a paper to the European Commission as delaying any movement until the wave force has built up to a sufficient level. The suggestion of Salter is that a hydraulic ram shows the way. This is a pump which receives the force of a large quantity of water and lifts a small quantity in response. The large quantity fills a tank until its pressure forces a valve to close behind it. The only escape is upwards. It would have to do that every few seconds to be useful in wave energy, as each wave arrived. Salter suggests that it could be combined with hydraulics. Latching, he says, could be applied to an OWC. 'The valve would have to be large enough to offer no pressure drop when open, strong enough to stand up to water impact when closed, and fast enough to operate in a second or less.' High-pressure oil, he says, could be used to activate the valve.[4]

The Norwegians have led the way in tackling this (still unsolved) problem. One of their colleagues, Even Mehlum, principal inventor of the Tapchan (discussed more extensively in Chapter 9), is the scientist who led the search for effective 'wave focusing'. This seeks to imitate nature. It has been found that there are 'hot spots' along any coastline, where the wave activity is stronger than elsewhere, and this is caused by the unevenness of the seabed. It has also been found that this is almost always the place where local fishermen congregate, because they have found, from experience, that that is where the fish are most numerous. The Norwegian plan to imitate nature was to build a water wave lens. Horizontal plates would be moored below the surface, to concentrate the wave energy at the site of a wave power station. The cost would be high but the yield in terms of electricity would justify this. It has not so far been built.

As to the buoy, it would have an installed capacity of 500 kW, so that a small power station of 200 MW would consist of an array of 410 buoys. Dr Falnes is a tall, white-bearded, distinguished person, who always appears to me to be a prototype for Dr Thomas Stockmann, Ibsen's 'Enemy of the People', the man who utters inflexible truths. He explained his system for controlled point absorbers to the Trondheim conference:

Consider a body which is making heaving motions in the sea. In regular waves it is fairly easy to obtain optimum motion of the body. All that is necesary is to tune the system in such a way that the natural period of the body is equal to the period of the wave. The system should be properly damped (sic). The damping may for instance be accomplished by an electric generator, delivering the useful power from the converter. Ocean waves are not regular. This makes it considerably more difficult to optimise the motion of the converter.[5]

The converter Falnes designed was a spherical buoy of 5 m radius, open to the sea at its base, with a pole passing through the centre down to the seabed, where it is held rigid. The buoy rises and falls freely on rollers, except during controlled intervals when it is clamped to the pole. This is phase control, which he says improves power absorption by a factor of five. How is it to be done? Dr Falnes said that there were two aspects of the control system. One was to predict the incoming wave; based on this information the buoy would be unlatched 'at a proper time relative to the trough or the crest of the wave'. Secondly, it would be latched 'as closely as possible to its extreme positions of heave oscillation. Thus, due to the latching, information is needed about the motion of the buoy. Typically, a combination of the measured values of its velocity and acceleration can be used for this purpose. This will not, however, be discussed in more detail here.'[5] It is clear that he was thinking along the same lines as Dr Nichols, about a combination of a forecast and a perception by mechanical or some other means of what was actually happening to the buoy.

In the neighbouring country of Sweden, a different approach has been introduced: the Swedes, at the Chalmers University of Technology in Gothenburg, have invented what they call the IPS Hosepump. It too has a width of 5 m, but it is 16 m long, weighs 50 metric tonnes, and is 21 m high, much larger than the Trondheim buoy. It differs from most of the devices in that it directly uses sea water (instead of converting it into an airflow), which will be directed on to a Pelton turbine, perhaps most familiar as the water-wheel type, with jets of water hitting rows of buckets which hang around the rim of a disc attached to the generator shaft. It is an impulse turbine and more suitable for the Swedish device than the Kaplan (which was invented by a Swede and has been chosen by the Norwegians for their Tapchan).

The Hosepump is highly original. A buoy floats on the surface and it is connected to a horizontal plate hanging in deep water, providing an artificial seabed and anchored to the real seabed. It is in effect a platform below the surface. The link is a hollow tube, the hose from which it gets its name, made of elastomeric material and filled with water and a piston. As the buoy rises and falls, the tube is alternately stretched and relaxed, and its diameter is reduced and expanded, like a sausage balloon. The movement causes a change of internal volume in the Hosepump. This is used to suck in sea water through a valve, pressurise it, and then pass it through another valve into a collection system. This collection system connects the outputs of several Hosepumps, thereby smoothing the flow of pressurised sea water to a central turbine and generator.

The significance of the plate floating between the surface and the seabed is that it frees the device from the tide. The plate stays at the same distance from the surface. One of its admirers is Salter, who believes that it is the device which could serve most easily as a display model and confidence-builder. He told me: 'It is easy to move around. It operates in any depth of water. You can work it in mid-ocean.'

Each buoy has an installed capacity of 50 kW and an annual output of 250 MWh. A commercial plant would consist of an array of several buoys, 10–20 m apart, with the pressurised water from each being manifolded together and feeding a common Pelton turbine and generator. The Swedes have tested it in Lake Lygnern and in the sea at Vigna, and have plans to station one in Donegal Bay, Ireland. The cost of electricity has been put by different authorities at between 2 and 4p/kWh. But the Swedes say, with exactly the right attitude at this stage of development, 'Little effort has been spent to find the most cost-effective dimensions of the buoy or the cost-optimum of the machinery.'

Almost unnoticed, an unexpected and extremely successful arrival in the wave energy family has been India. With government backing, the Wave Energy Group at the Indian Institute of Technology in Madras has built a 150 kW OWC outside a harbour at Vizhinjam, near Trivandrum. It was commissioned in October 1991, and the Wave Energy Group describe it as the first offshore power plant of its kind in the world, which is (just about) true. It is an OWC, and there have been others. It is not on the shore, but nor was the *Kaimei*, and nor are the wave energy buoys and lightships in the Pacific. However, it is the first one to be *standing* on the seabed, just off the shore, ahead of the OSPREY, though less than one-tenth of its size and linked to the land by a footbridge. But it is there and it is generating.

It was started in 1982, the year the British Government abandoned wave power—just the sort of gesture one hopes for and cherishes from a former member of the British Empire. The device consists of a concrete caisson, 17 m by 23 m, with an opening below the surface and a lip wall to separate the water column from the sea outside. It is designed for maximum efficiency in waves with a peak of 1.52 m but can take an extreme wave of 7 m. It has a Wells turbine of 2 m diameter with eight blades. It also uses the 'harbour walls' introduced by the Norwegians, an innovation which concentrates the waves at the entrance and doubles efficiency. The first Indian attempt failed because the caisson sank. A second attempt succeeded in 1990, and the plant was commissioned the following year.

The bottom part of the caisson, a concrete box 3 m high, was constructed first, in a pit 5 m deep on the beach, and other parts were assembled, with a temporary steel gate across the opening so that it floated inside the harbour basin. The gate was installed to close the front opening and ensure that the device floated, then the whole assembly was towed by tugs to its location outside the harbour. Ballast was added until the plant sank to the seabed. A steel bridge, 45 m long, linking the wave power station to the harbour, has been added. It is built entirely in India and is designed primarily to provide information on wave climate, pressure on the caisson structure, air velocity and pressures through the turbine, its speed, power, and the energy sent to the grid. The turbine has been self-starting and reached its peak power of 150 kW. Its average power is likely to be around 75 kW from April to November, and 25 kW from December to March. The entire operation has cost only £850 000.

One of the lessons learned has been the need to protect the turbine during what the team calls 'extreme wave climate'. The plan is to have two power modules in future units and to place them at each side of the water column instead of immediately above it. This will also facilitate maintenance and allow the modules to be run singly or in tandem to match wave power availability at different seasons. The intention is to build a full-scale station at the same site with a series of modular caissons and an installed capacity of 1.5 MW at an estimated cost of £3.9 million.

An unusual British device, which enjoys the cachet of being backed by the distinguished firm of consulting engineers and architects Ove Arup, is the Ecovision Lilypad, which uses the Swedish Hosepump. It looks like a floating mattress or Li-lo, 200 m by 60 m, and is built of flexible, reinforced rubber compounds. An identical-sized device is submerged underneath it. The two are linked by pumps. The upper mattress rises and falls, following the movement of the waves. The submerged one is anchored to the seabed, below most of the underspin of the surface waves and therefore not exposed to their force, and it remains largely static. Energy is extracted from the relative motion between the two mattresses. Its inventors are David Collier, a structural engineer working for Ove Arup, and Dominic Michaelis, a designer with an architectural background. Collier explained it at the Edinburgh conference.[6] They built a model using a sheet of sealed air bubbles reinforced by piano wire for the upper membrane, and mesh material for the lower one. When waves were created at one end of the tank, the upper membrane could be seen contouring and the lower membrane was relatively stable.

That was in 1979, and they approached ETSU, which asked RPT to assess the cost of electricity from the device. Unfortunately, RPT made the calculation on the assumption that the short side (the foot of the bedstead) would be facing the waves; it should of course be the long side because, as Collier said, it was a question of power per metre and the longer side had more metres, hence more power, hence cheaper power.

The project was dormant until 1990, when it was revived by building a prototype to verify the principle at sea. It was taken out in a fishing boat near Littlehampton, on the south coast, and it generated a strong jet of water at each wave. 'This was the qualitative result we had aimed at and delighted us as much as it did the fisherman and his mate.' Their paper said that as, typically, 80 per cent of the energy in a wave is to be found in a depth of one-sixth of the wavelength, the lower membrane would have to be at that depth. 'A device aiming to intercept 80 per cent of energy from 100 m long waves would need to have its lower membrane at a depth of 17 m or more.' The difference between the two, as the top one rises and falls and the lower one remains in place, is used to drive a series of pumps using either sea water or some other liquid, through a Hosepump which, as we have seen, has an automatic cut-off when the waves become too rough to be useful.

A lot has still to be done in developing the scheme, but Thorpe[7] estimates that a 200 m model would have an average output of 3.1 MW and an annual output of 27.2 GWh. The design team estimate the cost of 20 Lilypads as between £464 million and £1 116 million, which is obviously no more than a rough estimate. The cost of a unit of electricity is put at 7.5p/kWh, and with interest added on at a rate of 8 per cent it comes to 14.1p. (Thorpe, also using the discount rate of 8 per cent, puts the cost at 15p, almost the same as the device team.)

Collier does remark that the ETSU estimate 'assumes costs which contain no economies of scale and so it is, in essence, a prototype cost. The economic development work would therefore aim to study the manufacturing process to assess potential cost reductions as a result of mass production.'[6] (ETSU would say that economies of scale have been taken into account by its calculations.)

An advantage of the Lilypad, say its inventors, is that 'such a lightweight, flexible assembly floating at sea would present a lesser hazard to navigation than concrete or steel structures. A fishing boat would be brought to a gentle stop, while a supertanker would probably tear its way through.'

A disappointment has been the lack of progress in Japan, where energy is expensive and resources are scarce. It led the world with the invention of the Oscillating Water Column and the launch of the *Kaimei* in 1977. That was an early foray into chaos theory, pushing out the boat and waiting to see what happened, very different from the line pursued in most other countries which insisted on scientific experiments designed to anticipate every conceivable happening, heedless of the assertion by Sir Hermann Bondi that 'the sea always has a trick up its sleeve.' The Japanese have since carried out research into several devices in what they call 'exotic energy'. Some have appropriately exotic names and designs, but none of them is of significant size. Most of them are OWCs using Wells turbines, with outputs in kilowatts, and not many of those. One, built into a harbour wall at Sakata on the north-west coast, generates 60 kW.

In defence of the Japanese, it is said that the Sea of Japan has small waves and that there is not the scope for the 2000 MW power stations which are suitable for the Atlantic. But in fact the Pacific, to the east of Japan, can produce highly favourable wave climates, with averages ranging from 30 kW/m to as high as 70 kW/m. If the financial support had been available, Japan could have done far more. Dr Leslie Duckers of Lanchester Polytechnic (now Coventry University), reported to the Coventry conference on the Japanese situation and put the available wave energy at 2.7 GW. Japanese scientists and engineers, led by Masuda, reported to the Edinburgh conference on some of the devices they are developing.[8]

The Mighty Whale looks like a whale. It is produced by the Japanese Marine Science and Technology Center (JAMSTEC). It says that the coastal waters are used for aquaculture, and coexistence and harmony must be achieved between economic development and environmental conservation. The Mighty Whale swallows the waves into its open mouth and would, the

Japanese say, produce an area of calm water that would greatly increase the economic value of wave power, because it could be used as a floating breakwater and to supply compressed air to fish farms behind it.

Other Japanese devices include the Backward Bent Duct Buoy, which does actually bend over backwards so that its opening is facing away from the direction of the waves, towards the shore rather than the open sea. This innovation was suggested by Masuda himself and, according to Dr Tony Lewis,[9] has actually increased the power output, a surprising result confirmed by tests at University College, Cork. The Ryokuseisha Corporation, which has developed it, says that air output from the same air chamber is 13 times greater than from the *Kaimei*. It has been used in the Pacific for large lightships and navigation buoys, and generates at 10 cents (6.5p) a unit. It could be used for islands which are paying 50 cents (32p) for a unit of electricity from a diesel generator.

Another device is called the Pendulum.[10] It is a rectangular concrete caisson, open to the sea but for a pendulous flap hanging down. The standing waves generated inside the caisson make the flap oscillate, and this drives a hydraulic pump. All of the machinery is above the water line and therefore easy to maintain. It has an optimal power extraction of only 40–50 per cent and looks like some of the early designs investigated and rejected by Stephen Salter before he arrived at the Duck. If this sounds over-critical I would plead that it stems from disappointment: Japan made the original, absolutely crucial breakthrough in the early days through the work of Commander Masuda, but the Japanese programme has not developed significantly since then.

An invention which appeared on the scene just in time to be described at the Heathrow conference is the Bristol Cylinder. It is the only one in which the theory came first, in the shape of a scientific paper published in the *Journal of Fluid Mechanics*[11] by Professor T.F. Ogilvie of the Ann Arbor Department of Naval Architecture in Michigan. He discovered that if you place a cylinder in a narrow tank, like a rolling pin in a bath, and rotate it around a point below the surface, waves are generated in one direction only. The paper was profuse in abstruse mathematics and must have appeared at the time as simply an unusual observation, of interest to students of pure mathematics with no apparent application. But Professor David Evans of Bristol University, whose subject is applied maths, used the discovery to design a wave power station, safe from the turbulence on the surface.

He invented the Bristol Cylinder. It is a barrel-shaped object made of concrete, 100 m × 16 m, which floats on its side 3 m below the surface, held down by moorings to the seabed. It thus escapes being buffeted by the surface waves but benefits from their underspin, and rotates in what scientists call 'an eccentric orbit—an irrotational motion'. That is, it moves rather like a bottle floating on the waves, but under the surface, where the waves complete their orbit. It follows the same path as the particles of water, an up-and-down, rolling motion but without spinning, so the brackets on its side stay horizontal. The effect is to pull on the moorings which are linked to hydraulic pumps on the seabed. The pumps are pulled upwards as the Cylinder rises and then, as the moorings slacken, the pumps are pulled back into their jackets by springs. The effect is to drive sea water through pipes at high pressure, to a turbo-generator on a platform above the sea.

It is an invention that enjoys high respect from other teams, as does Professor Evans. He was a consultant to the Norwegians. Salter regarded the Cylinder as a partner to the Duck; it operates in a similar way, following the movement of the waves and generating electricity without the intermediate step of converting their movement into air.

Professor Evans says that it is the one device with 'two degrees of freedom—horizontal and vertical motions combined' (up-and-down and back and forth). The costs have been brought down from 9 to 6p a unit in the Thorpe report, with zero discount rate. Its disadvantage is that a 2000 MW power station is estimated to cost about £5100 million, and maintenance below the surface would not be easy—Thorpe suggests £93 million a year. Its moment may arrive if stations existing at surface level in the roughest seas recognise the value of going down below.

Denmark has been active in wave power. It has been developing a most unusual device, which could be regarded as a child, or at least a stepchild of the Cylinder, which it resembles in that it is a subsea generator. It consists of a floating buoy on the surface and a hollow concrete base, 9 m in diameter, with a submerged weight of 200 tonnes, sitting on the seabed in 30 m of water. There is an opening in the top of the base, and this is plugged by a piston with a submerged weight of 5 tonnes, which is connected to the float. When the float rises on the peak of a wave, the piston is pulled upwards and the sea floods in to the base to fill the area, spinning a turbine/generator as it enters. Then the float descends into a trough and the piston falls back into the base, driving out the sea water through an escape valve. Then the piston rises and there is space inside the base and the water rushes in again, driving the turbine, and so on. It is not an OWC, although it has a similar pattern of movement, but the OWC uses a stream of air to drive an air turbine, while the motive force in the Danish device is water.

The Danes built a 45 kW model off Hanstholm on the north-west coast, facing the North Sea, with a 600-mile fetch across to Scotland. It functioned for one month and was then taken ashore because the escape flap valves became damaged, and this prevented them from damping the pressure. As a result, in a strong gale the piston was pulled out of its cylinder. On the positive side, a lesson the Danes drew from the experience was that future models should have many relatively small valves rather than a few large ones. They also concluded that it was possible to construct large piston pumps which met the requirements of their invention, with great accuracy, small friction, and good wearability; that it was possible to use submerged turbine/generators with fixed speed connected to the grid; that fouling on the lining of the piston and its tube did not occur; and that sedimentation in the pump housing was negligible. They decided to build another model of 1–2 kW with built-in storage, and their leader, Kim Nielsen, insisted that this was not a scaling down, as the wave climate would be unchanged and they were prepared for 12 m waves.

And so to Michael French, inventor of the Air Bag, which led to a completely new area of wave energy leading up to the Clam; French then decided that the cost would be too high and that the prospect of full-scale Air Bags was remote with the receding of the energy crisis. So he switched to the Frog, 'a simple buoy reacting in heave against an internal moving mass', he wrote in a circular letter. 'Heave' is the up-and-down motion used by OWCs and the Falnes buoy; 'surge' is the horizontal motion. At the Heathrow conference, Professor Bellamy put it in this way: 'The surge strain due to horizontal forces is roughly twice as much as the heave strain due to vertical forces.'[12] French arrived independently at the same conclusion and changed his Frog to PS Frog (for Pitching and Surging, which has been mentioned earlier).

He explained his reasoning to the Edinburgh conference. He said: 'The advantages of heave over surge are: (a) freedom from directionality; (b) high wave force per unit area. The advantage of surge over heave is that the ideal power is twice as great.'[13] His reference to directionality concerns an issue that is important to all wave power stations, apart from point absorbers. The lines of devices facing the waves have to choose their attitude, and they will naturally choose to face into the prevailing wind force, from where the strongest waves come. But that can mean that they lose the chance of harvesting waves which come, as always happens for part of the time, from the 'wrong' direction. When the energy is being drawn from the up-and-down motion, that is to say from heave, this is less significant a factor.

And so to the French device. It is shaped like a paddle, which floats and (like a paddle) gets in the path of the waves and abstracts their energy. At the base of the paddle is a cylinder, 14 m × 9 m, containing a reaction mass of 1250 tonnes. As the paddle is driven by pitch and surge forces, the reaction mass slides along rails, backwards and forwards. Its movement is controlled by hydraulic rams which pump oil to drive a generator. There is an accumulator to provide storage. Thorpe has said that it resembles the early design of the Duck.[14] But it is a point absorber. French says that the Achilles heel of terminators (devices which face and absorb the power of the waves) is their large size, leading to high costs.[15] The paddle, made of steel, is 23 m high.

French said: 'In many ways, the most vital choice the designer has to make is that of the source of reaction.'[13] He is referring to the frame of reference, the upright equivalent of a wall or other stationary object which the moving device bounces against. His early device, the Frog (without 'PS') relied on heave, and this led at times to violent rolling. He then changed to PS Frog to take his power from surge. He said that the sea bed was unattractive because it required a stiff mooring to extract the power 'and a stiff mooring is a liability in storms, besides being expensive in itself'. Another possibility was 'amplitude diversity, the fact that the wave motion is less at lower depths and so a heaving body can react against another below it'. This applies to the Lilypad and the Swedish Hosepump, but it has 'inherent dynamic disadvantages', because the wave motion has the same direction at both levels—that is, the two bodies are being pushed in the same direction and this means a loss of some power.

Another method is an inertial mass within the device itself, and he is proposing to use this for PS Frog on rails which allow it to move in a prescribed direction. But the movement of the mass, he says, limits the capture of wave energy compared with what would be possible with a stiff mooring.

French concludes that the field for new devices is becoming exhausted but then, even as he writes, his natural optimism breaks through: 'In the course of writing this paper something quite new arose, which is probably not competitive with existing designs, but demonstrated once again how rash it is to conclude that the possibilities have all been examined.'[13]

References.

1. Falnes, J. (1993). Review of wave energy research in Norway. *Wave energy R & D*, pp. 125–8. Commission of the European Communities.

2. Thorpe, T.W. (1992). *A review of wave energy* Vol.2, C.xlii. ETSU R-72.

3. Nichols, N.K. (1993). Phase control in wave energy generation. *Wave energy R & D*, pp. 177–182. Commission of the European Communities.

4. Salter, S.H. (1993). Wave energy power-conversion studies. *Wave energy R & D* pp. 59–101. Commission of the European Communities.

5. Budal, K., Falnes, J., Iversen, L.C., Lillebekken, P.M., Oltedal, G., Hals, T., Onshus, T., and Høy, A.S. (1982). The Norwegian Wave-Power Buoy Project. *Wave energy utilisation proceedings* (ed. H. Berge), pp. 323–44. Tapir, Trondheim.

6. Collier, D. and Michaelis, D. (1994). Twin membrane wave energy converter. In *European wave energy symposium*, (ed. G. Elliot and Dr. G. Caratti). pp. 317–22. National Engineering Laboratory, Glasgow.

7. Thorpe, T.W. (1992). *A review of wave energy*, Vol. 1, pp. 106–11. ETSU R-72.

8. Miyazaki, T. (1994). Japanese wave energy devices. In *European wave energy symposium* (ed G. Elliot and G. Caratti), pp. 15–20, 323–37, 373–8. National Engineering Laboratory, Glasgow.

9. Lewis, T. (1993). Wave energy. Current research activities and recommendations for European research programme, pp. 18–22. (Distributed at EU conference in Brussels.)

10. Miyazaki, T. (1994). Japanese wave energy devices. In *European wave energy symposium* (ed. G. Elliot and G.H. Caratti), pp. 15–20. National Engineering Laboratory, Glasgow.
11. Ogilvie, T.F. (1963). First-and second-order forces on a cylinder submerged under a free surface. *Journal of Fluid Mechanics.* **16**, 451–72.
12. Bellamy, N. (1978). *Proceedings, wave energy conference. Heathrow Hotel, London, November 22–23 1978*, pp. 30–4.
13. French, M. (1994). The prospects for economical wave power and the quasiresonant point absorber. In *European wave energy symposium* (ed. G. Elliot and G.H. Caratti), pp. 397–401. National Engineering Laboratory, Glasgow.
14. Thorpe, T. (1992). *A review of wave energy*, Vol. 2, p. C.xix. ETSU R-72.
15. French, M. (1993). PS Frog Mk. 2. A promising design of wave energy converter. *Wave energy R & D*, pp. 171–6. Commission of the European Communities.

8 Scuppering the waves

The British Government decided in 1982 to abandon its programme of support for wave energy, once regarded officially as the most promising of the renewables. Why? Was the decision, as the French say, worse than a crime—a blunder? Or was it an act of perfidy? Or was it justified?

From numerous discussions with people in energy from the day the programme was launched in 1976, I became convinced that the comfortable, entrenched representatives of conventional and nuclear energy were not the sort of people likely to welcome the arrival of a new competitor on their parish. This was not a conspiracy but an instinctive reaction by scientists, engineers, and administrators with natural loyalty to their own subjects. They could see that the idea of drawing energy from the waves was popular; that the construction of 2000 MW power stations in the open sea would generate a great deal of electricity which they would otherwise supply; and that it would cost a lot of money which might have come their way. That was natural. But the outrageous fortune which followed was not. Let us examine some of the key events.

The public servant in charge of the wave energy programme, Clive Grove-Palmer, was banned from attending the meeting in 1982 of the government's Advisory Council on Research and Development (ACORD) which was to consider the future of the programme, an unprecedented occurrence.

The government's presentation of the recommendations made at that meeting suggested that the members of ACORD, scientists and engineers chosen as specimens of the great and the good, wanted the entire programme ended; they did not.

The Central Electricity Generating Board, the body charged with producing electricity for England and Wales, in an internal memorandum[1], which was wrenched out of secrecy into daylight with great difficulty, blurted out its policy: 'The use of renewable energy sources for electricity generation is likely to be less economic than nuclear power. Nevertheless, it is important to explore these alternatives in order both *to satisfy ourselves* (my italics) that nuclear expansion is fully justified, and to demonstrate this to others, since groups opposing nuclear expansion have made substantial progress in the past few years.' So one reasonable inference is that the CEGB set out on research in order to demonstrate how unpromising it was.

An even worse blow came from ETSU, the parent body itself, and its own consulting engineers, Rendel Palmer & Tritton (RPT), whose extraordinary estimates showed the cost of wave energy as ranging from 20 to 60 p a unit (1 kilowatt-hour) at a time when electricity was costing the domestic customer 2p (see Chapter 6).[2]

Once full-scale prototypes have been tested and proved in the sea, and serial production starts, the real cost will follow the example of hydroelectric power: major investment is needed at the outset to pay for the structure, but the electricity becomes progressively cheaper as the capital is paid off and the technology enjoys the benefit of free fuel. Yet in the Heathrow Hotel, before a single full-scale unit had taken to the water, the official consultants were making calculations based on a profound knowledge of the unknown. And, as we were later to learn, some of the premises on which those calculations were based were absurd.

The figures, index-linked, would now (1995) be about 60p–£1.80 per unit; no one would today dream of talking of such costs. And the reality is even more ludicrous, because RPT used a 5 per cent interest rate for its calculations. If that were changed to the later official fashion of an 8 per cent discount rate, in accordance with the figure introduced by John Major when he was chief secretary to the Treasury in 1989, then the costs would indeed go through the roof and into the stratosphere.

Today, there are few people who would justify even seeking, at such an early stage, such figures; cost was not the issue, credibility was. But the figures dealt a damaging blow to wave energy. Overseas businessmen started to move towards the exit—the hotel was conveniently close to the airport. And the press also started to slip away.

Perhaps the estimates had never been intended to be taken seriously. The range was 100 per cent—20p:40p and 30p:60p. Would one expect an engineer to work to a plan which says that the result may prove to be double the number he first thought of?

It has been argued by some critics, who support the idea that small is beautiful, that the fault lay in even thinking about a 2000 MW station. This I would resist precisely because wave energy grows, almost indefinitely, in modules. What was wrong was to link such a distant concept to a penny-pinching calculation at such an early stage of development, at a time when we did not have even one Duck in the water.

There was, with hindsight, one tactical error: Britain concentrated exclusively on what we now call offshore wave energy, which means going out to sea to harvest the tallest and therefore the most fruitful waves. The idea of onshore stations had not been considered. That came later, from Norway. We were right to concentrate on offshore wave power because we must eventually go away from the land, to the open sea and deep water, for the really significant contributions to large grids. But smaller units, on the beach, have a permanent role for small, isolated communities, and an interim role even for countries intending to seek large-scale generation for the grid eventually.

And it might have been the case that the energy establishment would have been less frightened if it had been possible to think of wave energy in the same way as wind and tidal power, as a potential small-scale contributor without emphasis on the 2000 MW stations.

The nearest that anyone came to an explanation for the high costings started as a joke. RPT had been the official consulting engineers for the Thames flood barrier, which eventually cost 20 times the estimate. So, it was whispered, they redressed the balance by adjusting the figures for wave energy in the opposite direction by the same factor of 20! Joke or not, it was not funny for the wave energy research teams.

These were critical events in the history of wave energy and the obstacles it encountered. There were many others, and it may help if the facts are gathered together and presented in sequence, including some that have not been published before, to help an understanding of how the establishment works. Wave energy will not be the last battlefront, and workers in other disciplines should gain from a study of these facts.

As a journalist, I have been able to watch events from the start. I discovered, on a visit to the National Engineering Laboratory in East Kilbride in 1976, that Britain was considering seriously this leap into unknown waters, and I broke the news in the *Daily Express* that the Government was to invest £1 000 000 in a wave power research programme. I was later to be the first to express publicly the suspicion that all was not going well.

The programme was launched in April 1976[3] and placed under the control of the United Kingdom Atomic Energy Authority (UKAEA, later renamed AEA Technology) and its satellite ETSU, both of which were based at Harwell, behind the barbed wire fence, guarded by the armed police of the AEA and with the AEA as landlord and employer. The apparent justification was that nuclear power was an 'alternative' (to coal and oil) and so it was natural to group all the alternatives together.

The early staff, including Grove-Palmer, who managed the programme, were 'nuclear people'. It took years before they appreciated that the renewable sources were in competition with nuclear power, the core activity of their own parent company. If that sounds naïve, I can only report that that was the mood at that time. The dominant feeling among conscientious people in energy was that, with world demand rising and Middle East oil supplies under threat, we needed energy, any energy, and every source was good. Atoms for Peace could live happily alongside wave power.

This was a time when Britain had a Government which had been brought to office in 1974 by a miners' strike and the three-day week, and so there was a general welcome for the development of any new source of energy. But officialdom was more wary and sought to play down its potential role. The first open indication of this came two years later, in April 1978, when the National Federation of Women's Institutes held an energy conference in Westminster. It was opened by the then Prime Minister, James (now Lord)

Callaghan and was part of a drive to make sure that an organisation such as the WI did not get anti-nuclear ideas.

A key speaker was Dr F.J.P. ('Freddy') Clarke, then Research Director at Harwell and Chairman of the Wave Energy Steering Committee (WESC); he later became the Atomic Energy Authority's corporate Director of Business Development, selling its technology to the world, and served for a time on Dounreay's Board of Management, seeking alternative employment for staff displaced by the abandonment of the fast breeder reactor. He was a charming person who told me: 'We were enthusiasts for the renewables who tried also to be realists.' Many of the wave energy people believed that he was an important ally highly placed inside the AEA. Grove-Palmer believes that his departure from the chair of WESC was one of the worst blows suffered by wave energy.

But in his speech to the WI, Dr Clarke gave the first public indication that wave energy was not going to go ahead as many had hoped; the fact that he was addressing a conference designed to promote the popularity of nuclear power makes the point that an energy policy had to be chosen.

He told the audience:

From a viewpoint of contributing to our electricity supplies, wave energy is the most promising of the alternatives since large parts of our seas are promising for the technology. Against this, it is certainly the one with the longest period of engineering development ahead . . . But because the ultimate contribution is high—100 mtce (million tonnes of coal equivalent) is not impossible—the Department of Energy is backing a vigorous programme in this area . . . It is not difficult to argue that the most promising of the alternatives is also the one with the biggest problems ahead.

He described the difficulties graphically, concentrating on the huge size of a wave power station with structures the size of aircraft hangars. 'One element of these devices could contain this hall' (Central Hall, Westminster). And he added that all forms of renewable energy were likely to make 'only a minor contribution to our energy supplies by the year 2000'. There could be a take-off in their use 'during the first decades [plural] of the next century'.

These statements had been carefully considered, as Dr Clarke showed when the magazine *Nature* misreported him.[4] It quoted him as having said that wave power might make a substantial contribution '*by* the year 2000'. Not so, said Dr Clarke. He sent a memorandum to the press section of the Department of Energy to put the record straight. He pointed out that he had actually said: 'We are most *unlikely* to get a substantial contribution by the year 2000.'

His speech was made in 1978, when the twentieth century still had 22 years to run. By insisting that there could not be a major contribution from wave power until the first decades (plural) of the next century, Dr Clarke was making it plain that official policy had allocated wave power to 2020 or later. That meant that it would not be a significant source of energy for at least 42 and possibly 52 or more years.

So, as early as 1978, when we were about to experience the second chapter of the Middle East oil crisis and the wave energy programme was only two years old, official opinion had already consigned it to the distant future. This was a political decision; there was, at that stage, no engineering or scientific scenario which would require another 52 or even 42 years of work in turning the knowledge that we then possessed into the practical action of converting the movement of the waves into electricity, if a will existed. In fact, the work was accomplished by the Norwegians by 1985 and could have been turned into 'a substantial contribution' at any time from then on.

Dr Clarke was a faithful scientific public servant and this was not a personal sortie by him; it was a policy that he was describing. It was the UKAEA's attitude, which meant the attitude of the energy establishment.

Was wave energy damaged by the fact that research was conducted under the umbrella of the UKAEA? The nuclear industry hotly denies this and insists that renewable energy is kept in a compartment totally separate from nuclear power. But it is difficult to see how the ETSU staff, employed by the UKAEA, working at Harwell, often themselves nuclear scientists by training, sharing the same background (and the same canteen), could be indifferent to the argument propounded by their own company and their colleagues that nuclear power was clean and safe and cheap. And if that point of view was valid, one might well wonder why, logically, anyone should seek an alternative to nuclear power.

ETSU itself has exposed the argument about separate compartments. Its staff move from nuclear energy to renewables and back again to nuclear. Dr Clarke himself went from wave power to Dounreay. And there is the case of Peter Davies, Wave Energy Programme Manager after Grove-Palmer had been driven out, editor of 'Wave Energy, ETSU R26',[5] which was intended to be the epitaph on the Government programme. It was published in 1985, and then Mr Davies was promoted to the position of UKAEA team leader at the public inquiry at Dounreay into the fast breeder reactor, which was then hailed as the key to our nuclear future.

Again, in Energy Paper 54,[6] the Chief Scientist's Group of ETSU produced (in July 1987) a table which declared that wave energy is 'U' (for Unpromising) and awarding it one star, meaning 'cost-effective in no scenario'. In the same table, the Magnox nuclear power stations are given three stars, meaning 'cost effective in all scenarios'. We are presumably supposed to believe that the two sections of the document were prepared separately, by different sections of the same department of the same organisation; that the two sets of conclusions came together by spontaneous cohesion without human intervention; and that the members of the Chief Scientist's Group gave a cry of surprise when they discovered that wave electricity was expensive and nuclear power was cheap.

It was in April 1978, the month of the WI conference, that the then Science Editor of *The Times*, Pearce Wright, referred to the internal memorandum which I have mentioned, which said that alternative sources of electricity were unlikely to contribute significantly, but that it was important to 'satisfy ourselves' that nuclear expansion was fully justified.[7] At the time, CEGB spokesmen denied any knowledge of the memo, and it is possible that the press department did not know about it—the CEGB, internally as well as externally, operated like the Kremlin before *glasnost*. What I could not reveal then was that the document had been handed to Mr Wright by the then chairman of the CEGB, Glyn England. It would have been a breach of confidentiality to disclose this at the time, but now that Mr England has moved on and the CEGB has been sold off, the disclosure can damage no one. Mr Wright, one of the best informed and most perceptive commentators on the energy scene, later left *The Times* after Rupert Murdoch had acquired it.

The report in *The Times* had been in indirect speech. I wished to quote from the original six years later at the Sizewell Inquiry where I was one of the objectors. But even then the CEGB tried to keep it secret and refused to make it available. Officials of the inquiry secretariat came to my aid. They were civil servants on detachment from the Department of Energy. They recognised that they had an independent role as Inquiry officers and, most helpfully, they made it plain to the CEGB that the Inquiry would, if necessary, exercise its legal right to require that a copy be produced. The CEGB was forced to comply but even then it censored the document, cutting out other, presumably more embarrassing, passages. But the sentence saying that it was seeking to 'satisfy' itself of its own view that nuclear power was better than renewable energy, and to demonstrate this to the public, was not deleted and it entered the public domain.

So 1978 saw the CEGB setting out to 'satisfy' itself that nuclear power was better than any of the renewables, and ETSU produced preposterous costings for wave energy. Soothing explanations were given at Harwell. These were early days, the costings would decline as the technology advanced and the presentation would improve to put the crude numbers in perspective. The impression was given that ETSU had understood the damage done to an informed public by the use of such numbers and that it would be more careful in the future. But 12 months later, in November 1979, the Department of Energy issued an official Energy Paper on wave energy.[8] It was the first major exposition directed at the public and it remains a valuable source, including its helpful remark that 'no major deleterious environmental effects could be identified'. No other renewable has been given that accolade.

But the preface, by Dr Clarke as Chairman of WESC, did the damage: it 'improved' on the Heathrow figures by saying that the cost was 20–50p a unit (it was the first time 50p had been mentioned). It ignored the estimate of 5–10p for one device. There was no press conference held to explain the costings. Instead, it was leaked in advance to what was then the most pro-nuclear newspaper, the *Financial Times*.

That year, 1979, a Conservative government took office. At first it did nothing about wave energy (probably it did not notice it). Then, in 1980, there was a significant happening: the Chief Scientist, Sir Hermann Bondi, a keen supporter of renewable energy, was moved on and a new man, Dr Anthony Challis, was appointed. He came from ICI and was reputed to have been picked by Mrs Thatcher, who wanted someone who would bring a business-like attitude to energy. Who better than a fellow chemist from industry? Challis was described to me, by a civil servant, as seeming 'more bureaucratic than the civil servants—unlike every other Chief Scientist'. This was surely unfair, but it is an indication of the combative mood inside the Department of Energy at that time.

It was the period when Mrs Thatcher devised her Ten Commandments—the nation needed 10 Pressurised Water Reactors and they were to be built, one a year, in the following 10 years. Energy policy was being directed towards the idea that nuclear power was the answer to all our needs. And there soon followed a number of rumours about what was going to be done to remove the threat of competition from such irritants as wave energy. I reported them.

I wrote in one of Michael Heseltine's magazines, *Engineering Today*, on 2 September 1980: 'The Government has decided secretly to cut back on its wave energy programme . . . The news was being witheld this week while the Department of Energy sought instead to obtain maximum credit' for new expenditure on Hot Dry Rock geo-thermal exploration. And three days later, in the *New Statesman* of 5 September, I wrote that the wave energy budget was to be slashed; and in *Tribune*, on 12 September, that a decision had been taken secretly to go slow on wave energy, and that John (now Lord) Moore, Minister responsible for renewable energy, had failed to disclose the information when questioned in the House of Commons by Frank Hooley, then the MP for Sheffield Heeley.

A few days later, I was surprised to receive an invitation to attend the opening of 'the Department of Energy Wave Tank Facility' at the headquarters of Sir Christopher Cockerell, inventor of the Hovercraft and designer of an elegant and much under-valued wave power device called The Raft. A large group of us went as Government guests to Southampton. On the edge of the tank stood John Moore. He declared: 'I am confident that, if solutions are possible, our wave energy researchers will find them. Whatever other problems they may face, lack of Government support will not be among them.'[9] That was on 26 September 1980. Eighteen months later, Government support was withdrawn and the official programme was dead.

There were divided views inside the energy establishment, and premature reports about the demise of funding for wave energy started to circulate. Such reports or rumours, whatever the justification or motives behind them, would give some indication of what the reaction would be to such a decision and they could be given the distinction of an official denial

Scientists expect wave power research to be cut or stopped

By John Ezard

Scientists working on Britain's officially-funded ... when the department reduced its original nine funded projects to four. These are Professor French's Lancaster Flexible Bag, which feeds sea-driven air pressure into a turbine on the bellow...principle; the Bristol Os ... uses cl ... produ ... genera ... turbine ... eering Water works Buoy, Belfast on the laborat ...

Wavepower studies may be dropped

By David Fishlock, Science Editor

...once believed ... the

Work on wave energy
May 27, 1981

From the Chief Scientist, Department of Energy

Sir,—David Fishlock's report on the UK wave energy research programme (May 13) is running well off the track when he says that it may be abandoned altogether by the Government next year. No deci...

NEWS

Acord evidence to remain secret

The Government is refusing to publish the controversial reports on which the Advisory Council on Research and Development (Acord) based its recommendations to curtail Britain's renewable energy programme (see *Electric* ... 1982).

David Mellor, the Un State for Energy, told a meeting of the Parliame. Group for Alternative Ener. (Parligaes) last week that the a "comprehensive technical and analysis" prepared by the Ener nology Support Unit and repor the various renewable energy committees—would not be made partly because it would be used in wha saw as a campaign of vilification be waged by some critics against Acord and i members.

However he did claim that the Government believed it has a renewable energy programme that "faces up to the challenge of the future. We are carrying out this work with enthusiasm and determination", he said. "I trust British industry will a

OBSERVER BUSINESS

Wave power switched off

by STEVE VINES

GREAT hopes of harnessing the power of the sun, wind, waves and other renewable energy sources were dashed last week when an official advisory body urged the Government to put all these projects into cold storage. The Development for Fuel and Power, delivered to the Government last week, takes the line that most existing research should be written up, a little more work could be done in areas like geothermal supplies and design of buildings to maximise the benefits of solar heating, but no fur- director of Lanchester Polytechnic's joint wave power project with industrial companies, says that £10 million is not an exorbitant amount for developing a device which we believe is capable of doing the job.'

Solar power is the only ...

Fig. 8.1 Headlines from (top to bottom) *The Guardian* (14 May 1981), the *Financial Times* (13 and 27 May 1981), *Electrical Review* (9 July 1982), *The Observer* (2 May 1982).

which would be truthful at that time. And then, seven months later, on 13 May 1981, it fell to David Fishlock, Science Editor of the *Financial Times*, to repeat the report that wave energy was to be dropped by the Government.[10] Fishlock had been seen the previous day at a lunch at the Institute of Energy addressed by David Howell, then Energy Secretary, and attended by Challis.

The Fishlock report, too, received the accolade of an official denial. Challis wrote to the *Financial Times*: 'Fishlock's report is well off the track. The UK wave energy programme—the biggest in the world—has produced a large number of possible solutions and there are grounds for cautious optimism.'[11] So now we had a second high-level denial.

Can it be sheer coincidence that Fishlock and I just happened to say what was to prove accurate a year or so later? I have since been told, by a good source, that the rumours which we were reporting were being initiated because of a folk memory inside the Civil Service which was haunted by a word: Concorde. The government had been involved in the decision to go ahead, with the French, in building Concorde. We had been prevented from pulling back by a legal commitment. The French did not intend to allow us to abandon the project and the costs rose and rose. The government was caught. Thousands of jobs and billions of pounds were at stake. When the plane was built, it lost money every time it took off. It was only years later that it started to pay. But at the time, the Civil Service was desperate to avoid being associated with a second, expensive disaster.

The fact that two of us, with very different contacts, were able to say in 1981 what became true in 1982 supports the view that the decision to abandon wave energy had been taken on policy grounds before the meeting of the Advisory Council on Research and Development, which was to be little more than a charade.

It took place in secret at the Civil Service centre at Sunningdale, Surrey, on 19 and 20 March 1982 for what the Civil Service calls a *tour d'horizon* and was followed by a formal meeting in the Department of Energy. Challis was in the chair. The members present included representatives of UKAEA, CEGB, British Gas, British Coal, Shell, British Petroleum (BP), the Electricity Council—all those who would not be enthusiastic about the emergence of a new rival to their own interests—plus a few independents.

The extraordinary innovation was the exclusion of Grove-Palmer, the wave energy programme manager. The more one looks back at it, the more outrageous it appears. He was the person in charge, the one who had guided the programme and had a grasp of all its details. He would certainly have argued fiercely for wave energy. The argument at that time was about whether only one full-scale prototype should be launched, or whether several should put to sea at the same time, and which ones should be chosen. The OWC and the Clam both had strong claims.

The members of ACORD were senior figures on the energy scene, not children in need of protection from uncomfortable ideas. Yet officials, led by

Challis, were not prepared to allow Grove-Palmer to make the case for wave energy. It says much about the character of the members of ACORD, including the independents, that they were prepared to be treated in this way and go through the motions of considering wave energy in the absence of the key figure who wished to make the case for continued support and for going ahead to the next planned step: the building of a full-scale prototype at sea. Grove-Palmer decided immediately to resign, three years before retirement age.

I have been told that the objection to his presence was personal—that he was not competent, according to one distinguished participant. I do not doubt that he had made enemies with his single-minded support for wave energy, which would have made it difficult for those who wished to use the available money on other projects. Knowing him well, I can understand that he would have fought hard for wave energy, regardless of the seniority of the person with whom he was arguing. If his ability were in question, then the right place to expose the fact would have been before the experts at a private meeting. There were people there with sufficient understanding of the issues to come to a conclusion on the merits of the case, and the best way of winning the support of ACORD would have been to admit him and confound his knavish tricks, as the loyal saying goes. By keeping him out, his critics were damaging themselves by raising questions about their own case.

At the time, I reported on the basis of good information that ACORD had given the Government a disagreeable surprise: there had been an unexpected backlash against the Government's wish to kill off the wave programme. That was printed in several publications including the influential *Electrical Review*. It was never denied. It was based on information from people who were present at the secret meeting. One difficulty was that ACORD worked on the Cabinet principle of not taking votes but simply collecting opinions, and it was not always clear to everyone what the consensus was. The meeting was followed by an official silence lasting for 38 days with the Department of Energy fending off inquiries. As late as 26 April, David Mellor, then Energy Minister, was writing to Leslie Huckfield, then an MP, that Dr Challis would be submitting recommendations 'shortly'. The Minister was apparently unaware that the recommendations had already proceeded so far through the Civil Service and political machine that there would be a release the very next day—or else one must assume that Dr Challis required 38 days to write down the recommendations and that he kept them to himself, not telling even the Minister or discussing them with fellow civil servants. Dr Challis would then have delivered his document to the Department the very next day, 27 April, and only a few hours were needed for his report to go right through the procedures of the Department and receive the Minister's approval for release. That sounds unlikely, and we must therefore conclude that either

Mellor did not know, or he was misleading Parliament knowingly; either way, it is obvious that there was a mighty battle going on inside the Department of Energy.

On the morning of 27 April, the Department's press office still did not know that a statement was about to emerge. Later that afternoon, some of us journalists discovered by chance that a document would shortly be available. It was announced (by Mellor) in a written reply, the method regularly chosen by Ministers who do not wish to take the opportunity of expanding on their decisions—those who, contrary to biblical advice, and in contrast with the usual custom of politicians, are actually anxious to bury their light under a bushel. Most newspapers did not receive it until 18:30—too late for publication on a massively busy news day at the height of the Falklands crisis. This was the government machine attempting ruthless action and producing instead a shambles.[12]

The statement was released without the members of ACORD being consulted or even informed of its content (again, for the first time). Indeed, they had not even seen the Minutes of their meeting. This is important because, with ACORD not taking votes, interpretation of the mood is decisive. Some of the members were surprised by the content of the statement, as their impression of what they had agreed was different. But they were in difficulty as the proceedings are covered by the Official Secrets Act. For several days they had no copy of a statement issued in their name, and some of them had to ask me what it was that they were supposed to have decided. One might have thought that courtesy alone would have ensured that they did not suffer such an embarrassment.

It is particularly surprising when one appreciates that the information about the proceedings, on which the statement is supposed to be founded, had been available for most of the 38 days. Was it feared that some of the members would have objected to this account of what they were supposed to have decided, if they could have done so while there was still time to prevent the issue of misleading information?

I am convinced that the Government decided to massage the view of ACORD and to try to pretend that it was acting in accordance with the opinion of a committee of experts. A decision in principle had been taken a year before to shut down the programme. But the ACORD meeting, most unusually, had attracted attention and publicity. Then the members proved less tractable than expected, even without Grove-Palmer to make the case. Reports of dissent began to slip out. I now know that the CEGB, which was among the best informed on wave energy, did not wish to see the programme ended. Nor did some from ETSU. Nor did RPT. Nor did Challis. And ACORD did not intend to end the research. It said in its advice to the government that the programme should be continued with the minimum funding necessary, perhaps £150 000–300 000. Stopping the programme altogether was not justified, said ACORD.

So who did want to end it? There was an implacable force inside the Department of Energy which did not intend to be thwarted. It had a policy and wave energy did not form a part of it. And so a decision was taken for political reasons, but it had to be presented as an energy decision. Nigel Lawson was the Secretary of State and Mellor the Under-Secretary. Faced with the unhelpful attitude of ACORD, the Department hesitated and then, when Parliamentary Questions started to appear, it rushed and stumbled. It found a complaisant MP (Gary Waller, then Conservative Member for Brighouse and Spenborough) to put down a question, and Mellor gave a written answer which was released late in the day.[12]

Mellor said that he had placed 'a summary' of ACORD's main conclusions and recommendations in the libraries of both Houses of Parliament and that these were being considered. The 'summary' was signed simply 'Department of Energy' with no indication who had compiled it. It was only five pages and it could easily have been circulated first to the members of ACORD, had the government wished to. Then they could have said that it had been approved as a fair and full account of what happened. Mellor, by choosing a written reply, reduced the likelihood of anyone asking whether this was the case.

The device of a written answer late in the day, designed to escape attention, was used on another three occasions over renewable energy by one of Mellor's successors, Tim Eggar: first when the Government, after long delay, released the report of the Renewable Energy Advisory Group and the Thorpe report on wave power, in response to two Questions from Michael Stern, Conservative Member for Bristol North-West, on 17 December 1992, which just happened to be the day that Parliament rose for the Christmas recess and the lobby correspondents vanished to do their shopping; and on 31 March 1994, the day that Parliament rose for the Easter recess, when Eggar announced that no further work would be undertaken on wave energy in reply to a Question from Julian Brazier, Conservative Member for Canterbury. Plainly, someone inside the Civil Service, attached to energy matters, has a sentimental attachment to this way of avoiding attention to renewable energy. The MPs who allow themselves to be used in this way must believe that this is what MPs are for.

It has now passed into history that ACORD recommended that the wave energy programme should be ended. We had to wait another two months to hear it from the mouth of a government source. Mellor attended a crowded meeting of the backbench, unofficial Parliamentary Liaison Group for Alternative Energy Strategies with about 150 of us packed into a committe room of the House of Commons on 29 June 1982. This was an odd setting for such an announcement. The reason was that, with the Falklands war in progress, the Commons had little interest in anything else. So the Government was able to take its disgraceful decision without harassment on the floor of the House. But there were still people who cared, and Mellor was persuaded to talk to them. We were an unusual gathering: concerned back-bench MPs, environmentalists, journalists, and academics holding a parallel 'parliament'.

Mellor arrived with a typescript. His case was that wave energy was likely to be more expensive than wind, hot rock, tidal, coal, or nuclear. Wave energy, he said, did not appear sufficiently attractive to justify 'the commitment of a large sum of money to a major sea trial'—which was what Grove-Palmer would have advocated, had he been allowed to do so. Meanwhile, 'no new development work will be initiated, although plans are being drawn up for a limited programme of research to explore possible improvements in the technology . . . Even if more money had been available, they (ACORD) would not have changed their recommendation on wave energy.' This claim has been strongly challenged to me by an exceptionally good source inside ACORD.

Mellor said the budget for wind energy would be about £3.2 million and it would be 'in the forefront' of the programme. 'I would like to think that our positive commitment to wind might get just a little share of the columns currently devoted to our caution on wave.' The biggest expenditure would be on 'the exciting development' of Hot Dry Rock geothermal energy, which would get more than £3 million, and on geothermal hot water for aquifers. They were also giving 'the most careful consideration' to the Bondi report on a Severn tidal barrage.

And then what happened? Tidal was abandoned. Wet geothermal was abandoned. So was Hot Dry Rock. Projects to gather wind energy offshore were abandoned. The only one which survived was wind energy on land and, as the Department of Energy knew, in Britain, with its high density of population, it would meet with objections on environmental grounds and could never be developed into a major provider of electricity to the Grid.

And what of wave energy? Mellor said: 'I should emphasise that ACORD's advice on wave energy was quite clear-cut and taken with a high degree of unanimity.' A *high* degree of unanimity? How high can unanimity be? Almost unanimous, more or less unanimous, or unanimously unanimous? This is how Whitehall says that something was *not* unanimous. As I suspected, and said, at the time, we were not being given the truth and the '*quite* clear-cut' decision was never actually taken. That was why Mellor used the adjective 'quite'. In this context, it meant 'not quite'. We were being given the smooth sell. This was not a simple slip by Mellor; it was in his typescript.

Those were my conclusions and I decided to test them. After seven years, it seemed to me that the government might be ready to disclose the truth. At my suggestion, John Home Robertson, MP for East Lothian, which included Salter's home, asked the Energy Secretary on 22 February 1989 if he would place in the Library of the House a copy of the Minutes of the ACORD meeting. It did not seem unreasonable to let the public know what had happened after such a long period. But the decision was still sensitive enough for the Energy Under-Secretary, Michael Spicer, to take refuge in a written reply. He said: 'A copy of a summary of the main conclusions and recommendations of ACORD was placed in the Libraries of both Houses on 27 April 1982.'[13]

A written reply avoids a supplementary Question which could have been: 'Yes, we knew that seven years ago, but what we are seeking is the contemporaneous minutes of that meeting. We have been given only the Department of Energy's 'Summary'. Now what about the real record? Why are you pretending to misunderstand the Question and answer one that has not been asked? Can it be that the public and Parliament have been misled for seven years about a major decision of significance to all our energy futures and that the government is still not prepared to admit it?'

If we are to consider the facts about official policy on wave energy, and to separate the sensible decisions from the blunders, and the blunders from the deceit, we need to be told why there was so much evasion about a straightforward policy decision. If the authorities had wished to persuade public opinion that they had nothing to hide, they could have made a start by opening up the record and presenting with pride the arguments that had won over the distinguished members of ACORD. But they preferred to shroud the event in secrecy. I was convinced from the day of Mellor's statement that there was something that the government wanted to hide; since then, I have been able to confirm my suspicion. Wave energy was not discarded by ACORD; it was the victim of a political decision taken a year earlier inside the Department of Energy by the Civil Service and the politicians.

What was supposed to be the final curtain was dropped in March 1985. It was the fruit of three years of research, and was intended to provide justification for the closure of the programme. It was a publication, 'Wave Energy, ETSU R26'[5] and it was beautifully produced, with first-class explanation and description of all the main devices and excellent illustrations. Its authors had been important figures at various times during the programme: Peter Davies, Malcolm Cloke, Ken Major, D.I. Page, and R.J. Taylor. It was damned by one phrase: 'The cost of energy produced by the various devices was assessed by consultants using cost data from the 2GW reference designs. The assessment concluded that there was only a low probability of any design achieving an energy cost below 8p/kWh (in May 1982 money values).' That is now (1995) 14p and rising for ever.

Note the choice of words: a 'low probability' of *achieving* a better costing. That takes care of any future threat of wave energy returning to challenge the other sources of useful energy.

Wave energy was now becalmed, and for two years little happened. And then came hopeful news from Norway: an Oscillating Water Column was to be built with Government support. The news transformed the wave power scene and made a mockery of the government's decision to abandon the technology. Norway had ample supplies of very cheap electricity from hydroelectric power, it had vast wealth in North Sea oil and gas, and it had turned its back on nuclear power. Yet here it was saying that wave energy deserved development.

The OWC was launched in November 1985 (see Chapter 9). One of ETSU's leading wave energy figures, Ken Major, was among a handful of us from the UK who flew to Bergen for the event. He was officially there to represent the International Energy Agency, and he visited the site with me the day before the official launch. To everyone's surprise, he let it be known that he had to leave early next day and would be unable to attend the launch, which was the purpose of the visit. It went ahead with no official representative from Harwell. I can only assume that the fact that the Norwegians were succeeding in an area which had been dismissed by ETSU was too bitter a pill to swallow.

Despite ETSU, the Norwegian success had one important result in Britain. Eighteen months later, with the Norwegians delivering 'free' electricity from two generators on the other side of the North Sea, the Government found itself compelled to agree to support the building of a station on the island of Islay in the Inner Hebrides, one which had gained from the work done by the Norwegians.

The Norwegian example was not the only factor weighing on the government. Newspapers and television kept returning to the subject, the wave energy research teams themselves arranged conferences in Bristol and Coventry, and Stephen Salter maintained constant pressure. We know from his tireless research into those official documents which he has been allowed to see, and from his detailed accounts of what was wrong, that there are serious questions to be answered about the conduct of the wave energy programme.

He gave evidence to two Select Committees and to the Hinkley Point inquiry about the way wave energy was treated. He showed, to take one of the simpler examples, that a firm of specialist consultants named YARD, commissioned by ETSU, concluded that it was assumed that a non-return valve would fail once in a million hours in the hydraulic system of a wind turbine, whereas in a wave device the same valve would fail 68 times in the same period.[14] Salter said that his letter drawing attention to this anomaly had been withheld from the Wave Energy Steering Committee by the programme manager, Peter Davies.

Again, it was estimated by ETSU that building 10 wind turbines modelled on the 60 m Orkney machine would reduce the cost of electricity by a factor of three, but building 1000 wave power units would 'be unlikely to show great reductions from the manufacture of a single prototype'.

Salter told the Committee that the reliability of a marine cable needed to carry the electricity to the shore was expressed in terms of 'the year kilometres per fault' and government consultants in 1980 produced the figure of 300, 'so that for a 10 km length you expect 30 years before you have a problem'. This was reduced to 100 in 1982, which would mean only 10 years before there was a problem, and then in 1983 to 10, which would produce one fault every year.

Fig. 8.2 Headlines from (top to bottom) *Private Eye* (5 August 1988), *The Guardian* (16 February 1990), *The Guardian* (27 July 1993).

Salter said, 'My inquiries to establish the reasons for this change were blocked by specific orders of an ETSU official, confirmed in writing.' Replying to questions, he said: 'When I tried to find out why they had changed it, an official from Harwell blocked the discussion; he told the consultants they were not to answer my questions.' Salter added that the North of Scotland Hydro Board (later Scottish Hydro) 'operate about 80 marine cables, some of which have been without faults since the 1930s.'

The equivalent figure for Norwegian marine cable is 625 years. The leader of the Norwegian wave energy programme, Knut Bønke, wrote to Salter: 'If failure rates on sea cables in the UK would be as predicted, the UK faces no energy crisis, only a cable crisis.'

Salter also pointed out the folly of ETSU's way of calculating the 'average' cost of wave power: the cheapest device under consideration was costed at 4p, the most expensive at 12p, so the average was 8p. If someone had introduced a device costing, say, 24p, then the average would automatically have gone up to 14p.

There was one occasion when ETSU was forced to retreat. The Glasgow engineering consultancy YARD was instructed by ETSU to assume a 20 per cent load factor (a load factor is the amount of electricity that would actually be supplied, compared to the amount that would have been generated if the device had worked at full output all the time). This was an error, said ETSU, which came about because it was working on a report which did not include a figure for the availability of the Duck. However, said ETSU in its apology, it was now ready to accept 38 per cent. In cost terms, this meant that a unit of electricity came down from 9.8p to 5.2p (in 1986 values).

Another engineering consultancy, Whessoe, assessed the cost of steel lining at £850 a tonne for 300 tonnes needed for each Duck. ETSU rejected the figure, insisting that the figure to use for electrical plant was £10 000 a tonne. This increased the cost per Duck by £2.7 million. A similar absurdity was encountered by Professor Michael French of Lancaster University, inventor of the Air Bag, who was proposing to use scrap iron as ballast. The official estimate costed it at £3000 a tonne when the normal price was £100.

Salter commented: 'I discussed these and many similar points with officials from the Department of Energy. Their defence was ingenious. For each single point they would offer no resistance but would ask only what per centage difference to the overall conclusion each individual objection would make. As each of the many was not on its own decisive, they argued that it was safe to ignore each in turn. The ETSU officials have told me privately that they are being forced to make the facts suit the policy.'

Salter said his device was 'rather futuristic' with 'lots of very advanced technology items in it'.

The consultants working for ETSU were really civil engineers and so they thought that a lot of the hydraulics and electronics we were using were a bit too complicated for them to understand—I think they were accurate in this opinion. So they appointed a sub-consultant whose name was Gordon Senior. He was the person who actually did most of the scrutiny of our designs, sat in on cost estimating meetings, and he really put us through the mill in a much more rigorous way than the previous consultants had done. He wrote a report . . . He then handed this report in to the main consultants, his employers, Rendel Palmer & Tritton, and they reproduced it with a number of 'nots', just simple negations . . . They reversed his conclusions. He was very annoyed about this. It would be very good for wave energy if you could take evidence from him.'

The committee did so and Senior replied with written evidence. He recounted an extraordinary series of events. He said that he was appointed by RPT with the approval of the Department of Energy in August 1981 to evaluate the Duck. The report, like six others on different devices, would have common chapter headings including Design Philosophy and State of Development, Engineering Appraisal, Inspection and Maintenance, Appraisal of Reliability and Availability, Performance and Productivity, and so on.

The format of the reports and editorial presentation were defined by RPT in agreement with ETSU. The Duck report was one of this series and did not carry my name (by agreement), although it was well known to Department of Energy and ETSU that I was its principal author. I submitted drafts of the various sections and chapters in manuscript to RPT which were typed onto their word processor and passed back to me for correction. I then discussed them with the RPT Project Manager and agreement was reached on the final copy.

The members of the Duck Team were Professor Stephen Salter, John Laing and Son Ltd, and McLellan & Partners, consulting electrical engineers. I met the members individually and together on many occasions . . . I found the Team always willing to respond to my questioning. When they failed to convince me of the validity of their ideas, they were also willing to retract and modify their design . . .

My conclusions were the last part of the report to be formally drafted . . . My final draft of these sections was submitted in May 1983. I expected a response from RPT within days to discuss these, consistent with our established practice. When this was not forthcoming I telephoned the RPT Project Manager to be told that the report had been completed, was to be submitted that night and could not be discussed.

When I pressed, I was told that the conclusions had been altered. When I asked for a copy to examine what changes had been made, I was told that no copy had been allocated to me and that copies were in short supply. When I pressed harder, I was offered a copy on loan. I found that most of the text of the report was as I had drafted, but the key conclusions had indeed been changed and even reversed. I objected and asked for my views to be made known to the Department of Energy, but was told that this could not be done and that I was bound by client confidentiality to RPT not to reveal my disagreement. I was also advised not to have further contact with the device team. It was and still remains my considered opinion that some of the conclusions in the report on the Duck device as submitted to Department of Energy cast unfair doubts on its long term viability.

ETSU banned Salter from talking to RPT to work out what had happened and RPT, as we have heard, told Senior to have no further contact with Salter.

Senior was also warned that client confidentiality to RPT meant that he must not reveal his disagreement (even to Salter!). This was supposed to be part of a disinterested scientific inquiry.

It is possible to argue that Salter was a disappointed inventor and therefore a prejudiced party. But Senior, who had worked for government departments as a consulting engineer and had been recognised for his distinguished work with the award of the CBE, had no axe to grind. On the contrary, he was risking his career by telling the truth. And since these events he has had no further commissions from the Government.

Reading through the extensive submissions by Professor Salter, and his exchange of letters with ETSU and RPT, it is difficult not to feel fury at the way in which the government side behaved. It was determined to press ahead with its policy of shutting down wave energy research. In one letter, John Dennis of RPT said: 'As regards the further data which you require, I have discussed this at length with ETSU and they are against the principle of our sending details of our computations to development teams, as this is likely to lead to lengthy and detailed discussions when there is neither time nor money to support such activities.' ETSU confirmed this with a letter to Salter from Ken Major: 'I have advised John Dennis (of RPT) not to carry out any special work in order to fulfil your request for further information.' Salter replied: 'I would have thought that the extra information could be supplied as a photocopy of the hand-written worksheets which they must have produced in order to reach their conclusions.'

The Select Committee invited a response from the other side. Peter Clark of RPT said that he had never been put under pressure from ETSU or the Department of Energy 'to bias my assessing or reporting in any way'. As to Gordon Senior:

. . . in common with most consulting practices, RPT from time to time have staff engaged on a self-employed base, who are classified as consultants. These individuals work as part of our team, responsible to our project managers and project director. They make inputs to our studies and their input, along with that of all the other members of the team, contributes to a final report. These individuals are most definitely not sub-consultants in the normal usage of that term, and they have no more status than any other employee. Gordon Senior was such an individual, taken onto our team to increase its strength at a period of peak workload; competent clearly, but not more so than some half dozen other members of our team, including myself, who all had a longer-standing familiarity with the engineering of Stephen Salter's Ducks.

This did not deal with Senior's point, that he was appointed specifically to evaluate the Duck and, as he put it, 'it was well known to the Department of Energy and ETSU that I was its (the report's) principal author'.

The head of ETSU, Dr W.M. Currie, said that the technical and commercial content of ETSU programmes was not controlled by the UKAEA. ETSU staff worked directly to the instructions of Programme

Directors in the Department of Energy. He added, most oddly: 'To avoid any possible conflict of technical or commercial interest, ETSU staff devote all of their productive time to Department of Energy programmes; they do not split their time between Department and UKAEA programmes', which no one had accused them of doing. He said that more than half of the professional staff had never worked on UKAEA programmes but had been recruited directly from industry, academia, and elsewhere. 'Fitness for the job is what matters.' On the question of 'the cost-effectiveness of wave power', Dr Currie said, 'there is usually much argument and the argument is often prolonged, in some cases interminable. Nevertheless, decisions have to be made.'

The process of 'reaching agreed final figures' had not been 'fully completed' at the time of the ACORD meeting, 'so it was the device teams' own capital cost and productivity estimates that were presented by ETSU in evidence to the Council.' Dr Currie continued:

The implication in Professor Salter's submission is that ETSU had a major hand in the decision to curtail the wave power R & D programme. ETSU's role in this respect was strictly limited. The Wave Energy Steering Committee, comprising government officials, independent advisers *and ETSU staff* (my italics) was in fact supportive of a continuing wave programme. In the event it was ACORD, with its wider responsibilities which, having weighed all the evidence, concluded that the substantial resources being devoted to wave energy could be better employed on other R & D programmes.

It is difficult to understand how ACORD could have even considered such a decision against the opposition of not only the CEGB, but the Wave Energy Steering Committee and 'ETSU staff'. We have also been told by Peter Clark, in a statement to the wave energy conference in Edinburgh in August 1993, that he, too, had defended wave energy and 'if you had seen my defence of wave energy before ACORD you would all have been cheering.' (He has since failed to respond to my invitation to him to expand on this statement). These facts raise the question of who could have advised ACORD against the wishes and views of the two groups which had carried out research on wave energy (CEGB and WESC) plus ETSU staff and RPT, the official government consultants. Who is the secret villain—British Gas?

Salter noted that neither of the replies to his evidence even attempted to deal with his detailed allegations concerning such matters as the reliability of cables and the cost of steel lining.

And the exchange left unanswered one question which the ETSU spokesman carefully ignored: why was Grove-Palmer, the man in charge of the wave energy programme, excluded from the meeting at which he could have voiced, better than anyone, an informed defence of wave energy and the reason why the programme should continue, an objective which ETSU itself is said to have wanted.

Why did the ETSU staff, who are said to have wanted the same decision, agree to go ahead when their chief spokesman was not allowed to join them? Why did they not say, 'If Clive is not admitted, then we are not going in, because he is the man in charge of wave energy who must be allowed to make his case.' And why, when the question of his exclusion had been raised before a Select Committee, did ETSU volunteer not a word in explanation of this bizarre decision?

Grove-Palmer was kept out so that the decision to shut down the programme, which had been made in advance, could be pushed through with the minimum risk of an open revolt developing among the members of ACORD. Even without his presence, ACORD did not roll over; but it did apparently conclude its discussion on a note sufficiently vague to allow the Government to end the programme.

The most measured response to the Government came from Grove-Palmer himself. His distinguished career had been summarily ended three years before time and he had been driven into what he called 'premature retirement'. He might well have been goaded into launching bitter attacks on those who had destroyed his programme. Instead, he remained the same courteous scientist that I had known since the first time that he invited me to Harwell, to instruct me in the rudiments of wave energy. He responded to the Government's attack on wave energy by writing a scientific paper for the Second International Symposium on Wave Energy Utilisation at Trondheim, and flew off there to deliver it in June 1982.[15] He began with an apology: 'It may be that I was too close to the heat to make unbiased judgements. History alone will decide.' He compared the present time, when 'we are consuming our energy sources more rapidly than nature is replenishing them' to the period when primitive man was 'operating a life-style which archeologists call "food gathering". They were consuming the food faster than nature was replenishing it. Something had to be done. It was: they developed agriculture. We have to ensure an inexhaustible supply of energy.'

He revealed what was then his own bias in favour of nuclear energy, saying that the fast breeder reactor 'is an inexhaustible energy source', but warned that its engineering problems 'might take longer to solve safely than thermal systems could cover'. (He has since revised his pro-nuclear view and the fast reactor is an abandoned hope in most countries.)

He noted that during the previous 100 years there had been a wide variety of electric generators driven by sea waves, but none on a large scale. One man 'who spans the time between small power units and the search for economic, large-sized power stations' was 'our well-loved friend Commander Yoshio Masuda, who patented and built a wave-powered navigation buoy in 1947, and who is today one of the world's leading authorities on full-scale wave power stations.' After that tribute to a pioneer who had not figured in the Harwell programme, Grove-Palmer noted that Cockerell and Salter had followed and been awarded 'somewhat grudging official recognition and a ridiculously small amount of funding'.

He defended the choice of Harwell as the site for the Wave Energy Steering Committee. 'I have heard remarks about putting Dracula in charge of a bloodbank.' But Harwell was earning half its funds by selling its expertise as contract research and development, and a whole infrastructure of supporting services and people were available.

The principal theme of the management style of these people was to give the research teams the maximum freedom to innovate. We wanted to engage people to apply their minds to the problems, not just to act as additional hands to the plough. It is a style of management which calls for a close rapport between all the parties and it is one whose delicate balance can easily be upset by heavy-handed bureaucracy. It was this style of management which Harwell was called upon to apply to the new technology of wave energy which Dr (now Lord) Marshall (then Chief Scientist) wanted us to develop.

Grove-Palmer recalled that the Select Committee on Science and Technology had criticised the wave energy programme for not spending money fast enough, as did the Press, and they replied that it was still an infant technology in the research phase. But the Select Committee was not impressed, and one member 'suggested that we were a cosy little group lacking drive'. They reponded by bringing in engineers from industry and outside consultants and set up Technical Advisory Groups of specialists. 'Although they caused me personally some aggravation, they did a splendid job in ensuring that all the many parts of this multi-faceted technology were fully examined.' They were given 'enthusiastic leadership' by Dr Freddy Clarke, who had taken over as chairman of the Steering Committee.

In 1978, they asked ACORD for three years' funding but were given only one year's money. 'We reported to ACORD early in 1979. Our funding for the ensuing year was approved and again we were advised of the importance which the Council attached to a sea trial at full-scale.' (If only they had said it publicly! Why did ACORD treat this and so many other matters as a secret?) 'In late 1980 and early 1981, the wave energy programme suffered its worst blows. Sir Hermann Bondi retired from his post as Chief Scientist and Dr Freddy Clarke left his position as chairman of the Steering Committee. With the loss of these two great men, we lost that intellectual perception of the significance of what we were trying to do.'

The programme was given funding in June 1980 for two years, which would culminate in a recommendation of which device, if any, should be taken to prototype sea trials. But in March 1981, ACORD tried to shut down the work immediately. After discussion, it granted a reprieve for a year but warned that ACORD would then want costings which 'looked encouraging'. What sort of costing would that be? 'In answer to my specific question, I (Grove-Palmer) was told about 5p/kWh.' The reprieve was not allowed to run its course. It was cut short, three months early, in March 1982, when the programme was closed down.

Grove-Palmer presented to the Trondheim conference a paper which he had drawn up while still at ETSU giving costings for all devices and backed up by detailed consideration of all the elements involved. It gave the research teams' estimates as well as those from RPT, and a third figure from Grove-Palmer himself, applying a rigorous method of calculation which produced a result close to that of RPT. Then he added a separate table showing 'development potential', meaning the cost once more work had been done. It should have been handed to the ACORD meeting and it would have made a profound impression. For example, the figures for the Duck were given as 5.6p RPT; 5.5p Grove-Palmer; and 3p device team. After development, Grove-Palmer put it at 3p. Most of the devices were costed at over 5p in 1982, but on development these came down sharply to 3–4p. All of the costings were explained in great detail. Grove-Palmer concluded:

Having spent £15 million and a huge amount of intellectual input into this work for the past seven years, it seems to me to be a criminal waste to stop now, when we are within months of being able to specify a prototype. We cannot be sure what the shape of future energy needs will be and must pursue any goal which could lead to an inexhaustible source of energy.

As we know, his words were ignored by Government, and years went by without funded development. Then the House of Lords Select Committee published its report on 27 July 1988[14] declaring itself 'concerned' about the ending of support for wave energy and saying there was a 'serious conflict of interest which only an independent review could resolve'. The Government responded, after a pause of eight months, by announcing in the House of Lords on 6 April 1989, 'a study'. It was due to last two years, which many researchers considered a needlessly long period, given that most of the information required was known and available. In the event, it took even longer, over three-and-a-half years. Some suspected that its original reporting date, the summer of 1991, had been designed to tide the government over until after a general election, which was at that time expected in the summer of 1991. When the election was delayed, so was the report.

The task was assigned to ETSU, which appointed two of its scientists to do the work. One of them soon resigned, and the Government rejected a call in Parliament by John Home Robertson, MP, for him to be replaced. So the survivor, Tom Thorpe, was left to do the job alone. It turned into a back-breaking task and damaged his health. He was required to investigate all the main wave energy inventions and seek an agreed costing. Then he had to take the figure to a Wave Energy Steering Group, which included one of the hardliners from the Department of Energy. It subjected every detail of his findings to a penny-pinching scrutiny, questioning the cost of every nut and bolt, sending him back again and again to visit the research

teams and try to arrive at a precise mathematical conclusion about an un-
tried technology, and one which satisfied wave energy's critics inside ETSU.

The result was released on 17 December 1992, the last day of Parliament
before the Christmas recess, when it was calculated to attract least attention.
For those who knew how to read it, it was a vindication of wave energy. It is
the best existing survey of the scene.[16] It will not surprise readers to know that
the work has never been made available to the ordinary book-buying public,
or even to HMSO; instead, it can be obtained only by those who know about
its existence and who ask for a copy from ETSU (which has 'published' it
free). Many people interested in wave energy have had great difficulty in
obtaining it because they did not know where to apply.

There was also a report by the Select Committee on Energy. It had a pro-
nuclear Conservative as chairman but it expressed

regret that instead of continuing R & D in order to reduce the uncertainty, the
Department (of Energy) withdrew all funding on the ground of an assumption which it
knew had been, in the words of one official, "picked from the air". We consider that, in
the past, the Department has attempted to establish costs at too early a stage in a
technology's development; to draw final conclusions from tentative assessments; and
placed too little value on continuity of funding. It is difficult to regard the history of
renewable R & D funding in the UK as other than a history of *volte-faces*, premature
judgements and plain errors . . . In view of the unhappy history of wave energy R & D
in the UK, a substantial increase in funding for wave energy R & D would be a
particularly strong signal of the Government's increased commitment to renewable
energy.[17]

The strong signal did not come.

Looking at this evidence, it is difficult to avoid concluding that whatever
ETSU, the 'Support Unit', was providing, it was not support. I have always
resisted the idea of a conspiracy, because I cannot believe that reasonable
people, many of whom I know and like, who have chosen to work in the public
service, are either villains or criminally insane; or that if the occasional one is
afflicted in this way, there are not others who would restrain him.

What I think is more likely is that public servants in the Department of
Energy and at ETSU were taken aback as they contemplated the enthusiasm of the public for renewable energy. They would have been especially
worried about wave power because it attracted such favourable publicity;
because everyone in Britain loves the sea; because wave power (unlike wind
and tidal) would not attract any protests on environmental grounds; and
above all because its potential was almost limitless and it was directed
towards the construction of 2000 MW power stations in the open sea. That
meant spending money. So it may well have been felt, at one of those
gatherings of leading civil servants known unofficially in Whitehall as a
College of Cardinals, that the wisest course was to discourage public
opinion. And once they and their followers had started to present the
case against wave energy, they soon found themselves compelled to slide

deeper and deeper into the quagmire, to sustain their views and also their reputations.

The most charitable explanation came from Salter. He said:

To make an accurate estimate on incomplete information requires the errors of optimism and pessimism to be evenly distributed on either side of the truth. The final answer is the result of a chain multiplication which is very sensitive to cumulative bias in sub-estimates. And every single input to the 1978 calculations happened to be wrong in the pessimistic direction.[18]

And so wave energy, like so many inventions throughout history, found itself up against a determined group of established authorities who at first expressed scepticism and then slipped deeper into error as they tried to demonstrate that they had been right from the start, when in fact they had been consistently wrong.

References

1. CEGB (1978). In *Extracts from CEGB Report on Long Term Research on Novel Methods of Electricity Generation and Storage.*

2. ETSU (1979). *Proceedings of the wave energy conference, Heathrow Hotel, London November 22–23 1978.*

3. Department of Energy (29 April 1976). *Press release 109.*

4. Walgate, R. (1978). Little renewable energy until next century. *Nature*, 272, p. 661.

5. ETSU R26 (March 1985). *Wave Energy.* Department of Energy's R & D Programme, 1974–1983.

6. Department of Energy (July 1987). *Energy technologies for the UK: 1986 appraisal of research, development and demonstration*, p. 21.

7. Wright, P. (11 April 1978). Electricity Board's aim to use underground turbines. *The Times.*

8. Department of Energy (November 1979). *Wave energy.* Energy paper number 42.

9. Department of Energy. (26 September 1980). *Press release 191.*

10. Fishlock, D. (13 May 1981) Wavepower studies may be dropped. *Financial Times.*

11. Challis, A.A.L. (27 May 1981). Work on wave energy. Letter from the Chief Scientist. *Financial Times.*

12. Department of Energy (27 April 1982). *Summary of Advice to the Secretary of State.*

13. Spicer, M. (22 February 1989). *Official report* (Hansard). col. 643.

14. House of Lords (27 July 1988). *Alternative Energy Sources.* Select Committee on the European Communities, p. 178 et seq.

15. Grove-Palmer, C. (1982). Wave energy in the United Kingdom—a review

of the programme. In *Wave energy utilisation* (ed. H. Berge), pp. 11–37. Tapir, Trondheim.
16. Thorpe, T.W. (1992). *A review of wave energy*, vols 1 and 2, ETSU R-72.
17. Select Committee on Energy. (11 March 1992). *Renewable Energy*. Session 1991–92, pp. *XXVII* and xl. House of Commons.
18. Select Committee on Energy (25 February 1982). *Minutes of evidence taken before the Select Committee on Energy*. Session 1981–82. House of Commons.

9 Norway to the rescue

Wave energy appeared to be dead, except in dreams and theoretical papers, after the British government's rejection of the idea in 1982, and it remained in the doldrums until April 1984, when word came to me that in Norway, the unlikeliest country of all, a wave energy programme was going ahead. Norway was the richest country in Europe where energy was concerned, with hydro-electric power providing virtually all its electricity, and North Sea gas and oil for export. It has no nuclear power because it has never needed any. But its government was now investing in wave power, with one of its largest commercial companies, Kvaerner Brug, as a partner, and building two units. I was given the news by David Evans, Professor of applied mathematics at Bristol University, who had been attached to the Norwegians as Visiting Senior Scientist.

It was a serious blow to the anti-wave energy camp. ETSU was preparing the energy paper, ETSU R26, published in March 1985, which was designed to be the obituary of wave energy[1]. A draft was actually distributed saying that Norway, like Britain, was closing its wave energy programme. This had to be hastily removed from the final, printed version. As Salter commented to a Select Committee hearing, 'it was all the more embarrassing because the cost of the two units, 600 kW together, was only £1.1 million—less than ETSU had paid Rendel Palmer & Tritton to tell them that waves were no good.[2]

It is agreeable to recollect the delight with which the Norwegian news was received in Britain. It was the first real breakthrough after the appalling decision of the Department of Energy to shut down the whole programme, which was being used by the International Energy Agency and the European Commission as justification for rejecting wave power.

But Norway pressed ahead regardless. Her inventors, led by Dr Knut Bønke, had carried out their own research independently. They had good relations with British researchers. Dr Bønke, in his first letter to me, agreed readily to provide information about his device: it was a time when there was a refreshing freedom of information. 'Your book, *Energy from the waves*, is well known to me and some of your rather sharp comments on the politics involved have given me a lot of pleasure,' he wrote. We thus started on good terms.

Apart from restoring credibility to wave energy, Norway contributed three major innovations: building harbour walls, detecting 'hot spots', and focusing the waves. The first is strictly speaking a misnomer because in normal use the walls of a harbour are designed to produce a sheltered area of calm water; the

Norwegians adapted the concept so that it reached out at an angle into the sea and almost doubled the catchment area, without removing the turbulence and therefore the energy. This was the result of model tests and theoretical predictions by two scientists, Kjell Budal and Johannes Falnes, from the Division of Experimental Physics at the University of Trondheim.

They also discovered the existence of 'hot spots', caused by wave refraction. As waves approach the shore, the shape of the seabed affects their power. Where the topography is favourable, the wave power is greater and at the best sites double the energy of the 'normal' sea. The places can be discovered by computer-aided study of the seabed; a simpler way is to observe where the local fishermen gather because this is almost invariably the site of a 'hot spot'. They (and the fish) found the sites many millions of years before the scientists.

Norwave, the company which invented and produced the Tapchan, has fed a computer with details on depth variation, the coastline and the topography of the seabed, and from this has produced print-outs as a colour-coded map showing at which points on a coastline the energy is concentrated. That is where the fishermen are to be found. Stephen Salter has explained it in this way:

The propagation velocity of waves in shallow water depends on the depth and so an uneven bottom can act like a group of optical lenses. This has the effect of producing some sites with unusually high energy and others where energy is unusually low. Norwave has developed computer techniques to predict the enhancement ratios from the soundings on charts. Every wavefield so far examined has 'hot spots' with annual energy input double—sometimes three times more than—that in the open sea . . . If you want a quick indication before spending money on the Norwave survey fees, your own fishermen will tell you where to look.[3]

The third contribution was an artificial means of creating 'hot spots'. Dr Falnes explained the idea to the Cork conference of 1992. He said:

The phase speed of waves is reduced as the waves enter into shallower water. The phase speed can also be reduced intentionally by putting submerged plates or other objects in the sea. By properly shaping such submerged objects, ocean waves may be directed to a focal area, analogous to the focussing of light waves by means of a glass lens . . . The lens could be designed to have its focal area at the entrance of a Tapchan.[4]

This has been done in a large outdoor wave tank but not yet in the sea. All these methods increase the efficiency of wave energy converters and reduce the costs, once the initial investment has been made.

These were among Norway's particular contributions, together with the courage, and the government support, to go ahead at a time when Britain, which had been regarded as the lead country, was running away. It was, as the *Financial Times* remarked, ironic that the device to be used by the Norwegians derived from the pioneering efforts of Britain: an Oscillating Water Column developed by the National Engineering Laboratory, and a Wells turbine, invented at Queen's University, Belfast. It is also a fact that, in addition to

Professor Evans, Brian Count of the CEGB was attached to the Norwegian programme as a consultant on hydrodynamic studies for five weeks. He tested a model of their device on the wide tank built by the Department of Energy at Sir Christopher Cockerell's headquarters near Southampton, and the CEGB, to its credit, gave the Norwegians the data without charge. (Since then, the wide tank has been drained and turned into an office, the CEGB has been privatised and split into two, and the idea of scientific collaboration without charge would be risible.)

But it was Norway's project and it would be wrong to imagine that it was a spin-off from the British programme. Norway's interest in wave energy began as early as 1968 with the issue of a theoretical document from the University of Trondheim, followed by numerous scientific publications from Budal, Falnes, and others. The first experiments on OWCs were in 1978, and two government surveys of their programme were published in 1979 and 1980.[5] The first of these notes: 'The total energy content of the ocean waves that roll in annually towards the Norwegian coast is estimated to be in the region of 600 TWh. Compared with solar and wind energy, wave energy is more concentrated . . . has higher energy density . . . In Norway there are two large and promising projects. The government have given this work high priority.'

Norway was frequently ahead of Britain, as in the development of harbour walls and 'hot spots'. The two countries worked in parallel, usually separately, sometimes in collaboration. In the end, it was Norway which won the race because her research teams had the idea of a small-scale start on the coastline, and her government and industry backed them.

What of the cost? Dr Bønke was, as always, modest. He said that this would be 'more confusing than helpful, as there is too large a difference in the way costs are evaluated in different countries—different interest rates and depreciation rates, different costs of labour and material.' He suggested that the realistic figure was about 30 per cent of the price calculated for the OWC designed by the NEL, but he thought that 50–60 per cent was fairer. Dr Falnes calculated that the 'recovery time' for the energy invested was about two years. Note that he was using the method of measurement favoured by many environmentalists of calculating the 'cost' by reference to the energy expended on building the device and the energy that it would repay, instead of thinking in money terms.

He appeared at a British wave energy conference at the Open University on 13 July 1984, organised by Dr Michael Flood of the Alternative Technology Group and Friends of the Earth. It was an important event because it was the first opportunity for the principal wave energy figures to compare notes since funding was ended in Britain. As Dr Flood reported, 'Most device teams have reduced manpower and scaled down operations considerably. Some have given up altogether. Morale is low. Furthermore, Britain is rapidly losing its technological lead to groups overseas.'[6] There was a brief nod to the work

Fig. 9.1 The Oscillating Water Column, built with investment from the Norwegian government and the leading engineering company Kvaerner.

being done in Norway, but there was no realisation at that time just how significant it was to prove.

The next development was a well-timed intervention by a scientist from the Coventry team, Dr Peter White, who specialises in turbine design. He asked ETSU to send him to Norway to see what the Norwegians were doing and

ETSU, perhaps surprisingly, agreed. He was welcomed by the Norwegians in the winter of 1984. They opened their books, and their construction sites, to him and he reported back to ETSU. The reaction was interesting: ETSU declared that the information was 'commercially sensitive' and refused to disclose what was in his report or to allow him to reveal it. I pointed out that the only information it contained came from the Norwegians and that they were happy to have it released. But ETSU was adamant. Soon after, Dr Bønke visited London, was amused and amazed to learn of ETSU's attitude, and happily gave me a copy of the report.[7] I could then see why ETSU had been anxious to keep it secret: Dr White's careful analysis showed that the Norwegians would be able to produce a unit of electricity for 3.4p, in a country where wages were higher than in Britain. This was less than the cost of electricity at that time from the most efficient coal-fired plant in Britain. Such information was certainly 'sensitive', but not commercially; a better description would have been 'politically embarrassing'.

The next move, clearly, had to be a visit to Norway, and I flew in for the launch of the world's first wave energy station on 13 November 1985 on Toftestallen, a small island 35 miles north of Bergen. The sea was splendidly rough the day that I arrived, and the two power plants (an OWC and the Tapchan) were on great form. The OWC was a 19.6 m steel tower or chimney standing on the seabed in water 7 m deep. There is an opening in the side, 1 m above and the same distance below sea level, admitting the waves. As they rise to a peak outside, the column of water inside the device rises in sympathy, pushing a pocket of air up inside the chimney and out through an air turbine into the atmosphere. As the water level falls into a trough, air is sucked back in from the atmosphere to fill the vacuum. The stream of air drives the turbine— a development of a Wells turbine, invented by Professor Wells at Queen's University, Belfast, so that it revolves in the same direction whether the air is coming from above or below. It can accept a burst of energy up to 1000 kW and revolve at up to 1500 rpm. On the day in question, it made a booming – sighing sound, like two elephants engaged in copulation, as the air rose and fell inside the tall canister and set the turbine spinning.

Nearby was a gap in the cliff, blasted by 15 tonnes of dynamite which took out 2000 m^3 of rock in one blast. A 90 m concrete channel has been built into the gap, 3 m wide at the point where it meets the sea, gradually narrowing until it comes to a pointed end at 0.2 m in a reservoir at the top of the cliff, 3 m above sea level. The waves ride uphill, inside the channel, gradually gathering speed as they are squeezed into a diminishing space, bubbling up in apparent fury, spilling over the sides, and finally hitting the end of the channel and rising in a man-made geyser, reaching in a good sea as much as 27 m, the height of a nine-storey building.

Next morning, for the day of the launch itself, inevitably the sea turned unseasonally calm, fulfilling the Norwegian formula: the height of the waves is inversely proportional to the number of VIPs present at the site. Also rendered as: the number of politicians times power output is a constant.

Fig. 9.2 Exploded drawing showing the inside of the OWC, with Wells turbine and generator at the top.

Work on the site started in May 1984. 'It is an unideal place,' Dr Bønke told me, 'but we chose it because it is easy to reach from the airport for visitors. It has only a 64° degree window to the Atlantic (32° each side of a line at right angles to the coast) so you get only 10–15 kW/m. With an open coastline, 180°, you would get 25–35, and in the Hebrides you would get 40–50.' This made particularly unfair a remark by David Hunt, then British Energy Minister, during a debate in the House of Commons on 25 October 1985, that the Norwegians had chosen a 'particularly favourable cliff face location'. This information must have been fed to him by ETSU, as a shameful excuse to explain why Britain had been so obviously overtaken from the leading position it once held.

Dr Bønke said that they were being handicapped by an 'Arctic wind sea, a local wind sea, and this means very small waves with low energy and too high frequency—5–6 seconds. We want 8–9 seconds, which requires a swell from the Atlantic. The incoming energy is somewhere between half and one-third of the average. Our device is not designed to work well if the waves come outside the angle W-WNW.' (West to West-North-West, which is 270°– 292.5° out of the full 360°.)

The fact that the wind was coming from the Arctic was apparent as I edged round the narrow walkway on the side of the OWC and could actually *feel* the reverberation as the pocket of air rushed up and down inside the steel chimney. It was a wonderful moment.

But back to Dr Bønke. He said that the device could have been insulated for noise but there was no need at the isolated site on Toftestallen. The sound did not travel far in the air and did not go down into the water very much. 'People fish at this site, and they will continue to do so. The sound does not disturb the fish. The biggest problem for them is acid rain'—which comes from the tall chimneys on the power stations of England and Scotland.

Dr Bønke said that for the turbine,

we learned basically from the Wells people, but we have a different aerofoil profile. The shape is different. The thickness is different. And we have guide vanes, which they do not—the air will contain some rotational energy after leaving the turbine and we reuse it. We get twice as much out of it as the British, while a Japanese turbine of almost the same dimensions had an output of 50 kW maximum.

The OWC was plugged into the local grid of 50 MW and it produced something like 1 per cent of the output—enough, said Bønke, for 1000 families in a developing country. Its output varied from 100 kW to 500 kW. And what is the cost? Dr Bønke said it worked out at 3–4p a unit at different sites along the coast, depending on the value of the site, with interest at 7 per cent. In the UK, it was then 5 per cent, which would bring down the price. But he did not seek to make a big point about the cost of electricity from a prototype, and his calculations were based on a 25-year design life. This, alas, was not to be.

The other device, alongside it, was a novel design which no other country, as far as I can discover, has used. The name Tapchan comes from the English words Tapered Channel. It is a development of an idea pioneered by Walton Bott (see Chapter 6.1) for Mauritius but never implemented there. A major difference introduced by the Norwegians is the invention of the tapered

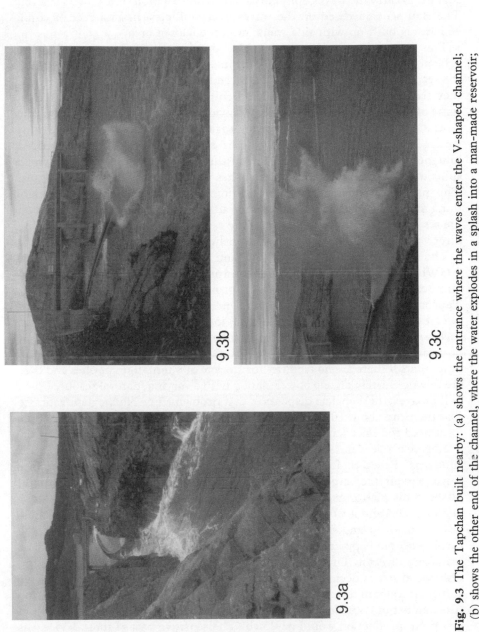

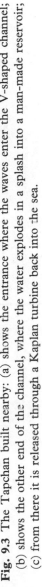

9.3b

9.3c

9.3a

Fig. 9.3 The Tapchan built nearby: (a) shows the entrance where the waves enter the V-shaped channel; (b) shows the other end of the channel, where the water explodes in a splash into a man-made reservoir; (c) from there it is released through a Kaplan turbine back into the sea.

channel to carry the waves uphill to a man-made reservoir 3 m above sea level. The Bott scheme relied on the waves over-spilling a natural reef of coral, which was built up with side walls into an enclosed area.

The Tapchan uses a concrete slope or channel 90 m long called the collector. The skill lies in choosing the most favourable dimensions to make the sea travel uphill. The waves are forced to proceed up the slope because they are being pushed by other waves behind them. As the channel narrows, some of the water splashes over the sidewalls and the rest hits the end of the tapered channel and rises in a fountain, to fall with a splash into the reservoir, which is 5500 m^2 in area. The water is released through the only exit, a 'plughole' filled by a low-head, Kaplan turbine linked to a generator which spins with the turbine as the water rushes through, back down into the sea. This part of the operation is a conventional hydroelectric plant ('The only thing that is unconventional is that, instead of letting God rain down water on the reservoir, we lift the water out of the sea,' said Per Anderssen, managing director of Norwave, a company established to build Tapchans.)

The installed capacity is 350 kW and estimated annual production is 2 GWh. The waves arrive unevenly and need to be 'smoothed' every 5–10 minutes, which is where the reservoir provides a unique service, giving the Tapchan an advantage over other wave energy devices: it serves as a store and releases the water in a regular flow, giving a stable supply of water to the turbines. It is a scheme particularly useful for small communities with little or no back-up from a grid or fossil fuel stations. They always face the risk of power cuts if there are no facilities for storage or alternative supplies and they are relying entirely on one power station with a varying, natural resource such as the waves; the Tapchan disposes of that problem. The Norwegians estimate that there are about 10 000 sites in the world with suitable topography and a local need for electricity.

Norwave's leader is Dr Even Mehlum from the Central Institute for Industrial Research in Oslo. His company received backing from Selmer Furuholmen, the largest civil engineering group in Norway, who build offshore oil platforms, and the government. Construction finished on 30 October 1985 and it went directly on to the Grid on the first day. The turbine has a 3 m drop and, explained Mehlum, 'a higher drop would make the turbine people happier, but the cost of civil engineering would go up'. His managing director, Dr Anderssen, was Dean of the School of Marketing in Oslo when it was decided to set up Norwave. He said they expected to have sufficient water in the reservoir to run the Tapchan for 5000 hours out of 8760 (the number of hours in a year). With a 2 m head, the number of hours would go up but production would go down. The sensitive part of their device was shielded from the sea, namely the generating station. The rock and the concrete took the load. 'It can operate unmanned and is idiot-proof when scientists are not available. We realised that you could not sell new technology until you had demonstrated it,' he said.

Fig. 9.4 Even on a calm day, the effect of squeezing the water in the narrowing space of the channel results in it gaining speed and fury, overtopping the low walls of the channel and finally hitting the end of the channel and soaring up like a fountain.

I returned to the site a year later, in December 1986, when the Norwegians invited a group of 70 energy experts, MPs, and others from the UK and flew us there for a one-day visit. In the party was A.N. Walton ('Noel') Bott, then aged 79. The Tapchan was being fed with small waves (about 2 m). He glowed with pleasure as it converted them into a jet of water five times as high, and then showered us with icy water and a rain of stones which it was picking up from the seabed and flinging through the air. Bott was impervious to the cold, the wet, and the danger. He had always vowed that he would not die until he had seen wave energy working. But he had to come to Norway to do it. 'It's Mauritius!' he kept shouting and he was largely right; the Tapchan was a development of his vision.

The Tapchan continued and has become the most successful wave power station in the world so far. Norwave was (at the time of writing) engaged in negotiation to sell it in the Pacific. But the OWC was less fortunate. It survived three winters and then, on 23 December 1988, it was hit by a record storm. Waves up to 20 m battered it. The Norwegians went out on Christmas Eve to inspect it and, as it appeared to have survived, they returned to their Christmas celebrations. But three days later, a second extraordinary storm occurred. Andreas Tommerbakke, of Kvaerner Brug told me: 'We had the most terrible hurricane. We did not have time to make a full inspection after the first storm. The very unfortunate thing is that there were two storms close to each other. The first one loosened the tower and the second one banged it against the rock again and again. People on these islands say that they have not experienced weather like this in their whole lifetime. We will learn from this.'

They had not appreciated that the first storm had loosened the bolts holding the plant to the cliff face, and the second battering, so soon afterwards, was just too much. The Norwegians did learn from the accident. They resolved that future models would be built of concrete and that they would design them so that the turbine and generator were sited on land, so that if a chimney fell, the mechanical and electrical plant would not be lost.

It was not a disaster. A prototype can be expected to suffer mishaps; that is what it is for. But with the world's immediate demand for more energy diminishing, Kvaerner decided not to replace it, for the present at least. The experience has not ended hopes of OWCs and, at the time of writing (1995), one is working on the island of Islay in the Inner Hebrides, and work is going ahead on building a new one in nearshore waters off Dounreay.

For those sceptical souls who may suspect that the severity of the two storms is being exaggerated, I consulted the UK Meteorological Office. Their records show that waves of 21 m were recorded near Thistle along with a Force 12 gale with gusts of 80 miles per hour. Towards midnight on December 22, a deep low of 944 milllibars north of the Faroes was moving very quickly north-east, in excess of 30 knots by 0600 on the 23rd. A wind of 50 knots stayed westerly right through the day, a violent storm force 11, perhaps into hurricane force with gusts of 80–5 mph. The significant wave height was between 9 and 10 m which, said the Mef. Office spokesmen, 'would give you an average maximum wave of 16 m and the extreme storm wave of 20 m'. There was a lull on 23 December and then another depression on 24 December with winds which by mid-day reached 55 knots. The speed never dropped.

Even the more experienced oil industry suffered. A floating oil collection platform, a former 200 000-tonne supertanker, broke free, and three oilfields producing 210 000 barrels a day had to be closed down. The waves would have increased as the wind roared across the North Sea to Norway.

The fact that it has not prevented further work being done on OWCs, and at Dounreay on one which will be more exposed to the weather, as it will be offshore, is a defiant answer to those who say that wave energy must be pursued in the laboratory for fear that accidents at sea will be damaging.

References

1. Davies, P.G., Cloke, M.S., Major, K.A., Page, D.I., and Taylor, R.J. (ed.) (1985). In *Wave energy*, ETSU R-26. ETSU for the Department of Energy, Harwell., p. viii.
2. *Alternative energy sources* (1988). House of Lords Select Committee on the European Communities, Session 1987–88, p. 196.

3. Salter, S.H. (1988). World progress in wave energy—1988. *Int. Journal of Ambient Energy*, **10**, pp. 3–24.
4. Falnes, J. (1993). *Wave energy R & D*, p. 126. CEC, Luxembourg.
5. Royal Ministry of Petroleum and Energy, Oslo (1979–80). *White paper no. 54*, Chapters 5, 10, and 12.
6. Alternative Technology Group working paper (1983). Open University.
7. White, P.R.S. (1985) *Report on discussions*.

10 Survival of the fittest

Norway launched the world's first wave power station on 13 November 1985, with the British government ostentatiously absent. But word of the event reached Whitehall. The tone changed and the Department of Energy was soon uttering favourable sounds about a project by the Queen's University of Belfast to build a wave power station on the shore of Islay in the Inner Hebrides. The British government had said in 1982 that it was abandoning wave power, and the first draft of the ETSU 'obituary'[1] actually cited the 'decision' of the Norwegians to do likewise in support of the British decision; this was hastily changed when it became plain that the Norwegians were going ahead. And when they succeeded, the British government had no excuse left.

The power station was built on Islay by a team from Queen's University, Belfast, and the manager of the project, Dr Trevor Whittaker, said that 'the best way of describing the device is that it is really like a hybrid between the two Norwegian devices',[2] meaning a combination of OWC and Tapchan, with modifications. It is a concrete box about the size of a garage and, as Whittaker put it to the Coventry wave energy conference in 1989, 'it has to withstand a demolition squad every 10 seconds', a reference to the pounding of the waves which deliver pressure of 40 tonnes per square metre. The front wall is open at the base to admit them. They have been captured in a natural V-shaped gully which accelerates their movement as it narrows. The waves race up to the top of the gully, enter the OWC, and drive upwards a pocket of air which in its turn rotates a turbine.

Why was it on Islay? The more obvious site for a Belfast university project would have been in Ireland, except that the entire western coast of Ireland, right up to the northern tip, is part of the Republic and therefore a foreign country so far as Britain and Northern Ireland are concerned. This fact had, from the start of the wave power programme, caused Britain to produce maps which suggested that the waves stopped when they touched the northern tip of Ireland, for fear that Dublin might regard it as an incursion on its territorial waters if scientists were even to display the great wave power available to the republic from the Atlantic swell. For Queen's University, the politics meant that they could not go west because Northern Ireland has no west-facing coast. So they had to think of using the west coast of Scotland.

Dr Whittaker is a pure child of wave power. He was born in 1954, the year when Walton Bott was starting his work on Mauritius, and became the first student of Alan Wells, inventor of the Wells turbine. Whittaker's Ph D thesis was on the hydrodynamics of the OWC. In 1983, after the British Government had withdrawn support from 2 GW stations in the open sea, Whittaker started to contemplate a smaller station on the shore. By coincidence, Dr William B. Cranston, a native of Islay, had contacted Queen's to ask if work was continuing on wave energy and if consideration had been given to onshore devices for island communities. He had been pottering round the shore with his son on holiday at Port Charlotte, on Islay, and had noticed the magnification which occurs when a wave is squeezed into a gully. He was also a director of the Cement and Concrete Association in England.

Queen's financed an aerial survey of the north coast of Ireland and the western Scottish isles and Islay was identified as being the most suitable location. Its gullies are, as Whittaker put it, 'subjected to vigorous wave action' (there is open sea all the way from Newfoundland). The loss of energy from friction in shallow water off the coast meant that 70 kW/m in the deep sea was reduced to 8 kW/m inshore. But with the gully the energy rose again to 20–30 kW/m. The gullies act as fortuitous collectors or focuses of wave energy, provided free by nature.

Whittaker started work with a handful of money from Queen's. A friend offered him a lift in a small plane, and they identified a suitable site close to Portnahaven. Then a feasibility study was launched, with funding from the Department of Energy (£62 000) and from the Cement and Concrete Association which, apart from Dr Cranston's personal interest, was aware that its product had a promising future in wave energy.

The design and feasibility study was completed in January 1987, and the government then approved a second stage, at a cost of £280 000, of which 93 per cent came from the Department of Energy and 7 per cent from Queen's. It covered work starting on 1 April 1987, although, 'unfortunately', as Whittaker said, 'we were not told until July 1'. This was not untypical of the way wave energy researchers were treated by officialdom. The funds covered the civil engineering (the concrete box which was to house the machinery) and the monitoring of the power output which, in the absence of the turbo-generator, meant measuring the flow of air. It was completed in April 1989 and resulted in one major change of plan. The original idea, based on testing a 1/50th scale model in a wave tank, had been to instal a 150 kW OWC. But, in real life, observations had shown that strong tidal currents, plus the turbulence caused by the unevenness of the gully, reduced the power levels. Also, the chamber had to be built further back than originally planned, to facilitate construction, so it was in a narrower part of the gully with reduced plane water area, and the water column was smaller. So it was decided to instal a 75 kW machine.

And then came the third phase, which started in the Spring of 1989 and was completed in December 1991, at a cost of £322 000, and involved the installation and testing of the Wells biplane turbo-generator.

The Thorpe report[3] comments that it was an experimental prototype and not an optimised design. It was designed to test various aspects of wave devices, in fact a demonstration project rather than a generating station, although it does supply the local grid. Thorpe notes that the highest average over a 15 minute period has been 17 kW, and for short periods it was in excess of 50 kW. It remained operational through severe storms and gave insight into construction techniques *in situ*. But Thorpe (and Whittaker) admit that output has been less than originally expected. Thorpe puts this down to the following factors: the wave climate was less energetic than originally estimated due to the strong effect of tides, which reduced the average wave resource by 20 per cent with the greatest reduction (60 per cent) at low tide. The lesson was that OWCs should be built in deeper water. (I would add that the tidal problem will not arise at all in the open sea.) Turbulence caused by the roughness of the gully walls caused considerable energy loss. Smoother gully walls (such as a designer gully) would improve performance. The turbine was only 50 per cent efficient, and guidevanes to a conventional turbine instead of a Wells turbine or variable pitch turbine blades, would ease that situation. A different design of generator would also reduce losses.

Whittaker estimated, at the European Wave Energy Symposium at Edinburgh in July 1993, that power output could be doubled simply by building 'harbour walls' which increase the catchment area.[4] The effect is to put a wider-angled V-shape at the entrance and draw in energy from a larger surface area, squeezing the waves even more as they enter the tapering area. For a nearshore OWC standing just off the coast, the harbour walls should increase output by a factor of four, he said.

After completion, a further phase of monitoring and 'optimisation' cost £223 000, taking the total to £887 000. As it is described as a 75 kW machine this figure, if taken crudely at face value, would suggest that the Islay station cost about 10 times as much as the target figure of £1 per watt. That might appear to support the complaints of the energy establishment that it was too expensive. But, considered fairly, the cost is inflated because this is an experimental prototype, burdened with machinery to monitor not only the electricity but also the air flow before the generator had been installed, and computerised controls never previously used for this purpose, and that the further period of monitoring was added after the work had been completed. It attracted all the design and purpose-built construction costs associated with a one-off. Design costs are normally spread across many devices. Also, the builders had to cross a difficult stretch of water to prove that construction could be carried out on an island with minimal infrastructure, an important selling point for island communities. This entailed more costly construction. There is no indication that these facts were taken into account by Tim Eggar before he announced on 31 March 1994 that he was ending funding.

There is no way in which a price could be put on the lessons learned—for instance, that in future it will be better to have a 'designer gully', made of steel and dropped into place on the coast, rather than use the gully provided free by nature, which, with its uneven rockface, is less efficient as an aqueduct. As

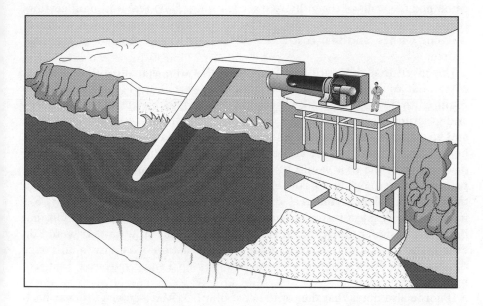

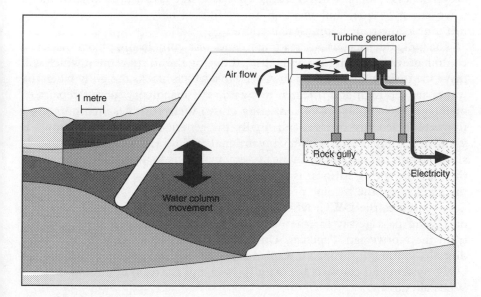

Fig. 10.1 Artist's impression of the Islay wave power station.

Trevor Whittaker has put it, 'We would double the power of the system if we smoothed the walls of the gully. We are learning.' The real lesson of 'costing' the Islay station is that the 'cost' can be adjusted and interpreted in whatever way one wishes, and that cost is not the proper way to assess a new energy source.

But given that there are people in authority who demand to know about cost, what *is* the price of a unit of Islay power? The Thorpe report was required to do this exercise as though it were a Stock Exchange investment and to assume discount rates of 8 and 15 per cent. It produced 'costings' of 6p and 9p a unit which, for a technology in its infancy, is good. The truth is even better. The Thorpe report also contained graphs which enabled readers to discover what the cost would be if the discount rate were set aside and the price estimated on the basis of cost of construction plus interest and maintenance. This is the real cost, and it has been described by ETSU itself as 'the simplest way of calculating the cost of wave electricity'. On that basis, the designer Gully would generate at a cost of 3p a unit. It would do even better and produce electricity for a small fraction of a penny a unit once the capital had been repaid and interest was no longer required, just like hydroelectric power.

Thorpe also notes that the capital cost of a 1 MW designer gully has been assessed at £1.4 million.[3] That would produce even cheaper electricity. Nevertheless, I persist in regarding cost as a side issue, even when it is on wave energy's side, and mention these figures only because others have introduced their misleading calculations.

The gully device consists, reading inland, of a gully leading from the sea; a column of water which rises and falls, producing the air movement which will drive the turbines; a butterfly shut-off valve which blocks the gully when the waves are too high and threaten to swamp the machinery, or for repairs or maintenance; a biplane rotor consisting of two Wells turbines incorporating a flywheel for energy storage; and finally the generator. Tom Thorpe puts it vividly by comparing it with a conventional engine. He says it constitutes 'a single degree of freedom dynamic system analagous to a mass on a spring. In this case the spring stiffness is provided by buoyancy, and the constriction of the air flow by the turbine provides damping.'[3]

It combines the OWC, which the Japanese invented, with the idea of a narrowing passageway for the waves which accelerates their force, derived from the Norwegian Tapchan. Unlike the Tapchan, which uses the water directly, sending it through a Kaplan turbine, the Islay station returns to the OWC system and converts the water power into a stream of air and drives a Wells air turbine.

Constructing it was a more difficult operation than might be suggested by the size of the project. Trevor Whittaker has described it. 'Working in real conditions and seeing Force 10 seas coming in is a sobering experience,' he said at the Coventry wave energy conference, which was organised by the

Solar Energy Society in November 1989. 'You get tremendous peaks within the average and water goes right over the top of the structure. The turbine blades can stall with a peak of wave power. The device has been in and out in one year—we had an unexpected problem when thunderstorms and electrostatic in the atmosphere knocked out our computers.'

Fig. 10.2 Waves breaking at the Islay wave power station.

That happened after they had surmounted the problems of building the station. He said: 'It is the size of a normal domestic garage, but it has to withstand a demolition squad every 10 seconds. It is all very well assessing energy in terms of money, but if this thing was run by accountants you would never do anything. Nearshore and offshore devices will benefit from what we are doing. It is easier to develop a shoreline Wells turbine and you know you can use it at sea.'

It is a 450-tonne structure, and 70 per cent of it was precast in northern Ireland and shipped in kit form to Islay. All the plant and materials had to be taken 30 miles overland by lorry, through the narrow roads of Islay, along with a mobile crane, a small concrete batching plant, a rock breaker, a tractor and trailer, a welding plant, a compressor, and hand tools. The main structure had to be divided into 54 prefabricated concrete beams, each weighing 6 tonnes, because of the limited capacity of the crane on the site. The first operation was to install a cofferdam across the gully to keep out the sea. The waves still washed over the top, and work was possible for only six months out

of 14 because of the sea and the weather. The experience forced a reconsi-
deration for future projects: they would dig a pit in the earth about 20 m
inland in the dry and lower into it a man-made designer gully, an OWC and a
turbo-generator—the entire power station. When it was complete, the bank of
earth separating it from the sea would be blasted away with dynamite. This
would remove the need to work in the difficult conditions created by the
waves in the course of their transposition from enemy to friend.

Fig. 10.3 Photograph of Colin Moynihan, then junior Energy Minister, conducting the
official 'opening'. (He is standing closest to the device and pointing. Next to him, on
his left, is Professor Trevor Whittaker of Queen's University, Belfast, who built it.)

Meanwhile, Gully One—how is it doing? It can claim, in the words of
Abbé Sieyès after the French Revolution: 'I survived.' The structure has
been standing in the face of the Atlantic for seven winters, from December
1988 until (at the time of writing) the spring of 1995, a remarkable
achievement for a prototype which is *almost* intended to be tested to
destruction. It taught Trevor Whittaker a lot about the loadings that
waves exert on the OWC, which will enable him to design a cheaper
one next time because—quite rightly, say his admirers—he over-designed
Gully One to ensure its survival.[4]

What of noise from the Islay machine? Trevor Whittaker put considerable
effort and expense into insulating it, after hearing criticisms that were made of
the Norwegian OWC, and he has reduced the sound. As you approach it, there
is a sighing sound which can be heard from about 200 yards back. But that is
on a calm day. What, ask visitors, when the sea is really rough—surely it must

get louder? That is not a question that would be asked by an islander on the Hebrides. Because in such conditions the blow–suck motion of the OWC cannot be heard above the sound of the waves crashing on to the shore and the roar of the wind. Gully One stands at the foot of the garden of a couple named Merrall, and they have no complaints about it. They have become supporters of wave energy.

But, bearing in mind the experience of the wind farms, what will happen when wave energy becomes a major supplier of the Grid, with 2000 MW stations? The answer is that they will not be on the shore. A considerable part of the appeal of wave energy is that its large units will be out at sea, disturbing no one because no one lives there.

But it must not be forgotten, amid all the argument about environmental advantages and problems, and about funding and costs, that the task of wave energy is to combat nature in order to gather energy in some of the cruellest and therefore most fruitful waters of the world, and that the sea can never be taken for granted. The most important aspect of Gully One is that it has taken the world a step forward, has taught engineers and scientists a lot more about the issues, and brought nearer the day when we start to enjoy the benefit of the waves.

All of the above appeared no more than an obituary to Whittaker's efforts in the autumn of 1994 when this chapter was being written and after Eggar had pronounced the obsequies for the British programme.[5] And then came two unexpected events. The Royal Society, Britain's ancient and most prestigious scientific academy, which awards honours for contributions 'leading directly to national prosperity', decided to present Whittaker with its Esso Energy Award for 1994, for 'outstanding contributions to the advancement of science or engineering or technology, leading to the more efficient mobilisation, use, or conservation of energy resources'. Such an award, from such a body, was plainly a rebuff to a government which had cut off support to his efforts. But the best was still to come. Whittaker was searching desperately for a new source of funding and he found it: the company which was in process of building the newest wave energy device, the OSPREY (see Chapter 12), designed for a site in near-shore waters off Dounreay, decided that it would also invest in a new, onshore Gully. This, it reasoned, would give it the ability to tour the world offering other countries, particularly islands depending on burning imported oil, the option of building a wave power station on the beach, or in the sea, according to the local conditions. The money was sufficient to satisfy Brussels that it should reinstate its investment and the contract was signed on the day of the presentation at the Royal Society (24 November 1994).

The guest of honour was to be the very man, Energy Minister Tom Eggar, who was, in the minds of many, the villain of the day. There are good grounds for believing that his Secretary of State, Michael Heseltine, had been ready to continue the small investment which the government was making in

Whittaker's pioneering effort, but that his junior minister insisted that wave energy investment must be ended. Eggar appears to have realised that he was unlikely to be popular with the distinguished audience, and his private office made discreet inquiries as to whether questions would be asked after his address. He was assured that there would be none, and on that basis he made a short address and a swift departure back to the House of Commons.

Gully Two is due to be launched in the summer of 1995 at Porto Cachorro on the northern shoreline of the island of Pico in the Azores, where the Portuguese have been monitoring the wave climate with a waverider buoy offshore. They have discovered a wave climate of around 20–40 kW/m and a 'hot spot' at the entrance to a natural gully, which has been chosen as the site. The device is similar to Islay's: it will be an OWC and is being backed by the EU and the Portuguese and Azores electricity utilities (Portugal has the good fortune of having electricity suppliers which have not been privatised). Joining them are two Portuguese technical institutes, an engineering consortium and the two Irish centres with experience of wave energy, the University College in Cork, which has made its wide tank available for testing, and Queen's in Belfast.

The plan is to build a concrete structure on a rocky bottom, in water about 7 m deep, over the gully entrance which has been identified as a 'hot spot'. A temporary cofferdam will shelter the construction site. It will be a 500 kW device, with two Wells turbines capable of rotating at a wide range, between synchronous speed and twice its value. This, say its designers, will enable the turbines to respond to a wide range of sea states and provide flywheel storage. It will have a peak output of more than 1 MW. The turbines will have fixed blades, but these could be changed to variable pitch later, if sufficient progress is made in EU studies on this question being conducted by Peter White of Coventry and Stephen Salter. The station will be similar to Islay but considerably larger (the water column area is 150 m^2 compared with 25 m^2 at Islay) and with improvements which have been learned from the experience on Islay. The Azores at present get their electricity by burning expensive, polluting, imported diesel oil.

It is the only device which has been the subject of regular reports to the wave energy conferences by a woman, Teresa Pontes of the National Institute of Engineering and Industrial Technology in Lisbon.

References

1. Davies, P.G., Cloke, M.S., Major, K.A. Page, D.I., and Taylor, R.J. (ed.) (1985). In *Wave energy*. ETSU R-26, ETSU for the Department of Energy, Harwell.
2. *Alternative energy sources* (1988). House of Lords Select Committee on the European Communities, Session 1987–88, p. 186.

3. Thorpe, T.W. (1992). *A review of wave energy*, Vol. 2, pp. Ei-Exli. ETSU R-72. Department of Trade and Industry, London
4. Elliot, G. and Caratti, G. (ed.). *1993 European wave energy symposium*, pp. 283–7. NEL, E. Kilbride.
5. Eggar, T. (31 March 1994) *Official report* (Hansard). **240**, cols. 1009–10. Written answers.

Brussels stumbles into action 11

With one of Norway's plants lying on the seabed, and wave energy officially rejected by the British government, there was little sign of activity in 1987 when I came across a strange document: 'Wave energy—evaluation for CEC' by Dr Tony Lewis[1]. It was published by a company directed at the institutional market and was not for the general reader. But it was music to this reader. It was a report, in old-fashioned typescript with unjustified columns, of an exercise carried out for the European Commission by Dr Lewis, oceanographer and maritime civil engineer at the Hydraulics and Maritime Research Laboratory of Cork University. It was, he said (rightly), the first systematic study of the European wave power potential. It found that 'the total power available at all coastlines is estimated to be 92 GW, and if the Iberian peninsula is included the total rises to about 110 GW. This is equivalent to about 85 per cent of the present EC electricity demand.' (The Iberian countries were not, at that time, members of the European Community; they have since been admitted.)

Dr Lewis's study gave a breakdown: 66 GW along the Atlantic coastline, 1.5 GW on the North Sea coasts, and 25 GW in the Mediterranean, which 'would need further investigation'. Many experts would agree that this last figure looks suspiciously high. But, against that, all the figures are underestimates because, by going further and further out to sea, in the way that the oil companies have done, one can add to the 'front line' of generators off the coast. In estimates for some of the countries, Dr Lewis puts the potential at: UK 30 GW; Ireland 25 GW; Norway 12 GW; France in the Bay of Biscay (which is known in other countries as the Gulf of Gascoigne) 11 GW. He puts Spain's potential at 3 GW and Portugal's at 15 GW.

Given that all the figures are estimates, no one should regard them as a precise statement of the electricity available. Dr Lewis had done an extremely important service by gathering the figures together in one volume for the Commission and making it plain that there was a huge resource waiting to be tapped.

His work was ignored. The EC and the International Energy Agency failed to respond. With Britain, the lead country, insisting that wave energy was likely never to be economic (ETSU R26)[2], it was a dead topic for Brussels. And then there came a strange event which was to transform the situation in a manner which can only be described as profound. It was certainly not anticipated.

Dr David Lowry is a research assistant to Llew Smith, the Labour Member of the Westminster Parliament for Blaenau Gwent and at that time also the Member of the European Parliament for Wales South-East. In September 1990 Dr Lowry drafted a Question for Mr Smith to put down in the European Parliament: 'Can the Commission indicate on what basis wave energy projects have been largely excluded from the research, development and demonstration funding in the field of alternative energy sources?' The reply was given on 28 September 1990 by the Vice President of the Commission, Sr Filipo Pandolfi. He said: 'Concerning demonstration activities on wave energy, a study was carried out for the Commission in 1985 by Professor (sic) Tony Lewis of Cork University with the aim of analysing the possibility of including wave energy in the Demonstration Programme on Energy Saving and Renewable Energies. This study confirmed that it would have been premature to start demonstration in this field.'[3]

Dr Lowry is a very close friend of mine and an indefatigable drafter of Questions for both the Westminster and Brussels Parliaments. He always ensures that I am informed of parliamentary activities concerning wave energy, and he duly sent me a copy of the Question and Pandolfi's reply. It struck me like a blow between the eyebrows. Having read the Lewis report (and I think that I am one of the few people ever to have seen it, so poor was the distribution), I knew that Pandolfi had got it wrong. The report had not said that it would be premature; on the contrary, it specifically recommended that two European sites should be chosen for demonstrations and an investment of 13.7 million ECUs (then about £9.5 million) be allocated. He specifically suggested the establishment of a Demonstration Facility costing 5.7 million ECUs and a medium-scale demonstration project for island communities costing 7.2 million ECUs where systems up to 1 MW should be demonstrated.

It was time for action. I wrote two articles, one for *Private Eye*,[4] the satirical magazine which has a wide readership among politicians and civil servants, and the other for *New Scientist*,[5] telling the above story. 'Filipo Pandolfi has been caught by the normally mouse-like European Parliament and is being summoned to appear before MEPs to explain himself,' said the *Eye*[4]. 'Llew Smith is in hot pursuit of the Commission. He has tabled a resolution denouncing Pandolfi's reply as misleading and calling on the Commission to implement the Lewis recommendations.'

Sr Pandolfi had unintentionally misled the Parliament and, to his credit, he responded quickly. He apologised handsomely to Mr Smith and to the Parliament and, even more importantly, announced the immediate allocation of 1.2 million ECUs to wave energy research and the calling of a seminar of wave energy experts.

It was held in Brussels on 25–26 April 1991, and those attending included Sr Pandolfi, Dr Lewis, whose report had started the EC's involvement, Godfrey Bevan, head of the Renewables section at the Department of Trade and Industry, Professor Stephen Salter of Edinburgh University and the inventor of the Duck, Professor Norman Bellamy of Coventry University and the inventor of the Clam, Dr Johannes Falnes from Trondheim University, Winifred Ewing and Llewelyn Smith, Members of the European Parliament (MEPs) who had been most active in promoting wave energy, and me. It was made plain that Sr Pandolfi's presence was a rare distinction at such a seminar; he was doing penance lavishly, a custom among Roman Catholics.

The discussion saw another round in the debate, by now 12 years old since the original Heathrow conference in 1978, about whether it was best to go to sea sooner or later. Professor Salter insisted:

I don't want to be the first wave power device at sea. I want to be the last one. I want to make all the mistakes in private, with instruments to tell me what mistakes I have made so that I don't do it again. I want to do all the difficult things in the laboratory. There was enthusiasm for airships, but the R101 crashed. Airships finally died when the Hindenberg died. If you had a spectacular disaster with one wave energy device, you could drag everything down, too.

Professor Salter, whose early experience was in aviation, has urged people to read Nevil Shute's autobiography, *Slide rule*.[6] Shute was a flying pioneer and engineer before becoming a novelist, and the book describes graphically the sequence of events leading up to the R101 disaster; it is well worth reading, particularly for anyone planning a leap into the unknown. It was first published in 1954, and one can imagine the vivid impression it would have made on the young Salter.

I have given his argument in detail because it is the one issue on which I have found myself in disagreement with his view, and it is important to be fair. The issue will be judged by what happens from now on. I thought, at the time of Hermann Bondi, when wave energy was new and adventurous, that a full-scale prototype should be built and launched and that, if it crashed, then the public would understand that early models do such things. Flying was not killed by the series of disasters which bedevilled the Comet jet airliner. The Oscillating Water Column survived the accident in Norway. As Per Anderssen said of the Tapchan (see Chapter 9), 'We realised that you could not sell new technology until you had demonstrated it.' But Professor Salter has shown inflexible determination in insisting that he will not be tempted into putting a Duck to sea before he is ready.

The conference concentrated on laying down the ground plan for EC involvement in the development of wave energy. Godfrey Bevan, apparently irritated at the contrast which was being drawn between EC munificence and Whitehall's inactivity, said that the British Government had spent '1000 times 1000 ECUs' on building the station at Islay. He was right—the figure is £887 000. Professor Bellamy said that he wanted to go to sea with the Clam, but Bevan replied that it was not ready for a full-scale prototype but was ready for testing of components. He thought that the one generic device on which sufficient work had been done was the OWC.

The one disagreeable note came from the representative of the International Energy Agency, Mr S. Wennenberg, who said the IEA had assessed wave energy and 'this assessment recognises that the contribution from wave energy is very low. It requires large and costly experiments. There is a long payback time. It is not for poor countries to invest in.' This was not a surprise to most participants who had known for a long time that the IEA was no friend of wave energy. Its view is sometimes cited by apologists for the British Government as supporting evidence that wave energy is not a good idea. But the reason that the IEA agrees with the British Government is that the British representatives *are* the British government—either from the Department of Energy (now part of the Department of Trade and Industry) or from ETSU. And because Britain is widely regarded as the leading country in wave power, the IEA accepts the British view. It is annoying for those who know the facts to be told, as though it was conclusive proof of something, that the IEA *also* said that wave energy was a poor choice.

Stephen Salter, in his evidence to the House of Lords Select Committee on the European Communities, said:

Britain is a member of the IEA and reports to it on British wave research. These papers, from ETSU, are circulated to research teams in various other countries who are in close direct touch with us. More than one such team was to ask us why these reports were so negative. I have seen extracts relating to our spine tests which I believe do not accurately reflect our results. My requests for the complete versions have been refused both by ETSU and the Department of Energy.[7]

So much for the IEA; happily, in Brussels its advice was not heeded.

Sr Pandolfi, summing up the EC's view of the conference, said that 'the fundamental thing, the most important thing' was to bring research centres together and provide a pool of information—something which has happened on an *ad hoc* basis only. He also made the point that there was 'no clear winner technology over others', and that it was important to keep 'the spectrum of options' as open as possible, which has happened. Thirdly, he wanted to see a strong contribution from industry. He thought that on financing, 'can I say we take two or three prototypes, not very expensive, in order to try and get close to how useful they are in comparative terms?'

Then, he made his financial proposal. 'The 1.2 million ECUs has to be used this year. Next year, I expect 2 million ECUs for the research programmes. We will spend more on programmes which look more interesting. If we can find a path that is promising, the ECUs will follow, particularly if we get strong industrial interest.'

The words were what had been hoped for. The money was insufficient, but at last there was someone with access to official funding who was prepared to invest in wave energy. Pandolfi's error over the Lewis report had proved a blessing in disguise. He had apologised handsomely and, even better, had produced money in support of his words. It would be a happy day when a misleading answer to a question in the London Parliament could be rewarded in such a style.

The next stop was Cork, for a conference on 1–2 October 1992 of 45 engineers and scientists from Britain, Ireland, Norway, Sweden, Denmark, Portugal, and Spain. It marked the signal for half-speed ahead. In retrospect, it was a masterly demonstration of the European Commission's power of control. It was represented by Dr Giancarlo Caratti, an Italian, enveloped in charm and quick intelligence, who surprised most of us by saying unequivocally what he thought and what he would recommend the Commission to do. This does not often emanate from civil servants who, in Britain at least, are more likely to avoid committing themselves, to put the responsibility on their political masters and say that they will inform the Minister of whatever it is that has emerged in any discussion. The different tone confirmed my suspicion that the Commission ran the Community and that the politicians were second runners—but it would be dishonest not to say that in the context of wave energy I welcomed what he said. This is a topic suitable for a thesis on ends and means and democratic control. On the practical level, this is what Sr Caratti said.

He gave a thoughtful analysis of the scene. He said that progress had been above the EC's initial expectations but there were too many devices and concepts and little use of common methodology. The research teams were working independently. Wave energy was still in the research and development stage, its economics were not yet reliable, and it needed public support. He insisted it was too early to go ahead to the 1 MW module based offshore—something which was then regarded as the logical next step. Wave energy, he insisted, was 'still very much an R & D activity' and should advance to a 500 kW OWC which would allow for the testing of new components—on the shore, not out at sea. 'We are ready to have full European cooperation on an onshore plant now,' he said. 'We need it in the water. Let us go for what is ready. I remain open to an offshore plant—as a second phase.'

He was met with sharp retorts from delegates, two of Salter's collaborators among them. Professor Denis Mollison of Heriot-Watt University commented that there had been an OWC of 500 kW built at Bergen as long ago as 1985. Dr Martin Greenhow of Brunel University, who was one of Salter's early research team, said: 'We have already had OWCs in Islay, Norway, and Portugal. We have got to go offshore with a floating or flexible structure, with mass-produced modules.' Dr Leslie Duckers of Coventry University, which wants to build a Clam at sea, said: 'The Japanese have already built four OWCs. Another one will have a limited contribution to make.' And George Elliot of the National Engineering Laboratory said that the studies 'will not produce a model that you can buy off the shelf'.

Ten months later, we all assembled at Heriot-Watt University, Edinburgh for a third EC conference, organised by the National Engineering Laboratory. Dr Caratti was there once more and his message was different: 'We want to put one foot in the water. We are on a very good train. I am very happy with the natural evolution of the programme. There is increased political support at the European level. We will give priority to the plans for three pilot plants.'

He offered an important advance in official thinking: 'Do not base a decision on future predicted costs.' At last! An organisation had recognised that there was life after debt.

This was the key to EC thinking, and it marked a qualitative change from the official attitude in the UK at least, where cost had been the decisive element almost from the beginning.

Dr Caratti said that the EC expected to make known its plans within three months, and it did so. It announced, in October 1993, that it was allocating 2.6 million ECUs (£2 million) to a near-shore station off Dounreay, where a device called the OSPREY and rated at 2 MW was to be built and stationed in the sea; that a new Gully was to be built on Islay, double the installed capacity of the present one; and a 500 kW device was to be built on the island of Pico in the Azores. All three are OWCs.

In addition, Coventry University was given money for turbine development, and the Danes for work on their device.

References

1. Lewis, T. (1985). *Wave energy: evaluation for CEC*. Graham & Trotman, London.
2. Davies, P.G. (ed.), Cloke, M.S., Major, K.A., Page, D.I., and Taylor, R.J. *Wave energy, the Department of Energy's R & D programme 1974–83*. ETSU.
3. Official report of European Parliament for 28 September 1990. European Parliament office, London,
4. Ross, D. (4 January 1991). Brussels sprouts, *Private Eye*.
5. Ross, D. (10 November 1990). Europe misled over wave energy. *New Scientist*.
6. Shute, N. (1954). *Slide rule*. Heinemann, London.
7. Select Committee on the European Communities (1988). Report of Session 1987–88.

12 The OSPREY takes off

As always with wave energy, just when a final blow to its hopes seems to have been delivered (usually by the British Government), something happens. In 1982, Nigel Lawson and David Mellor read out the obsequies. Then Norway launched two wave power stations, and Britain was forced to sanction the building of Islay One. In 1990, the European Commission misread its own report and said investment would be premature; it was then persuaded to reverse direction and out of it came substantial funding. In 1989, the British government was forced by reports of two Select Committees to set up a wave energy inquiry and concluded that, despite the report's favourable analysis, no more money should be spent on offshore wave energy. But in December 1993, the EC announced that it would back the building of two plants in the UK and one in the Azores.

This was too much for the latest Energy Minister, Tim Eggar, who said that no more money would go to wave energy, as though his words could halt the construction, in Scotland, of the first offshore device.[1] It enjoys backing not only from Brussels but also from organisations which are highly esteemed in Conservative government circles: GEC whose chief executive, Lord Prior, is a former Tory party chairman; British Steel, which was privatised by the government; Scottish Hydro, privatised as part of the electricity industry; the government's own QUANGO (Quasi-Autonomous Non-Governmental Organisation), the Highlands and Islands Enterprise; and AEA Technology, better known as the Atomic Energy Authority. The last-named is particularly interesting. It is owned by the government and contributing services and facilities worth hundreds of thousands to the OSPREY while the government, advised by ETSU, is saying that wave energy is not viable and never will be. Who runs ETSU? Why, AEA. ETSU is a subordinate branch of AEA. ETSU staff are recruited and paid by AEA. So the parent company is investing in an activity which its own sub-section, ETSU, which specialises in renewables, and the government, which subsidises AEA, say is not worth a penny. We have an Energy Minister without an energy ministry, who appears to be unaware or forgetting what his own department is subsidising. As Mr Eggar is discovering, and as King Canute could have told him, you may huff and puff as much as you like, but you will not stop the waves.

The newcomer is being built by an Inverness company called Applied Research & Technology and is called the OSPREY, a rather strained acronym from Ocean Swell Powered Renewable EnergY (the real osprey is a rare bird

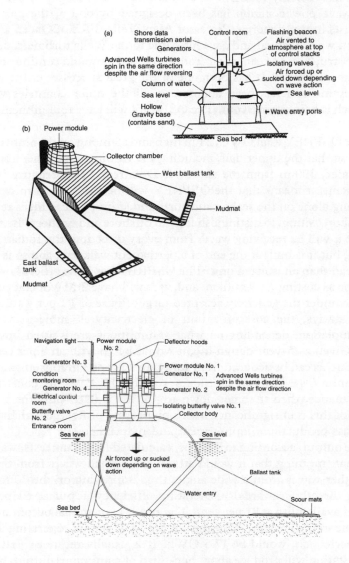

(a) Shore data transmission aerial
Generators
Advanced Wells turbines spin in the same direction despite the air flow reversing
Column of water
Sea level
Hollow Gravity base (contains sand)
Control room
Flashing beacon
Air vented to atmosphere at top of control stacks
Isolating valves
Air forced up or sucked down depending on wave action
Sea level
Wave entry ports
Sea bed

(b) Power module
Collector chamber
West ballast tank
Mudmat
East ballast tank
Mudmat

Navigation light
Power module No. 2
Deflector hoods
Generator No. 3
Power module No. 1
Condition monitoring room
Generator No. 1
Advanced Wells turbines spin in the same direction despite the air flow direction
Generator No. 4
Generator No. 2
Electrical control room
Butterfly valve No. 2
Isolating butterfly valve No. 1
Entrance room
Collector body
Sea level
Sea level
Air forced up or sucked down depending on wave action
Ballast tank
Water entry
Sea bed
Scour mats

Fig. 12.1 (a) the first design of the OSPREY was shaped like a bell with ballast in the hollow base. But tests persuaded its development team that it needed more ballast. They tried three spheres at its base but then adopted the design (b) which placed the ballast load in the protruding 'feet' facing the incoming waves. Finally, they settled for (c) with twin air 'chimneys'.

which has recently returned to Scotland after an absence of half a century). The wave power station has been designed by one of the most respected scientists in wave energy, Professor Alan Wells, FRS of Queen's University, Belfast, who invented and gave his name to the Wells turbine, a device which can be struck by a stream of air from above or below and continue to revolve in the same direction. It has been one of the great successes of the wave power programme and has been adopted in all the other countries where wave research is being carried out. The OSPREY will have four of them, each rated at 500 kW.

The OSPREY is an OWC, 28 m high and standing on the seabed in 14 m of water so that the upper half, including the turbines and generator, are above the water, 300 m from the shore off Dounreay. The distance is short but important: it means that the OSPREY will be the first wave power station standing alone on the seabed and surrounded by water. This is regarded as a 'nearshore' siting, to distinguish it from offshore and onshore. Its significance is that it will be receiving waves from every direction; the Indian OWC does so too, but it is built at the end of a permanent walkway, and so is more like a pierhead than an isolated unit. The OSPREY has been officially assessed[2] by Thorpe as costing £1.9 million, and, as it will have 2 MW installed capacity it will be under the generally accepted target figure of £1 per watt capital cost.

As always, the cost of a unit of electricity is subject to widespread contemplation, depending on what assumptions are written into the equation. Given a 25-year design life, it would be 7p with an 8 per cent discount rate. But, as can be deduced from studying Thorpe's graphs, if one ignores the discounting system and considers simply the costs of construction and maintenance, then it comes down to 4p. ART itself puts the cost at 3.1p. None of this is of significance with a pioneering prototype which offers scope for mass production, improvement and reduced costs.

The output, according to Thorpe, calculated from tank tests, was put at 115 per cent (meaning that it would attract some small waves from the shoreside and other waves from a wide angle, thus improving on the 30 m wavefront facing directly seawards). Generating efficiency is put at 60 per cent and annual availability at 91 per cent. The result is an annual output of 3.3 GWh. The theoretical maximum output of a 2 MW station, operating at unattainable perfection, would be 17.5 GWh. It is usually reckoned that a wave (or tidal) station will produce about one-third of continuous output, bringing the figure down to 5.8 GWh. So the present target for the first OSPREY makes generous allowance for losses in generation and other factors.

The success, so far, is due to the coming together of two men, Professor Wells and Allan Thomson, a welding engineer who ran a company with 500 offshore construction workers in North Sea oilfields. He knows the problems of survival in that environment and has capital of his own—and he was prepared to invest it in wave power. If OSPREY One is successful, then wave energy can really take off, because it provides the basis for a design that can be installed offshore by many countries—a flock of OSPREYs, as one of its backers put it. It will be modified according to the local wave climate, bringing electricity where it was previously unknown or providing it without pollution where oil and coal and gas were burnt. Thomson is on the road to being a universal benefactor and could be the first wave power multi-millionaire.

That is the good news. It would be misleading to hide the worries. He has saved on costs by building it of steel rather than concrete and by relying on gravity-anchoring instead of piling it into the seabed. This means it will stand on the soft soil in the seabed, making a dent in its own shape on being dropped down, and then will depend on a heavy load of ballast in its base to keep it upright. This saves a lot of money; the worry is that one huge wave—the 50-year wave, which seems always to happen more often—could push it over. Against that, there are the reputations of Wells and Thomson, both of whom know the problems and the sea.

Work on its design started in Inverness in 1990, and the first model was shaped like a bell. But tests persuaded the research team that the ballast might not prove adequate, so they redesigned the ballast tanks. It now looked like a bell with three spheres at the base to hold it on station. It was given tank trials at Queen's and at Scottish Hydro's laboratory at Pitlochry, and the team were still not happy. So a third design emerged. Above the water it looks like twin conning towers with a sphere under them, containing the collector chamber, 20 m wide, 20 m deep, and 20 m high, its roof above the waves. Inside it, the air rises and falls with the movement of the waves. A place has been left for the installation of a 1.5MW wind turbine to assist continuous output even when the sea turns dead calm. In the 'conning towers' are the power modules containing four Wells turbines and a GEC Flowpak generator, the controls for which are supplied by CEGELEC, a French company. They are designed to maintain a fixed power to the Grid and to permit the turbines to run at the optimum mean speed. The device weighs 70 tonnes without the ballast and 7000 tonnes fully loaded and lowered into position. The ballast tanks appear as graceful slopes on each side. The total effect is 'post-modern structural', as one academic described it.

Why did they change? Professor Wells told me that there had been a problem in accommodating 'enough ballast-mass to hold the thing down. The extreme wave forces are very high. If I say 10 000 tonnes, I don't think it would be an over-estimate for a 50-year wave. If it is anchored by gravity, it needs a certain volume of sediment and the bell would not have contained enough sediment to do the job. Therefore, you have to be very sure.' They had reached the conclusion that the ballast load must be placed as far forward (that is, facing out to sea) as possible. In the wave-breaking zones, he said, 'you have a temporary layer of deposited sand sediment, 1–2 metres thick. When the storms come, most if it goes into suspension so you have got to tap through and underneath it. Grout has to be introduced to make it cohesive. Schemes to do that have been developing all the time, with reference to grouting contractors and all the consulting sources we could find.' He said that the OSPREY still counted as a point absorber, accepting energy from all around, though the waves on the land side would be less ferocious and therefore less fruitful. When they went out into the more open sea, with later versions of it, they would need a modified type of device: 'the more one goes into this, the more one realises there are horses for courses.'

The big event was the decision of the EC in 1993 to give it funding under the Joule programme. This depended on OSPREY gaining backing from private industry, because the EC religion is that nothing may be invested unless the native governments, industrialists, or utilities are prepared to invest, too.

The device floats and it will be towed out to its site with the base partly flooded to keep it 'neutrally buoyant'. When it reaches the site, sediment is pumped in until the device just touches bottom but can rise and fall freely, making a depression in the seabed in its own image. Then more sediment is pumped in and it sinks into the depression it has made.

GEC Alsthom explained its involvement by saying that the OSPREY had at first appeared to be 'just another project to generate energy from renewable resources. However, on careful examination it was found that there was more potential for OSPREY than for earlier, less efficient schemes.' This is praise indeed from such a cold corner of the marketplace. The statement continued: 'The concept of generating constant frequency power from a variable energy source can now be achieved by the use of power electronics and modern electrical machine design techniques. ART and their partners have put together a robust and efficient energy conversion device, for which GEC Alsthom will supply the induction generators.' Thus speaks the company headed by Lord Weinstock, who has never been noted for sentimentality or for allowing his heart to rule his wallet. He and his company believe in OSPREY.

British Steel says it is providing the steel free 'as part of its commitment to the future of alternative energy', something which had not been very noticeable before. AEA Technology mapped the seabed near Dounreay, which it knows well from its studies of the consequences of discharges from the Fast Breeder Reactor, now dead.

Professor Wells designed the turbine for the first Islay device, and it has, as he put it to me, proved 'extraordinarily rugged'. It is a bi-plane design which has 'swallowed hundreds of gallons of sea water—it was inundated at times'. It is designed to take in air. 'Once, the butterfly control valves in its duct failed, it was a piece of work in glass fibre, it disintegrated and the bits went through the turbines and came out the other side, and the blades were not even dented. So what we got from the Islay experiment was an enormous push in confidence. That imbued us with the belief that we could go forward.'

He described the team producing OSPREY as

a very strong one because of complementary experiences and characteristics. My managing director is an ex-offshore steel contractor, very sound in commercial terms (Allan Thomson). We have a young project engineer who is marvellour at tugging us back to have our feet on the ground (Tom Heath). Thanks to the work of David Evans in Bristol, and a number of others in Norway, the studies on point absorbers showed that you could get capture factors exceeding one, with cylindrical structures. We have been able to verify that. We have a maximum capture factor which is about twice the diameter of the thing. That is really quite an important feature of the difference from the NEL device [which is part of a line of devices, facing one way].

As to costing he said: 'There are differences with Tom Thorpe, but there had to be because his criteria are the Department of Energy's and ours are commercial.'

The key to the success of the OSPREY was the commercial talent of Allan Thomson. By 1990, enough was known of wave energy for almost any knowledgeable insider to design a device which would work. The problem was finding the money to build it when there was a miserable, tight-fisted government with no vision ruling from Whitehall. Thomson, perhaps because of his experience as a businessman in the North Sea, was surefooted from the start. He managed the difficult operation of persuading me, and others, that he was confident that he would be able to put to sea, but at the same time, that he needed more money. And if the money did not materialise? 'We would have to look for other sources—a fresh injection from shareholders, or new shareholders, or merchant bankers or whatever. We are going for it, come hell or high water.' It was a difficult balancing act, insisting to sceptical onlookers that OSPREY would succeed, while continuing his campaign to get more backing on the grounds that it was needed.

He did not disclose that he had also been given sustantial support by a reclusive Swiss environmentalist, Stefan Schmidheiny, who lives in Zurich, 500 miles from the nearest sea wave. Schmidheiny's own representative, Hans van den Berg, was appointed to the four-man board of ART, providing a reassuring back up as well as investment. And in the end, the EU produced 550 000 ECUs (£435 000) and the project was on its way.

Postscript

The OSPREY was launched in blazing sunshine from UiE shipyard on Clydebank on 2 August 1995 with Caroline Thomson, wife of Allen, breaking a bottle of the local Orcadian Highland Park whisky over the stern, and with helicopters and balloons and a carnival atmosphere all around. Inevitably, there then followed problems. First, one of the tugs due to haul it to Dounreay suffered, of all things, an electrical fault, and the following day the tug had problems with its clutch. Another tug did the job two days later.

This provided a reminder that the best planning of the keenest minds in science, engineering and technology depends in the end on some ordinary, basic machinery.

But four days later more serious difficulties developed. While the OSPREY team were loading sand into the ballast tanks, the sea developed a three metre swell from Iceland which continued for six days, straight into the OSPREY. The chance of that sea at that season is 0.4 per cent, on the basis of weather reports from the whole spread of meteorological information for the north coast of Scotland. And it happened at the worst possible time, when the ballast tanks were still not fully loaded. The OSPREY was designed to face (and would have survived) such a powerful sea without difficulty if the ballast tanks had been filled. But with emptiness behind the casing, it buckled and tore and water rushed in.

The result is that a new structure has to be built. the electrical and

Fig. 12.2 Artist's impression of the OSPREY One.

mechanical equipment, including the Wells turbine, have not been damaged and the intention is to use them on OSPREY two. What makes this particularly frustrating is that during its short life OSPREY One performed wonderfully. the collector worked perfectly. The surge of air through its twin chimneys was up to the most optimistic expectations.

The incident can be seen as support for Stephen Salter's insistence on the advantage of working in the laboratory. But against that, it also supports Sir Hermann Bondi's view that it was necessary to get into the sea as quickly as possible because the real sea always has a trick up its sleeve. No-one could forecast a strong swell sea at precisely the time when the ballast was being loaded, but next time the OSPREY team will know that it can happen. Infuriatingly, they would have avoided the trouble if there had not been three days of delay at the shipyard before the OSPREY could sail.

They learned a lot from OSPREY One. They are determined to do better next time.

Fig 12.3 Photograph of the OSPREY as it floated in the Clyde at the UiE shipyard where it was built, on the day that it was launched, 2 August 1995, before being towed to its station off Dounreay.

References

1. Eggar, T. (31 March 1994). *Official report*, (Hansard), **240**, cols. 1009–10.
2. Thorpe, T.W. (1992). *A review of wave energy*, Vol. 2, pp. C.xxxiii–C.liv. ETSU R-72. Department of Trade and Industry, London.

13 The official view

Tony Benn was the Energy Minister when the programme was launched and he agreed to see me after an article, criticising the rate of progress, had appeared in the *New Statesman*.[1] He has since sent me his Diary entry for that day (14 September 1978). He described me as 'very anti-nuclear' which is, I think, a reflection of the fact that at the time he was very pro-nuclear. He wrote: 'His main interest is in wave energy and he thought what we were doing was too dispersed and not concentrated enough. He was a very decent guy, rather nervous, thought he was being persecuted a bit. I gave him my brief so that he would know what my official advice is and said I would arrange for him to talk to Sir Herman Bondi' (which he did). His action in giving me his brief was in line with his commitment to open government. It seems to me that the least I can do in response is to include the full text in this book and to hope that other Ministers and the Civil Service may one day appreciate that if they behaved with similar openness they might do their case some good.

The brief said: '*David Ross articles in New Statesman on wave power*

The Department gave generous background briefing to Ross but did not have a preview of the article. The article argues, in emotional terms, that the UK is not really trying to develop wave power rapidly whereas the Japanese are successfully doing so. He further argues that our programme is poorly motivated because of official and ministerial commitment to nuclear and coal.

The rate of build-up in expenditure from scratch on a new technology follows a natural growth curve. It is meaningless to compare spend on a 10-year project (fusion energy, which I had referred to) with expenditure on a two-year-old project. The programme on wave power has increased by about five times in the two years since it was first announced in April 1976, which is a very rapid rate of increase. In contrast, fusion research has increased by only about six times in the past 10 years in real terms. (A factor of 10 in 10 years might be regarded as a norm, although the Department could not substantiate such a figure at present.) The rate of growth of spend can be increased by accepting a greater risk of financial waste. Corners can be cut and programmes run in parallel, etc. The risks are justified in wartime situations but few would judge that the wave energy programme should be seen in such desperate terms.

Ross infers that the wave energy programme is now £2.9 million. The programme is actually £2.5 million *plus* the £2.9 million recently announced, i.e. about £5.5 million. Further the £2.5 million was the total programme size over three years to 1978. £2.9 m. is an additional spend for the year 1978/79; it is expected to increase substantially—subject to good technical progress—over the next few years.

The ETSU management team on wave power is now *outside* the nuclear perimeter and not involved in nuclear work at all. Many have been recruited from outside and *not* from the nuclear world.

The Japanese have pushed ahead rapidly with a single device and will be carrying out large-scale sea trials shortly. By contrast the UK has a more broadly based, scientific programme. It remains to be seen which approach succeeds but three points must be borne in mind.

(1) We have a stake in the Japanese work by virtue of our £300 000 contribution to the joint IEA (International Energy Agency) programme (they have no such stake in ours).

(2) Japanese industry has offered very low prices for plant because of low order books and this has contributed to their rapid transition to large-scale trials.

(3) The Japanese had many years' start on the UK because of Masuda's work on light buoys.

We have no evidence that anyone in wave energy work feels constrained by shortage of funds—which is not to say that they are all happy. Some are looking for long-term financial commitment by government to a wave energy programme. This is being considered, particularly by arranging things so that a team working on one device could be used on an alternative one if their own were closed down. It is inevitable and right that the number of devices being pursued should be reduced as the programme advances. Ross appears to praise Japan for single-mindedness and yet to decry any suggestion that the UK should reduce the number of options under investigation.

Furthermore on the question of timing of narrowing the choice of device-type, the wording of the White Paper is quite clear. It is expected to occur not immediately but over the next three or four years of engineering development.

Wave power at any cost is an objective that could very easily be achieved. It would not, however, serve the economic interests either of this country or even of wave power. David Ross appears quite unable to appreciate this fundamental point.'

References

1. Ross, D. (1978). Will Britain miss out on wave power? *New Statesman and Nation* (now *New Statesman and Society*), pp. 763–4.

14 The future

Where does wave energy go now?

There are two positive indications on the political map. The first comes from the British government. It set up the Thorpe inquiry into wave energy in April 1989, in response to the strong criticism that had been made by two Select Committees, and it camouflaged the news. It was announced by Baroness Hooper, the bottom minister in the Department of Energy, in the House of Lords, and it was buried in the last paragraph of an announcement about the allocation of a mere £87 000 to Queen's University, Belfast, to study the shoreline resource—by no means as important as the news that Britain was looking again at offshore technologies. There were suspicions about the government's motive from the start. The Secretary of State was John Wakeham, a former Chief Whip with antennas tuned in to public opinion. It was to be a two-year study which would have tided the government through the summer of 1991, which was then expected to be the date of the next general election. When the election was delayed, so was the report. It was eventually published on 17 December 1992, 18 months late, and on the very day that Parliament rose for Christmas and Lobby correspondents could be expected to be less attentive than usual. The minister, Tim Eggar, used the device of a planted written question to which he gave a written answer, so that he did not have to risk any supplementary questions.

The report was then left to gather dust for another 15 months, until 31 March 1994, before the government announced that it had decided not to fund any further work on wave energy. It had wasted five years, from April 1989 until the end of March 1994, in prevarication. And the day that it chose to release the news happened also to be a day when it was likely to escape attention: Maundy Thursday, as Parliament rose for Easter. It too was a written answer to a planted Question. This was a favourable indication, because it meant that the Government was persuaded, presumably on the basis of a private opinion poll, that wave energy was such a sensitive issue that it should seek, twice, to avoid attracting attention. Not many delicate decisions are awarded this accolade.

It means that in Britain there is a healthy awareness among the public of the importance of renewable energy and that the government is concerned that it could become a political issue which would force its hand.

The other hopeful sign from government was the statement by Tim Eggar on 17 February 1993. He was asked by Llew Smith, MP, what assessment had been made of the effect of the 8 per cent discount rate on public sector investment in energy technology projects. He gave the remarkable reply: 'My Department's investment in energy technology projects is for research or regulatory purposes, for which assessment on a discounting basis is not appropriate.' Eggar, a merchant banker, must surely have understood the significance of what he was saying. So, too, must the civil servants who drew up the reply. I am repeating it in full because of its importance. Somewhere inside the DTI, which is supposed to be trying to intervene to revive British industry, there is a policy of costing investment without imposing a discount rate to decry a project by making it appear expensive. That clearly is a policy waiting for a politically convenient time to be used in wave energy.

It is particularly important because of the study of wave energy which I mentioned at the start of this chapter. It is by Tom Thorpe, a scientist employed by ETSU, and it is the first major report from that body which has been well received by the wave energy teams since 1982, when ETSU said that wave energy was never likely to be viable, even in the future. Thorpe, a Cambridge scientist who had been working on North Sea oil and gas at Harwell, started work under unfortunate circumstances. The wave energy teams wanted money, not another study. When he appeared first before the teams at the Coventry conference in 1989, Professor David Evans said: 'It is very difficult to turn on a community which has been switched off for seven years. I would like to be assured that something will come out of this review. One needs to have a spark, a seed, that what happens is going to be taken up. Why should I think in wave energy terms? What are you going to discover about offshore wave energy that you did not know in 1982? What has changed?' That was the sceptical attitude of nearly everyone. But within a remarkably short time, Thorpe had won the confidence of the research teams. I believe that it is correct to say that he made no enemies during his long study.

More than that, his report has been well received by all of the teams. It is a scholarly work which does not say that wave energy is in perfect condition; it makes criticisms and suggestions (some of which have already been adopted by Salter to his design for the Duck). But above all it makes it clear that its author is not hostile to the concept. The one failing in the report is that Thorpe was compelled to apply a discount rate of 8 per cent to all his calculations and then, as though to satirise the situation, an extra rate of 15 per cent was added on, as though it was a supplement to the *Investors' Chronicle*.

What happened to Thorpe? How was he rewarded for bringing calm to the stormy waters of wave energy and ending the war between the research teams, Harwell, and Whitehall? Was he rightly regarded as having made himself one of our foremost experts? Was he not the person who could apply himself to the subject of bringing down costs even further, if that is what the government wanted? Was he not the person to continue his tour of wave energy research teams, applying the scrupulous scientific method that he had used, to ensure still better results? Not so far as Harwell was concerned. He was switched to other work connected to environmental matters, and well below his ability in the view of Salter. His offence, like Grove-Palmer's, was that he had believed that wave energy had a future and that the people carrying out research had something to offer the nation. He failed to say that it could never be worth while.

The final irony is that work is going ahead on the OSPREY off Dounreay. It is being helped by the company which has made available a sub-station at the site. That sub-station is worth, in the view of the OSPREY management, hundreds of thousands of pounds which they would otherwise have had to spend. It contains transformer, switch gears, control rooms and a link to the Grid.

And who owns it? Who has decided that wave energy is worth supporting and has invested such an important site in its future? Why, a company called AEA Technology, better known by its earlier name of United Kingdom Atomic Energy Authority, the parent company, the employer and the land-lord, of the organisation called ETSU.

During the past 20 years, much progress has been made; more should and could have been. In the future, we can be certain, public perceptions and pressures—and governments—will change, and the moment must come when countries recognise that they cannot go on burning up a dwindling stock of fossil fuels, polluting the atmosphere, and wasting money on nuclear power stations that become a dangerous blight on the countryside. When that happens, we will be there, because the waves go on for ever.

Appendix 1 Wave language

The key factor in assessing the energy in a wave is its height, just as most of us would imagine without any technical knowledge. It is the high wave which lifts us up as we swim and throws us the greatest distance. But there are other factors of significance. These are some of them. They are drawn mainly from the studies of the Institute of Oceanographic Sciences and the Hydraulics Research Station.

The *height* of a wave is the distance from the trough to the crest, not to the height above sea level. As the waves rise and fall, the volume of water above sea level is roughly equal to the volume of water below. The sea does actually rise and fall, just as it seems to be doing when we are on a ship.

The *Significant Wave Height* (SWH) is a term used for convenience which refers to the highest one-third of the waves. The earthy aspect of the science is that it has been discovered from practice that the SWH is almost identical to the ancient mariner's tale. When an experienced seaman reports on the size of the waves that he has survived, the figure he gives has been found invariably to be close to the highest one-third of the waves.

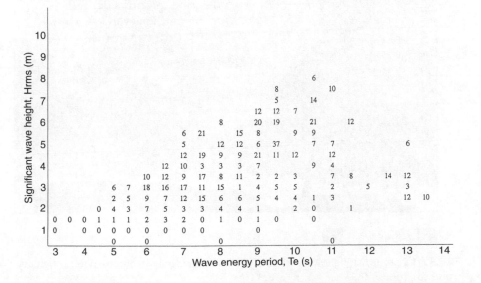

Fig. A1 Scatter diagram recording wave climate. The frequency of occurrence of each combination of height (in half-metre intervals, left-hand scale) and wave energy period (in half-second intervals, base line) is plotted in parts per thousand.

(a)

(b)

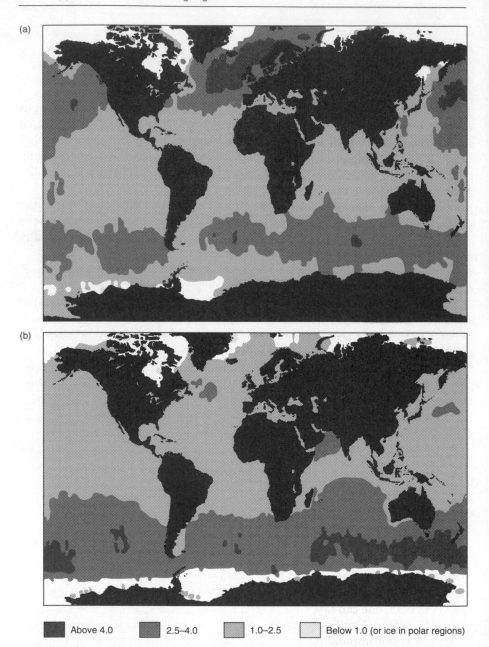

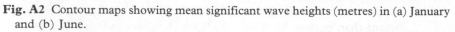

Fig. A2 Contour maps showing mean significant wave heights (metres) in (a) January and (b) June.

The *fetch* is the distance in nautical miles over which the wind has blown continuously on the sea before reaching the point under consideration—in our case, the line of wave energy generators. In general, the longer the fetch, the higher the waves. Strong winds of short duration can whip up higher waves than gentler winds blowing for a longer time; against this, a weaker wind over a greater distance can create very high waves. But it is still the length of the fetch which is the biggest factor.

The fetch is broken by any strip of land on which the waves break. Then a new fetch has to be calculated from zero. The fetch will also be broken by a line of generators which will absorb the energy and create a calm patch of water. There is some dispute about how much distance must be left between parallel lines of generators to enable the waves to grow significantly again. Many people believe that there will have to be a gap of 160 km but there is a growing feeling that an 80 km gap, followed by generators half the size contemplated, would make a significant contribution.

The *Zero Crossing Point* (ZCP) is an imaginary dot on a dead calm sea, something which we normally call sea level. It is roughly half-way between a crest and a trough. It is also used, horizontally, to measure the time and distance between waves.

Wave frequency is a term familiar to anyone associated with radio or, indeed, any form of noise. But it is best to avoid its use when discussing sea waves because they, unlike air waves, do not travel at the same speed. For instance, the longer the *wavelength*, that is the distance between the lines of crests, the faster the waves travel. A better way to describe the waves is to consider their *period*, that is the time between waves. A typical time is around 8 seconds. For those who feel more at home with frequencies, it may be helpful to note that the frequency is the inverse of the period. Thus, an 8-second wave has a frequency of one-eighth of a cycle per second.

The *power* in a wave can be expressed by the formula

$$P = 0.55 \ H_s^2 \ T_z kW/m$$

It is not as formidable as it looks. It means that power (P) equals 0.55 times the square of the SWH (in metres) multiplied by the Zero Crossing Period (in seconds). The result is in kilowatts per metre. Let us take an example.

Imagine a wave of 3 m height with a Zero Crossing Period of 6 seconds. Then the power equals 0.55 multiplied by 3^2 multiplied by 6. That is, $0.55 \times 9 \times 6$. The answer is 29.70 kW/m of wave front. And, given that we are dealing with a number of unknowns, it is safe to simplify the formula: instead of 0.55, one can say 'a half'. The answer, in the example given, would then be 27 kW/m. Until wave energy devices are operating on a large scale, the difference is not important.

What is important is to bear in mind that the height is squared. So height is more important than period. In the example given, a wave of only one metre more in height would produce the equation $0.55 \times 4^2 \times 6$, which would produce 52.80 kW/m. One metre more in the wave's height, the size of a child, and its power would be nearly doubled.

Another formula, enabling the wavelength to be calculated, is $L = 1.56 \, T^2$, where T is the time in seconds. This is useful where instruments exist to measure the period between waves, while the wavelength is more difficult to measure. The wavelength is an interesting figure as a description of a sea, particularly for those who go out in small boats. It is less significant for those dealing with wave energy, except for the Cockerell Raft; for most inventors, the height and period are the more important figures. For those who like to have a mental image of the sort of conditions we are discussing, under the formula quoted an 8-second wave would have a wavelength of almost 100 m. (99.84). A 9-second wave would have a wavelength of 126 m.

The waves are created by the wind. Its energy is transferred to the water at the surface by a method which is still not fully understood. But there is agreement among experts that the waves represent a concentrated form of wind energy.

A generally-accepted guide to the power in the waves is that they produce roughly 70 kW/m off the Outer Hebrides, 25 kW/m in the Irish Sea and off the north-east coast of England, and 50 kW/m off the Scilly Isles. As a convenient figure, it is usually the figure of 50 kW/m which is taken as the average and this gives 50 MW/km—kilowatts to the metre and megawatts to the kilometre.

Several attempts have been made to codify the types of wave power stations. A good description is given by Dr Tony Lewis in his book *Wave energy*[1], written for the European Commission. He divides them into *active* and *passive*. The first are those which move in response to the waves and do useful mechanical work against a stable reference frame. These include the Duck and the Raft. The passive devices are those which remain stationary, such as the Tapchan and OWC, and he includes the Air Bag and the Clam and the *Kaimei* because they do not have mechanical elements responding to the waves, but provide a frame for the air to move inside them.

The way in which they receive wave power has led to three types being identified. They are *terminator, attenuator*, and *point absorber*. The first are those which are at right angles to the predominant wave direction and parallel to the wavefront (the line of froth which one sees approaching the beach). That is, they lie across the path of the incoming wave which is stopped when it hits the device, hence the name. They would normally stand on the seabed. The attenuator lies nose-on into the waves and absorbs the energy as the waves pass and is therefore likely to have lower efficiency but is less liable to be wrecked; the *Kaimei* is an example of this. The third type, the point absorber, is small in relation to the wavelengths of the waves which it receives. The typical example is a buoy, which can receive wave energy from all directions, and the French Frog.

Latching and *phase control* are methods of improving the performance of wave energy devices by delaying the moment when the force of the water activates the device, with the help of valves and hydraulic rams.

Directionality is the word used to describe the fact that all the waves do not arrive from the 'best' direction, and some of the energy is lost by devices facing one way. The point absorber is one answer to this problem. Another is the Norwegian invention of 'harbour walls' which reach out over a wider area than the entrance to the device and capture much more of the available energy.

Variable-pitch turbines are being developed as the next generation, to succeed the Wells turbine. The hope is that they will be more efficient, starting to spin sooner, even in a comparatively calm sea, and then adjusting to slow down the passage of air which enables the generator to continue functioning when the waves rise to a peak. In the words of Stephen Salter, 'fixed-pitch turbines are only momentarily at their most efficient point,' and he is now devising a machine that will match the infinite variety of seas.

References

1. Lewis, T. (1985). *Wave energy: evaluation for CEC*. Graham and Trotman, London.

Appendix 2　Chronology

12 July 1799: First patent filed by Girards in Paris.

1945: Yoshio Masuda begins study of small-scale wave energy generators.

1954: A.N. Walton Bott investigates wave energy on Mauritius.

1973: Stephen Salter, and Government Central Policy Review Staff (the Think Tank) start, independently, to investigate wave energy.

February 1974: National Engineering Laboratory commissioned to carry out survey. Japan Marine Science and Technology Center (JAMSTEC) begins tank trials.

February 1975: NEL reports that wave energy could supply half of our electricity.

29 April 1976: Department of Energy launches wave power programme.

1978: First international conference at Heathrow Hotel hears that official cost estimates make wave energy astronomically expensive.

June 1980: ACORD (Advisory Council on Research and Development) recommends two-year programme to study Oscillating Water Column, Lancaster Flexible Bag, and Bristol Cylinder, at end of which one would be chosen for building of prototype and sea trials. Later that year, Sir Hermann Bondi retires as chief scientist, and Dr Anthony Challis from ICI takes over.

March 1981: ACORD meets for mid-term report and considers shutting down all work, but then agrees to reprieve the programme. But it decides that a decision will be brought forward to March rather than the June of 1982 previously agreed.

Mid-March 1982: Clive Grove-Palmer, Secretary of the Wave Energy Steering Committee, is told that he will not be admitted to the meeting. He decides to take premature retirement at the age of 62.

19–20 March 1982: ACORD makes recommendations. Contemporaneous Minutes of meetings kept secret.

27 April 1982: Government announces end to funding for wave energy, releasing only its own version of a 'Summary of Advice' of ACORD's views.

22–24 June 1982: Grove-Palmer tells international symposium on wave energy at Trondheim what had happened.

March 1985: ETSU publishes official 'obituary' of wave energy.

July 1985: Report to Commission of the European Community says that European resource is about 85 per cent of electricity demand and calls for 13.7 million ECU (£9.5 million) research and demonstration programme.

13 November 1985: Norway launches two wave power stations at a site near Bergen.

1 July 1987: Department of Energy allocates £230 000 to wave power station on Islay.

5 May 1988: Salter and Whittaker give evidence, and Department of Energy and ETSU reply to it, before House of Lords Select Committee on the European Communities.

27 July 1988: Select Committee issues its report, calling for an independent review of the conflicting evidence; and further evaluation of offshore wave power.

26–28 September 1988: Wave energy researchers organise their own conference at Bristol University.

15 November 1988: Stephen Salter and Peter White give evidence to the Hinkley Point C Inquiry, explaining how the British Government has blocked attempts to gain a new source of energy from the waves while seeking to build new nuclear power station.

16 April 1989: Baroness Hooper, Energy Under-Secretary, announces a review of wave energy, spread over two years, including offshore technologies (this became the Thorpe report).

30 November 1989: Solar Energy Society holds one-day conference in Coventry attended by ETSU representatives, including Tom Thorpe. Sceptical delegates questioned the motive of the British Government in launching another survey of wave power.

October 1990: Vice President of European Commission (EC), Signor Filippo Pandolfi, tells European Parliament that a study of wave energy carried out in 1985 had concluded that it would be 'premature' to start demonstrations of wave energy.

24 January 1991: Pandolfi apologises for misleading European Parliament and allocates 1.2 million ECUs for preliminary research and studies.

25 April 1991: EC holds one-day seminar in Brussels. Pandolfi hints that millions of ECUs will soon be available. Godfrey Bevan of British Department of Energy, says his government is 'strongly supportive'.

16 July 1991: Shoreline wave power system switched on by Energy Minister, Colin Moynihan, on Islay.

5 August 1991: Renewable Energy Advisory Group (REAG) set up by British Government 'to provide a focus for the future'. Report expected 'early in 1992'.

1–2 October 1992: EC holds conference in Cork and agrees to go 'half-speed ahead' with hopes for a 500 kW shore-based plant to test new components but refuses to go offshore yet.

17 December 1992 (the day Parliament rises for Christmas recess): British Government publishes Thorpe report, 20 months late, and REAG report, 11 months late. Tim Eggar, Energy Minister, says he will make a decision 'in due course'.

21–24 July 1993: EC holds conference in Edinburgh and says it now wants to put a foot in the water and support the first wave power station at sea off Dounreay; also a shoreline station in the Azores, and a new Gully station on Islay.

31 March 1994 (the day Parliament rises for Easter recess): Tim Eggar announces 'existing work on wave energy will be completed, but no further commitments undertaken as this technology has limited potential to contribute commercially to energy supplies in the next few decades.' This means that the Portuguese programme, supported by that country's electricity utilities, and the OSPREY, supported by such companies as GEC, British Steel, and the Atomic Energy Authority, will go ahead.

2 August 1995 OSPREY is launched on Clydeside but two compartments of the ballast tanks are damaged. It is hit by high seas before the sand ballast is loaded and the two compartments which were damaged are ruptured. OSPREY One is a write-off. Her backers vow to return with OSPREY Two.

Appendix 3   Further study

Readers wishing to pursue their interest should take advantage of just about the only contribution being made to wave energy by this government: copies of the Tom Thorpe report, *A review of wave energy,* are available free on application to: Renewable Energy Enquiries Bureau, ETSU, Harwell, Oxfordshire, OX11 0RA, tel. 01235 432450. It is a superb, technical survey of the whole field. Volume 1 gives all the basic information which most readers will need, but there is a second volume (also free) for specialist readers requiring greater detail. The only quibble that I have is that it uses the government formula of 8 per cent and 15 per cent discount rates to estimate costs, but it contains graphs from which a sensible reader can deduce what the real figures should be. Hurry to obtain your copy before the government discovers that it is doing something useful and puts a stop to it.

In fairness to ETSU, it should be said that the organisation has produced the other two surveys of the subject which contain excellent accounts of the technology, now dated, but still valid in everything except subsequent developments and costings. They are both called *Wave energy*. The first is Energy paper 42, published in 1979, and the other is ETSU R26 published in 1985.

Conference papers which I have cited are other sources of information, but usually available only through libraries. The best summary of the situation is by Professor S.H. Salter, *World progress in wave energy —1988*, which was first given in an address to the National Academy of Science and Technology of the Philippines in Manila and reprinted by the *International Journal of Ambient Energy*, vol. 10, number 1 in January 1989. It is a brilliant and sparkling read.

Readers will find that developments in wave energy are regularly covered in a magazine called *Safe energy*, published from 72 Newhaven Road, Edinburgh, EH6 5QG, obtainable on subscription. The same applies to an important newsletter called *Renew*, published every two months by the Network for Alternative Technology and Technology Assesment (NATTA) and available from NATTA, Energy and Environment Research Unit, Faculty of Technology, Open University, Milton Keynes, MK7 6AA.

The Open University also has available a research pack for tertiary education, no. T521, covering all forms of renewable energy. Details can be obtained from the same Energy and Environment Research Unit. A degree-level course in renewable energy is due to start in 1996.

Index